DUFFERS ON THE DEEP

First road in Spitsbergen Adams, Sverdrup and Brown

DUFFERS ON THE DEEP

by Winifred Brown

Pitchpole Books
Cheshire, England
pitchpole.co.uk

Published 2013 by Pitchpole Books
Cheshire, England
pitchpole.co.uk

First published in 1939 by
Peter Davies Ltd: London

ISBN 978-0-9575549-3-1

INTRODUCTION

TO THE PITCHPOLE EDITION

This edition of Winifred Brown's classic story of her first steps in yachting with her companion Ron Adams is based on the book published by Peter Davies in 1939. The text closely follows the original so that, for example, Norwegian names are rendered in the same way as they are there with aa where å would be used today and ö where ø would be preferred. The layout of this edition generally follows that of the Davies one. The Davies edition did not have an index but this one does.

There seem to be no extant negatives or prints of the photographs so these have been scanned in from the book and, where possible, improved but inevitably their quality is not of the best. All of the photographs reproduced here were taken by Win and Ron. One photograph, of them taken on deck before they departed on their adventures, could not be reproduced for copyright reasons.

The two maps have been redrawn and the drawings of *Perula* contained in the Appendix, originally on a fold-out sheet, have been separated and printed on succeeding pages. The writing on these is sometimes difficult to read but it seemed a pity to spoil them with modern labels so they are printed as they were. All the information is elsewhere in the Appendix.

The edition is produced with the permission of Tony Adams, Winifred's son.

Win and Ron made a third voyage to Norway in 1939 with Europe on the brink of war. They sailed to the Ålesund area and Win then took a steamer to visit Einar Sverdrup in Spitsbergen, leaving Ron on *Perula.* Win and Sverdrup had corresponded as she wrote Duffers over the winter of 1938 and when he visited England in early 1939 they became, briefly, lovers. The visit to Spitsbergen was not a success—after a few days Sverdrup told her to leave—and she and Ron returned, reaching home waters just as war broke out. She was never to see Sverdrup again and he was killed in 1942 leading a force seeking to retake Spitsbergen from the Germans. The story is told in her other books and in the biography published by Pitchpole as *Winifred Brown: Britain's Adventure Girl No.1.*

CONTENTS

PART I: IGNOTUM PER IGNOTIUS
THE BAR PARLOUR AT THE GAZELLE....3
THE "L" YACHTSWOMAN....11
LAYING UP AND FITTING OUT....20
VISITORS ABOARD....26
COMPASSES TO OYSTERS....36
WRECKING THE CALEDONIAN CANAL....44
THE NORTH SEA....53
THE "ENGINEERS"....60
FJORDS AND INDRELED....69
MAINLY ABOUT ANCHORAGES....80
A SAGA AND THE SOGN....88
HOMEWARD BOUND....95
"WHERE ANGELS FEAR TO TREAD"....102

PART II: HORRESCO REFERENS
OUTWARD BOUND....116
NORTH OF SCOTLAND....125
BACK IN NORWAY....133
SUNDRY BOTHER....142
IN THE ARCTIC....151
THE PARIS OF THE NORTH....161
SVALBARD SEAS....170
THE "OUTSIDE" WORLD....185
BY THE GRACE OF GOD....205
THE ROOF OF EUROPE....220
TROMSÖ TO AALESUND....234
ABSENCE MAKES THE HEART GROW FONDER....252
APPENDIX....265
DRAWINGS OF *PERULA*....273
INDEX....277

ILLUSTRATIONS

First road in Spitsbergen Adams, Sverdrup and Brown................*front*
Perula's second voyage to Norway..2
Perula from mizzen (top) and masthead...43
At Sundal..68
Washing day at Romsdalfjord and *Perula* under Seven Sisters, Geiranger..78
Gudvangen, Naeröfjord and Florö..79
Perula's second voyage to Norway..114
Look out for ice; Brown in Main Street, Longyearbyen and Lapp settlement at Lyngen...184
Perula at foot of glacier; Perula at Isfjord, Spitsbergen....................204
The diver at Tromsö and Tromsö — *Perula* looked small and white among the whalers...218
Perula at Jokelfjord...219
Hammerfest - midnight (the northernmost town in the world) and North Cape at midnight...233
The Saltstraum near Bodö...251

Sketches by the Author pages 115, 121, 144, 152, 175, 211 and 240

PART I: IGNOTUM PER IGNOTIUS

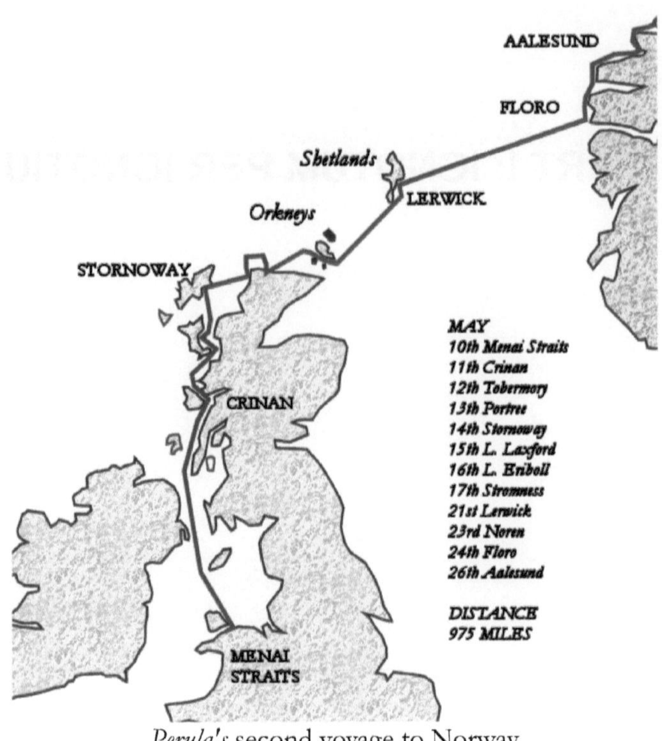

Perula's second voyage to Norway

CHAPTER I

THE BAR PARLOUR AT THE GAZELLE

A cold grey twilight had settled on the Menai Straits, the Welsh mountains loomed darkly up into scurrying clouds and the lights of Bangor gleamed out from across the water. Dai put down his book, yawned and stretched himself Nearly opening time. He threw another log on the fire that smouldered in the open brick fireplace, kicked it into place with a sandaled foot, and felt in his pocket for a match. "Damn these oil lamps," he said. "Wish they would hurry with the electricity." The lamps gave a soft yellow light, cast shadows from the oak beams and reflections on the rows of tankards and bottles. A cheery little room, the bar parlour of the Gazelle; it spoke of the sea and those who go down to the sea in ships. That old-fashioned "log" over the bar, the port and starboard lights, large copper lanterns; what stories could they have told of the sailing ships that had once carried them across the oceans. There were souvenirs, too, the things sailors collect in foreign parts: when you wanted to know how capable you were you counted the swordfish teeth; nobody was ever sure how many there were, as the number seemed to increase as the night developed. The bar door opened and admitted a rush of wind, followed by three figures in oilskins.

"Pa Hwyl, Dai," they said, for Welsh is frequently spoken in the Gazelle.

The skippers sat down round the fire and ordered their nightly "pint." Soon others would join them, Scotch and Irish skippers, men from the south coast, for most yacht owners have their fad as to the part that provides the best crew. Fishermen would come, too, and perhaps some local farmers. Until 9 o'clock they would sit and discuss the things that formed their world. Sometimes they sang, but mostly it was discussion; the merits of their own particular boat; the deficiencies of someone else's rig; the latest method of removing varnish without scraping and, last but not least, the yacht owners themselves.

In the spring of 1936 they had plenty to talk about. A new owner was arriving. This in itself was a thing of interest, and called for discussion as to who would be skipper and who crew, would the job be worth having and what was the owner like? Owners that remained at moorings and hardly ever came down were, of course, very much preferable. Then the bombshell fell. A big man drained his tankard and announced in a singing

Welsh voice: "Indeed, there will be no job on the new boat for any of us, the owner, she is a bloody woman and she is not having a skipper or crew."

"What!" gasped the horrified company. "The boat is a 30 tonner—you must be wrong, man."

"Indeed, I am not," he replied. "I have it from the yard and I have seen it in the newspapers."

From his pocket he produced a tattered cutting: it read as follows: "Airwoman to take up sailing: Miss Winifred Brown, the Lancashire airwoman, has purchased a 45 foot yacht and is planning to sail round the world. In an interview Miss Brown told our reporter she has no sailing experience whatsoever, but she does not intend to employ a skipper or crew. Miss Brown has named her ship *Perula*, after a South American goddess, believed by Indians to aid the sick, guard the sleeping and cheer the disconsolate. Miss Brown will require all *Perula's* supernatural powers . . . ."

It was the horrible truth. I had obtained a boat; I did not know the first thing about one and I had talked of a world cruise. Quite a lot of people do this, but my case was rather different, for I had not wanted a boat, had no desire to know anything about one, and as for the world cruise idea . . . . But I had better start at the beginning.

It was all *Perula*'s fault. She started life in 1932, built as a fishing boat by A. M. Dickie & Sons, Bangor, for Captain Randalls of Fleetwood. In those days she was a sturdy little ship costing some £1,100, with her 4 cyl. R.N. diesel engine. She could hold her own at sea with the larger trawlers, often visiting far distant banks, but she was found to be too small to be practicable; her fish-holds not large enough to warrant long passages. So *Alec Randalls* lay in Jubilee Dock, Fleetwood, unwanted, neither one thing nor the other.

In 1935 she was converted to a yacht and renamed *Monavic*. The new owner was a house builder, and the conversion seemed largely to have been done by house builders, for *Monavic* resembled a "modern detached" more than a ship. She was now yawl rigged, and a contraption mostly of glass, popularly referred to as the "Tomato House," rose some 6 feet high between the masts. This was as I first saw her in the summer of 1935, when I grudgingly accepted an invitation aboard.

I had always hated small yachts since my father, in his younger days a keen yachtsman, had taken me at the age of twelve on a rough passage to the Isle of Man and fed me on a mixture of sardines, condensed milk and chocolate, with results that "brought out" the worst in me.

Fate thrust *Monavic* upon me. I had no intention of buying her, yet circumstances arose in the autumn of 1935 that led me to being landed with her.

I surveyed my new possession with mixed feelings. I could not afford to run a yacht and an aeroplane. The obvious course was to sell the yacht, but this was easier said than done.

We discovered the engine was completely seized up; the white-metal bearings looking as if the rats had been at them. There were also other snags too numerous to mention, and as a grand finale the dinghy was seized by a gentleman who apparently had more right to it than I. In other words I appeared to have paid £300 for a glorified houseboat.

There is something pathetic about a boat out of the water. She looked so funny with her comic deck structure and dirty paintwork; like a stray puppy, you don't want the damn thing, yet something makes you keep it. I invariably make decisions and think afterwards.

"I'll keep her," I said to my friend, Ron Adams, and instructed Messrs. A. M. Dickie & Sons to carry on with the necessary work.

Most yachtsmen know the cost of fitting out, especially when it involves practically pulling a boat to pieces. I did not know, but I soon found out! Making *Perula* seaworthy cost me £584 15s., of which £161 10s. went towards reconditioning the engine. I had to raise money somehow, so in January, 1936, I made my last flight, a demonstration of the aeroplane presented to me by Sir John Siddeley, after I won the King's Cup Air Race in 1930. With the new owner's cheque in my pocket I sadly left Woodford Aerodrome. For ten years I had been an air pilot; I had sacrificed everything for a boat I did not really want.

I think now that it was inevitable, that the sea was in my blood, perhaps inherited from my father. At the time, however, I felt it was the end of everything, and turned recklessly to the wildest scheme I could think of

Never enter the yachting world in a blaze of publicity and rash statements; other yachtsmen don't like it. One night I sat in the bar parlour of the Gazelle and listened to a man discussing me. Unfortunately, someone informed him he was addressing his remarks to the very person he was talking about. I was very much amused, but he, poor man, departed in considerable embarrassment; even leaving his beer.

Perula was launched on 10th June, 1936, and very neat and trim she looked. Few would have recognised her as the old *Monavic* . The tomato-house had been removed (before a wave did it for us) and replaced by a teak wheelhouse, aft of which was a small cockpit, lead-lined and self-draining. Her rig was now a Bermudian yawl, with a new mainmast, but the old mizzen. New sails gave an area of 563 sq. ft. It was not very much, but considered by Dickie's to be sufficient for Adams and myself to handle. Her decks had been recaulked and cleared of obstructions, the old skylights and hatches either removed or replaced. A companion ladder from the wheelhouse led to the new engine room, the old one having been completely gutted. We had sacrificed a good deal of space to *Perula's* engine. Some considered it foolish, but for ten years my life had more or less depended on engines, and I felt the engine room should be one of the most important parts of my ship.

A low coachroof had been built to give full head room, and we had plenty of space to get at any part of the engine with ease. There was a work bench with a vice, racks of tools and sufficient equipment for various repairs that might be necessary at sea.

On the port side of the engine room were racks for luggage and the toilet compartment. Lavatories are not a very delicate subject, but ours is worthy of mention on account of the extraordinary difficulties it presented, both to Dickie's and the plumber. The thing simply would not work. For some time everybody pondered on the great problem, then a lampshade was unearthed from its "innards." How it got there will always remain a mystery.

On either side of the engine were passages leading to the saloon. The saloon had been left more or less as before and was large for *Perula's* size, panelled in walnut plywood, complete with fawn carpet. The upholstery had worried me a good deal; it always reminded me of a third-class railway carriage. Being under the impression these cushions had been specially made for *Monavic* at great cost I felt it would be wicked to scrap them. It was not until later I discovered the labels: "S.S. BALTIC THIRD SALOON."

In the saloon we had fitted two root bunks; canvas stretchers that could be set into three different notches, according to the state of the weather. Aft of these bunks were two large cupboards, one a wardrobe and the other a "wireless room" for the receiver we rented from the Marconi Company at the cost of £16 per year, which included installation and service.

The fo'castle, which had previously been the owner's stateroom, had been converted into a cabin-cum-galley, an ideal arrangement which enabled me to cook breakfast without getting up. There were two built-in bunks with spring mattresses, a large sink (which also acted as our wash basin) and two stoves, one a Lathom paraffin with three burners and an oven, the other a gimballed primus. The cups and jugs which swung from the beams still bore the name "Monavic," but we expected to break them by the end of the season. There was also a teapot which was to form a useful alarm, for on the approach of bad weather it invariably flew off the rack and hit me on the head.

So on that June morning Adams and I found ourselves aboard the new and very strange floating home.

"What do we do now?" he asked, as we watched the retreating form of the gent in the blue jersey, who had piloted us across from the yard, moored *Perula* and left us, for the first time in our lives, to cope with 45 feet of yacht.

"Let's go for a sail," I suggested, with a bravado born of drinking the launching champagne (such a waste to break the bottle on the bows).

"No," replied Adams, who represented the Insurance Company. "Wouldn't look well to wreck it the first day."

"All right," I agreed. "We'll have food instead."

Lapse of ten minutes.

"Say, Win, can you light a primus?" "A primus?" I said with scorn. "Anybody can light a primus. You just pump." Five minutes later: "Where did we put the fire extinguisher? Oh! Ron, just look at the nice new paint—ruined! That steak would have been good, too; still, we have some biscuits." Lapse of thirty minutes.

"Go ashore? O.K.! Can I what? Can I row? Oh! row! Er . . . yes . . . I can row, at least I have done . . . once."

Twenty minutes later.

"I don't know, Win, but it does seem to me that if you sat facing the back of it, instead of the front, we might go in the right direction."

"If you know so much about it, Ronald Adams, row the blasted thing yourself!"

It seems incredible that two able bodied persons could be such idiots. For two days horrified members of the *Royal Mersey* watched the club burgee flying upside down on *Perula's* mainmast. I, of course, had let go the flag halliards. I thought nothing of going alongside the jetty on the windward side and, with the aid of a friendly wave, arriving on top complete with dinghy.

Adams developed the habit of reading up yachting hints which, although they stood him in good stead later on, at the time only landed us into still further trouble.

We had pondered deeply on why the dinghy had suddenly become so hard to pull, just when we felt we were getting on with it so well. One day, I really lost my temper. "You haven't the strength of a mouse," I said, as poor Adams pulled against wind and flood, without perceptibly moving the dinghy; "take the thing inshore out of the tide." He did so, but it was even harder; he pulled and pulled but we got no further.

"Give me the oars," I said in disgust. After pulling for about ten minutes, I suddenly said, "What's that rope?"

"What rope?" asked Adams.

"The one on the back," I replied.

"Hell!" he said. "It's the bucket."

"Bucket?" I questioned.

"Yes," he explained, "the one the book said we were to hang on the dinghy to stop it bumping at night."

It was full of mud. For twenty minutes we had been dredging the Straits.

Of course, tying the dinghy up to the jetty was always a snare and a delusion. The tide either came in or went out, and even when we had grasped which it was going to do, we invariably forgot we had a dinghy. On the morning of the 11th of July there happened an occurrence that shook to its very foundations the tradition and dignity of the sailing world; it even shook the general public, for at 3 a.m. a yachtswoman was seen in the Straits, clad only in pink undergarments.

We had a visitor aboard, a very posh visitor. He had come straight off the *Queen Mary*, heralded by a telegram: "Sailing weekend would be delightful—shall I bring dinner clothes?" He duly arrived, and being an American promptly remarked, "Say, that Gazelle is a cute little joint; reckon I'll take it back to Hollywood." The owner, Mr. McNeil, had other ideas; however, he did consent to sell our distinguished guest some of the old wine from the cellars. We went ashore about 7 o'clock, and Dai carried up the bottles: old ports, sherries, etc., on which our guest insisted we should pass judgment by tasting. After some hours of this he suddenly said: "Say, I think that draught beer your guys drink is kinda cute—I'll have some of that, too." So there followed a long argument, with samples, on the relative merits of mild and bitter. By this time we had, of course, completely forgotten the dinghy.

When we were eventually thrown out, all we could see was a small black shape some fifty yards from the shore; the tide had come in and the painter was a good ten feet under water.

I was, however, in no mood to be dismayed and promptly rose to the "spirit" of the occasion. "Say, bo," I remarked in my best American, "hold my pants" and, clad in pink undies I dived into the five knot tide. Fortunately, I am a strong swimmer: in the ensuing battle I had to be. I reached the dinghy and tried to pull myself down the painter, and as my head alternately rose and disappeared beneath the water there was a loud shriek from the Gazelle.

"Help!" yelled a dear old lady from her bedroom window. "A woman is drowning." The commotion that followed is best unrecorded. Next morning our distinguished visitor returned to London without even waiting for breakfast, and I have never heard from him since.

So the yachtsmen at the Straits spoke mournfully of the good old days before I came, and in the bar parlour of the Gazelle, skippers sadly shook their heads. One night I arrived to hear the large gentleman exclaim: "Women are no bloody good! Thinks because she can fly an aeroplane she can 'andle a boat—says to 'er myself, t'aint the same up there as it is down 'ere . . . Oh! . . . Good evening, Miss Brown. Thanks, don't mind if I do—mine's a mild."

At least I knew "where I stood." They were good lads at heart, though, always ready to give me a helping hand. Sometimes we used to argue on navigation, and one night I said: "Tell me, skipper, why do you think navigation is so different in the air from on the sea?"

"Oh!" he replied promptly, "t'aint the same up there as 'tis down 'ere."

"Well, ask me a question," I persisted.

"All right," he replied. "We're sailing to the Isle of Man. Half-way there it gets foggy, what would you do?"

"What would I do to what?" I asked ungrammatically.

"What would you do to the compass course?" he said.

"To the compass course?" I repeated, puzzled. "What's happened? Has the wind changed? Has the tide turned?"

"No," he said. "Everything is the same—it's just got foggy."

"Then," I replied, "I'd make no alteration to my compass course."

"Ah!" he chuckled knowingly, "that's where you're wrong. I knew it weren't the same up there as down 'ere."

"I give it up," I said. "What would you do?" "Add 14°," he exclaimed in triumph, "for magnetic variation.

Granted it was late in the evening, and we'd all "had a few"; but I went out of the bar with a new hope.

CHAPTER II

THE "L" YACHTSWOMAN

On June 18th we made our first solo. That is to say, we took *Perula* to Puffin Island and back, all by ourselves. Previously we had hired one of the local skippers to take us out in his free moments.

After two or three of these lessons I really felt I knew all there was to know about the Menai Straits. For example, I knew that I must not cross the banks unless the water was up to the dirty mark on the lighthouse; what I should do if they ever painted the lighthouse was shrouded in mystery. I had written out lengthy instructions for myself which ran as follows: "If on starting the engine it begins to smell and a lot of smoke comes out, you have probably forgotten to turn on the water. Leave the sails severely alone. Decide in good time what you are going to do with the dinghy; this is the most difficult problem. If you decide to tow it behind, it makes going backwards frightfully difficult, and if you decide to leave it on the moorings, you probably sink it when you come back. On leaving the moorings cast them overboard with reckless abandon; if in the middle you hesitate to wonder if you will ever pick them up again, you'll probably go with them.

"The next step is to pray and hope the tide will take you clear; never try to steer a boat backwards, they don't go where you think and other boats are sure to be near. If you see a race in progress, return to moorings at once. If you see the Liverpool steamer coming, pray, even harder.

"Red buoys are kept to 'Anglesey', and black ones to 'Bangor and the Great Orme'. If you don't think of them like this , they change round coming back. If you want to be 'posh' and talk of 'port and starboard' wear a green sock on one foot and a red one on the other. In the first instance they can be put on by reference to the light boards which are painted in these colours. Otherwise you can think of port and crème de menthe. Bad port is light red and 'left'; crème de menthe is green and usually all 'right'."

With these excellent instructions before us, our first solo was successful. We even picked up our moorings again, at the third attempt.

We began to look for fresh worlds to conquer, and the Isle of Man seemed a good place. We took a friend with us named Alfred. Alfred was our one hope of salvation. He had been in the Navy, and he felt the responsibility keenly; so much so that all the way from Manchester to the Straits we kept stopping the car to obtain "courage" for him. As a result we arrived at the Straits rather later than expected, and Alfred began to wonder if we ought to set out.

"Well," I said, with great logic, "we've never been to Douglas in the daytime, and as we don't know what it looks like, we might just as well go in at night."

We arrived off the harbour entrance about midnight.

"Is there a midnight boat out?" asked Alfred.

"Heavens!" I cried in horror. "Suppose we met it in the entrance?"

So we sat outside Douglas for about an hour, waiting for a steamer that never came. We spent the time studying the Sailing Directions, which, as usual, cheered us up immensely, describing in detail the Tower of Refuge which "forms a safe retreat for the crews of shipwrecked vessels."

At last we went in. I had been left at the wheel, so that Ron and Alfred could attend to the anchor. I have never been so frightened in all my life. Boats seemed to leap out of the darkness on every side.

"Mind the Lady of Man," howled Alfred in agony, as I endeavoured to ram the company's best steamer.

"Drop the anchor," I shouted back imploringly. Down it went, but promptly dragged into the middle of the harbour.

"You can't anchor there," roared an enraged voice from the jetty.

At last, having disorganised everything, we got more or less tucked away in a corner.

"Better put out a kedge," said Alfred, and after much difficulty it was achieved.

"Better keep an anchor watch," said Alfred.

"All right," I said, "but I'm going to bed."

We all went to bed, and had got nearly to sleep when there was a frightful crash. "We've dragged," I yelled, rushing out of my cabin and descending to the floor with an awful bump. For the next five minutes the saloon was a mass of cursing humanity, odd chairs, a table and some flower vases. The crash was due to Alfred falling out of his bunk , and in the darkness both Ron and I had fallen over him.

It did not seem worth going to bed again, so we dressed, had breakfast and spent the morning sitting on a horsetram to mend our shattered nerves.

Back in the Straits we felt very superior, and Adams and I even went solo to Holyhead, although with my usual objection to rocks I did go right round the Skerries. Coming back we even put the sails up and, thoroughly delighted with such progress, we both went below to have lunch; for Adams had read in a book that you could leave a boat to sail itself. We enjoyed our lunch very much, but on returning to the wheelhouse something seemed terribly wrong with the coast line.

"Ron," I said, "Wasn't it on the other side of us when we went below?"

Perula had turned completely round and we were nearly back in Holyhead.

About this time my father came down; I don't think he had trusted us before. Our moorings were rather a long way out; it being considered safer to keep me well away from anything else. Taking pity on the amount of rowing we had to do, father bought me an out-board motor for the dinghy. It duly arrived, complete with the instructions in French. We fixed it on the dinghy: Adams sat aft to work it, while I sat for'ard with the instructions. I'm not very good at French, but I struggled nobly, translating as I read. Suddenly there was a frightful roar; Adams had been following my instructions and the motor had started.

He had no idea how one steered, and we were charging straight for *Perula*.

"Quick!" he yelled. "How do you stop the thing?"

As *Perula* loomed closer every word of French I knew went clean out of my mind. Adams wrenched the steering lever, the dinghy nearly turned over. I turned over completely. It must have been a terrible sight; up and down the Straits we charged, everything that could fled before us, the rest we missed by a succession of miracles. At last it stopped, no thanks to me, merely of its own accord.

Outboard motors are not things to be treated lightly; when being taken from a yacht to a dinghy, or vice versa, they should always be attached to a piece of rope. We discovered this the following day. Adams was stepping from *Perula* into the dinghy, the outboard in his arms. He had not noticed the Liverpool steamer passing and the wash had just reached us. He told me afterwards that as he fell one thought ran through his mind: "Hell! there goes £15." So with an effort worthy of a contortionist he threw the outboard safely into the dinghy and himself into the Straits.

He was all dressed to go ashore, complete with oilskins, and the tide was running at about 5 knots, but he looked so funny that instead of helping him out I simply sat on deck and howled with laughter. Fortunately he came up alongside the dinghy and managed to grab and clamber into it.

The following day he had his revenge. We were leaving the moorings, and having "got above" my instructions, I clean forgot the dinghy tied aft and put *Perula* astern. I glanced back to see if we were clearing the other boats, when to my horror, the dinghy started to come towards us; the propeller had caught the painter.

For a moment I watched fascinated, as more and more rope got wound up, then, stirred to action, I leaped to the gear wheel. But Adams was quicker; knife in hand, he took a flying leap into the dinghy and cut the painter just as the bows were being dragged under. I felt I could weep; here we were out of control, with lord knows how much rope round the prop, and not the slightest idea what to do. Fortunately, we were only about a hundred yards from the mooring, so wrongly or rightly, we decided to risk using the engine to get back to it. In this we succeeded, and then the debate started: how to clear the rope. We tied a knife to the boathook; we turned the shaft; we tried to get at it from the dinghy; it was no use. There seemed to be only one course, other than grounding *Perula*, and that was a spot of diving.

"Well," said Adams with a nasty gleam in his eye, "*I* had my swim yesterday!"

"O.K.," I said, "I can take a hint; in any case I'm a better swimmer than you." And with my nose in the air departed below to change. I think I was in the water for an hour.

With my legs wound round the rudder, I sawed and sawed at the mass of rope until I thought I should blow up. After a few dives I would have to climb back on deck and lie there gasping. I cleared a good two and a half fathoms of it; then Adams went in (with two bathing costumes on because he thought it would make him sink better) and cleared the few remaining feet. After we had consumed large quantities of rum to restore our circulations, we decided to continue our sail. We had not proceeded far when one of the mainsheet blocks flew to pieces and the boom shot aloft. Fate was definitely against us; we returned to our moorings.

It was about this time we met the "friend in need." We called him that because for some time we had wanted to sail to Heysham, but had not found anybody to accompany us; not when they knew where we wanted to go. "Morecambe Bay?" they said, "Very unfortunate, but we are engaged this week."

One night the "friend in need" came strolling into the bar.

"Morecambe Bay, Winnie bach?" he said. "Nothing to it." So off we set, full of optimism and without a chart. The "friend in need" had said he would bring one, but presumably the owner had locked it up. The remarkable part was we got there, both the crew and the weather being in a complete fog.

The foggy weather actually helped us, for other ships were going so slowly they could be followed, until, with great inconsideration, they "turned off" for Fleetwood. This was rather a set-back, but undaunted we seized the Sailing Directions and drew a pretty picture of what we thought Heysham lake would look like; if we could see it. As we could not see it we felt very pleased with our effort and proceeded with the utmost confidence. Although it was afternoon, the buoys were lighted, and every time we saw one we went up to it, looked at the number, noticed if it was flashing or occulting, and then crossed it off our "chart." In this way we eventually arrived in Heysham harbour.

I don't think the Railway Company were exactly pleased to see us, but after a gentleman had shouted at us through a megaphone, porters arrived and *Perula* was finally moored to a kind of raft at the lower end of the harbour. The local boatman promptly seized the golden opportunity to row out holiday makers, at threepence per person, to view "th' lady and 'er yatch." As the holiday makers insisted on having their full three pen'orth, the procedure was not without embarrassment.

Heysham is a nice harbour, but care is needed with a dinghy. We went ashore, tied ours by the steps and returned to find it gone. A waste pipe, situated just above it, had been busily belching forth and sunk it. The "friend in need" quickly rescued it. He was a great asset, always charming and cheerful, even when he fell down the harbour steps after the dinghy. Above all, he had a deep and tender thoughtfulness for my welfare.

The next morning he came to me.

"Winnie bach," he said, "you're not looking so well this morning."

"No," I said, "I don't feel so good."

"Could you use a couple of chickens for lunch?" he asked. Dear, kind, thoughtful boy!

"Yes," I beamed, "I certainly could." Then as an afterthought added, "But where from?"

"Oh," he replied innocently, "I've just been snooping around the quay; some lovely packing cases of chickens, one just goes ashore in oilskins . . ."

"Come on," I interrupted hastily, "We're leaving Heysham."

When we got back to the Straits I saw a chart of Morecambe Bay. The goddess *Perula* had certainly used her supernatural powers.

These short cruises had stirred our enthusiasm; we would do something bigger; go away for ten whole days. With tender memories of our first cruise to Douglas, we naturally turned again to Alfred and the traditions of the Navy. He was delighted to accompany us, and on September 16th we set out for Falmouth. In a stiff breeze and with darkness rapidly approaching, we sailed out between Puffin perch and Trwyn Du light-house. We had talked of taking the shorter passage through the Swellies, but thought better of it.

Everything went well until it was discovered *Perula* was heading for Dublin instead of Milford Haven. Moral: never have two navigators, one is bound to change the course of the other, if only to "show him, like." Alfred and I were both navigators. I thought I was better than he, and naturally he was quite certain he was better than I. It was left to Adams, who knew little of navigation, to keep the peace and devise an arrangement whereby Alfred was asleep when I was on watch and vice versa. In this way courses were only changed once in four hours; but Adams got no sleep, for Alfred had wisely insisted that at night, at any rate, two of us must always be on watch, and Adams had to sit up with each in turn.

In fact, poor Adams had rather a thin time. He never knew where we were going. On the afternoon of the 17th, he remarked: "Never knew Milford Haven looked like this."

"It doesn't," I replied, "I've decided to put into Fishguard."

On the afternoon of the 18th he remarked: "Shouldn't we be at St. Ives by now?" "We've passed it," replied Alfred, "that was Win's idea; I've decided to carry on to Penzance."

On the morning of the 19th he remarked: "Aren't we passing Penzance?"

"Yes," I snapped, "that was Alfred's idea, I'm going on to Falmouth." So we arrived at Falmouth at 5.30 p.m. on the 19th, and moored close by H.M.S. *Dart.* As bugles blew and guns boomed out, Alfred, his Navy blood afire, made us line up and hoist or lower colours. "We'll show them," he said, "that we are no scrappy yacht." Better not repeat what I said on being dragged out of a warm bunk or cosy evening at the local, all in the name of flag etiquette.

At Falmouth we filled up with fuel oil; we wanted 70 gallons. With some difficulty we tied up alongside a steamer quay; the stone wall towered up above us, but there was no sign of our oil. Suddenly there was a puff, snort and a whistle, and with a hiss of steam a railway engine pulled up above us. "Good gracious!" I said, "what has that come for?" We soon found out. A huge pipe was unhitched from one of the wagons and hurled over the quayside. A shower of Diesel oil covered us from head to foot. After considerable bad language and a frantic hunt for a funnel, *Perula* (and the harbour) were refuelled. I happened to mention we could do with a little water, so off the train went to get us 50 gallons.

The passage homeward was enjoyable but rather misty. We anchored off St. Ives, and Alfred rowed off to a fishing boat to obtain some breakfast. He returned in a state of agitation.

"Have you been altering the compass again, Win?" he asked.

"No," I said.

"Can't understand it," he continued, "When I asked the fisherman to sell me some fish, he replied: 'No speaka de Englesh'." However, we were at St. Ives and the fishing boat merely a "Frenchie" after pilchards.

St. Ives is charming, but it is a great pity the anchorage is so exposed. There is, of course, the small harbour, but the idea of negotiating *Perula* round the narrow right-angled bend filled me with terror. As we had been warned that ships are apt to bump if any sea is running we deemed it safer to remain outside, much to the grief of the kindly old Cornish harbour master.

Newquay was our next port of call, and again we were fascinated with our surroundings. We decided to dine ashore, but on enquiring the way to the hotel we were informed: "It's just up there, but," with a glance at our still oily clothes, "they would not serve you. It is select."

After a night at Holyhead, and a morning cleaning away the mud that comes up with the anchor, we arrived back at the Straits, with some relief.

Towards the end of October we decided on a final cruise, to end the season—Ireland and Scotland. It sounded mad at that time of the year, but I felt I must definitely test *Perula's* seaworthiness, before spending more money on her. In short, I was out looking for trouble. I found it!

After some debate we decided to take a professional skipper, for, as I pointed out, "we should learn the correct way of coping with a gale." He duly agreed to come for fifteen shillings a day. That showed what he thought about it; but he had the reputation of being the best man in the

Straits. We set off on the morning of October 23rd. My log book records a wind of force 6. I thought it a nice gentle beginning of our training, but the skipper thought otherwise. In fact, he refused to go to the Isle of Man, which we had decided would be our first port of call. Now, some of my ancestors were Scots, and I refused to pay fifteen shillings a day to sit in the Straits, so after some argument we went to Liverpool. I thought the skipper knew Rock channel; he doubtless thought I had a chart, and in consequence we went down it in the dark on a falling tide, with Sailing Directions, more pictures and the grace of God.

Next day it was really blowing: I rubbed my hands in glee—here was my gale. Again the skipper refused to contemplate the Isle of Man, but after more argument we agreed on Fleetwood. "I'll get him away bit by bit," I said to Adams craftily, for I knew that most skippers were loath to leave home.

It was bad in Queen's Channel; *Perula* was shipping a good deal of spray. We went up on the wrong side, with Cunarders hooting their sirens at us in rage. The skipper had evidently decided we were not going far, for he had not reefed the mainsail and the anchor was hanging over the bows. However, I was quite unaware of his intentions, and while I thought it a bit odd, it was not for me to question my teacher.

"Better put back, Miss Brown," he said.

"Why?" I asked. "This is what we've come for."

"The tail shaft is leaking," he continued.

"I know," I said cheerfully, "but it's not much."

"Put back to the Mersey," he implored. "Let's have it seen to there."

Again the fifteen shillings roused my Scotch blood. "Listen," I said, "if the boat isn't right we'll take it back to the Straits to be seen to."

"We can't," he said, "not in this."

"Can't we?" I said, "Watch me." And I turned *Perula* into the wind and seas.

The skipper sat with his head in his hands.

"What's the matter?" I asked.

"Flu," he groaned. "I think I'll lie down."

So he departed below and reclined on the saloon settee, while the teapot, sundry plates and numerous apples and oranges leaped wildly about the floor around him.

By this time Adams and I were having a pink fit; the wind was increasing rapidly and the waves getting larger and larger. It seemed that at any moment the anchor would go through the planking, but in the nick of time a kindly wave picked it up like a feather and deposited it correctly in its chocks on deck!

We dared not attempt to get the mainsail down, and reefing was quite beyond us. The sail lacing broke, and although at the time we considered this a catastrophe, it is probably as well that it did break and leave us with a loosefooted sail. The wireless aerial came down and the sail battens tore out, but we were beyond caring about such details, it was taking us all our time to steer *Perula*. The steering was of chain and wire and very heavy. On we struggled, using engine, and endeavouring to tack; this in itself was rather alarming to us, and the boom swung over in a series of horrible crashes.

The passage took us 17¼ hours, and we had no nourishment except a bottle of rum and some biscuits. Every time a wave hit the wheelhouse with a resounding crash, I had another go at the rum bottle and the weather seemed to improve like magic. Once off Ormes Head I succeeded in putting poor *Perula* broadside; the wheel spun out of my hands and for a horrible moment everything was water, but she shook herself like a wet spaniel and on we went. As we approached Puffin Island we were surprised to see a blaze of lights.

"Good gracious!" said Adams. "Everybody is up late in Anglesey." It was then about 2 a.m. Closer inspection, however, proved the lights to be those of ships sheltering from the gale. We, of course, had been far too occupied to light our own navigation lights.

We aroused the skipper to pilot us down the Straits. I don't think the poor man had ever expected to see them again, and I'm quite sure he never wanted to see me again.

The gale did us a world of good. It gave us confidence in ourselves, but more so in *Perula*; we felt that no matter what daft things we did she would somehow see us through. It was the beginning of a bond between the three of us—*Perula*, Adams and myself

"Ron," I said, "I'm glad I sold my aeroplane—*Perula* is worth it."

CHAPTER III

LAYING UP AND FITTING OUT

Laying up a yacht for the winter is always a sad affair, but I did not yet know this and wondered why such an air of gloom had settled on the Straits. The question "When are you laying up?" was on everybody's lips. The yacht owners became more and more miserable as their boats were stripped in readiness to go into the yard. The barometer was watched with anxiety, and any mention of strong easterlies made everyone groan; for it is almost impossible to get a ship into Dickie's yard with winds from this direction.

Perula was last out, and no longer were there cheery crowds in the bar parlour of the Gazelle. Adams, Dai and I would sit in front of the fire, joined perhaps by a farmer, or a skipper who had come across from "the other side."

The day before we were due up the slip we began to understand the gloom, only in our case it was intensified. We had little idea how to go about the numerous jobs, let alone work to a system. Sails to unbend, rigging to dismantle; of course we never thought of tying labels on things at the time, and afterwards we could not remember where all the "wretched ropes," as I called them, had come from. The deck became littered and the wheelhouse quite un-enterable. The saloon was a complete jumble, packing cases, parcels of crockery, everything carefully wrapped up in newspaper, ready to be stored for the winter. With carpet up, curtains down and cushions packed, it looked a complete picture of desolation. I was tired out and filthy; there was nowhere to sit, everything I touched was covered with Vaseline and we had but one plate to eat off, and we only had that because it had been left out by accident.

The barometer was falling and the wireless said a deep depression was coming. As far as I was concerned it had come already. I thought of the morning, looked at the tide tables for the twelfth time, and wondered if I should put *Perula* aground on the banks by starting too soon. Happily I remembered that the other yachts had left when the water reached the flagpole on the jetty. So next morning I sat in a fever of anxiety watching the flagpole through the glasses. I hope they never move it, for I use it to this day.

When we got alongside the dock, dozens of men in large boots leaped aboard. They hammered and banged, pushed me aside until I did not know where to put myself and my heart bled for my poor boat. Out came the masts under the eagle eye of Mr. Dickie, leaving two gaping holes in the deck. Every time I went below I fell down a corresponding hole in the saloon floor. I was not trusted to put *Perula* on the cradle this first year, so I stood wretchedly in the cockpit, feeling certain she would fall off. At last we were on, most of the men swung down the trestle framework into a waiting boat, and the big winch was started and slowly pulled us up on to dry land.

Adams and I had thought we could stow the gear all by ourselves during the afternoon. We were soon enlightened. For one thing we had forgotten how high the deck would be from the ground when *Perula* was propped up out of the water, and in consequence we had not unloaded the really heavy gear at the quayside as we do now. When we did, obtain a ladder, it was, as borrowed ladders usually are, quite unsafe. Hour after hour I either climbed or fell down it and trudged off across the yard, winding my way between masses of boats and endeavouring to avoid the tin cans and various assortments of rubbish that absent-minded seafaring gentlemen will still persist in tossing overboard when they are on dry land. On my head were perilously balanced sundry cushions; from my shoulders hung coils of rope or wire; under my arms were parcels, mops and brushes, and in my hands buckets, lamps or life belts. Naturally, there was a long flight of steps up to the store and, of course, it rained. It usually does. We let some of the gear down from the deck, but if our "knots" did not come undone, the rope broke. I had skilfully purloined a wheelbarrow for the heavy stuff, but it was a massive affair of iron and I soon discovered that wheeling it, especially over bumpy ground, was an art in itself.

Darkness came. Everyone went home and we toiled on. At last it was all in; and so were we. We gazed at it in wonder; however had all that stuff come off our little boat?

We went back to take a final look at her. How bare and empty she was, stripped of all her gear; her cupboards and lockers propped open. "Good-bye, *Perula*," I whispered, then hurried back to the car before I wept, and in the early hours of the morning we drove back to Manchester.

I discovered that no sooner is a boat laid up than you start planning and preparing for the day when you launch her again, in the following spring. It is all terribly exciting. You add up your money and decide how much you can afford to spend on her: then promptly arrange for work to be done that will cost at least twice that amount. You pore over charts and atlases and decide where you will go next summer. If you happen to be a woman you will also design your new yachting costume. If you are new to this great sport of sailing, as Adams and I were, you will probably spend the winter evenings deep in study, trying to make yourself worthy of` a boat that has suddenly become your entire world.

Well, I counted my money and decided how much I could spend on *Perula.* I had not nearly enough for what I wanted to do, so the more important items had to be picked out. After the gale episode, I decided that new steering was essential, and held long consultations with Mr. Dickie and Mr. Campbell, his designer, on the merits of chain or wire.

"Chain is heavy," I said, "and it clanks."

"What about wire, then?" suggested Mr. Dickie with a smile. But I would not have it unless I could see it all, I knew too much of the wire controls of an aeroplane. No matter how good the fairlead, wire ultimately frays.

"Then," said Mr. Dickie, "it's going to be expensive. What about rods and bevelled gear?"

So completely new steering was duly made by Reids and proved a very fine job. The wheel could be flicked round with a finger, yet once in place "stayed put." I felt it was fifty pounds well spent. A new rudder of naval brass replaced the old one, in readiness for the day when we won a football pool and could scrap *Perula*'s iron-fastened pitch pine planking for teak and copper sheathing.

Two new 160 gallon fuel tanks were also made, shaped to the hull and fitted on either side of the engine room. This gave us a total fuel capacity of 430 gallons and an approximate range of 3,000 miles. We also discussed our water tanks, one of which we suspected of being a house cistern. Still, they gave us a capacity of 100 gallons, and although the water which came out of them was usually a dirty brown, Adams and I had both drunk the waters of the Amazon and were not unduly disturbed. In any case, undiluted water "rots the boots" and should always be suitably sterilized.

The next question was where to go. The world cruise had, of course, been shelved. We realised now that it would take years of hard work to fit ourselves and our boat to make a success of such a venture. Some day, perhaps. Most of us have dreams and ambitions: life is not good without them.

For the coming season we decided on Norway, as it was it one of the few countries we had not visited.

My father looked a bit doubtful when I told him of our intended cruise, and suggested we should sail round England before attempting to go foreign. But Norway had been my idea: I liked it, and to Norway I intended to go. The fact that Adams and I had never been further than Holyhead by ourselves did not worry me, for "where ignorance is bliss, 'tis folly to be wise."

In the evenings we studied. My department was to be navigation. In my early flying days I had attended the Manchester Nautical Academy, under the instruction of Captain A. W. Dobson. I went to the academy after making the horrible discovery that there were no railway lines across the English Channel. In those early days navigation was still rather a mystery to many civilian pilots and we resorted to what we called "Flying Bradshaw." I had followed various trains all the way from Manchester to Folkestone, much to the annoyance of the engine driver. whom I playfully swooped down upon. If I got lost, I merely flew low over a, station, read the name and caught the next connection. The Channel was, of course, a complete set-back. I looked down at the ships below me and realised for the first time the immense oceans they crossed, all without a single landmark. If I could learn what those seamen knew, then I too could navigate.

Captain Dobson agreed to take me and substitute the word aeroplane for ship; but the very first morning I think he regretted his decision. I had never done trigonometry, never done algebra; geometry was a complete mystery and I added up on my fingers. If the horrible truth were known I had been hastily removed from school at the age of 14, before an enraged headmistress could throw me out. Shortly afterwards the War broke out and saved me from any further education of the right kind.

So I sat with glee, the only woman amongst all the lads studying for their mates' and masters' tickets, and completely disorganized the class. Fortunately, Captain Dobson was not only a very able teacher, he was also a very persistent and patient man. It was mostly due to him that in 1930 I adjusted the compass of my three-year-old aeroplane and flew round England at an average speed of 103 m.p.h. As the top speed of this aeroplane was only 105 m.p.h. and the King's Cup Race was on handicap, I came in first, much to everybody's astonishment, including my own. In fact, I couldn't believe it until a little cockney newsboy thrust a paper into my hand and remarked before departing without the customary payment:

"'Ere ye are, Miss, read all abart yerself for nuffink."

In the winter of 1937, I once again delved into Nories, the Nautical Almanac, and my latest treasures, the Admiralty Manual of Navigation, volumes 1 and 2. I could not understand volume 2, but it looked well and gave me a feeling of great superiority.

Not only had I to fit myself mentally to *Perula*, but bodily as well. I weighed fourteen stone! The maximum load figures of my aeroplane had had to be altered specially, and when I played hockey in a short gym tunic, small boys cheered wildly for the fat ladies' team. Once when staying in digs in London a maid asked me if I wanted "a penny or tu'penny bath." When I paused wondering whatever she meant, she looked at me again and added: "But I don't think a penny 'un 'ud cover you, mum!" Apparently it was a sort of slot-machine geyser.

All this, of course, has no connection with sailing, but it shows what the dinghy had to put up with, and it will be understood that there were various parts of my ship into which I could not penetrate. I therefore went on a diet, and when *Perula* was launched again I was the classical weight of ten stone.

Meanwhile Adams was deep in his "hints" on seamanship and various text books on diesel engines. Engine work was not entirely new to him, in fact, we both had a slight knowledge of petrol engines. At one time we spent some weeks in an engine shop at Croydon Aerodrome, and it had been a very instructive and profitable experience. The very first morning I learned a lot. One of my fellow workers, at the sight of my nice new white overalls, turned to his mate and remarked: "Gor blimey, Bill, she thinks she's in a bleeding bakery!" I was promptly sent off to dismantle an engine that had been buried in the Sahara Desert for two years. But I liked the engine shop. There were so many nice new shining connecting rods, valves . . . so useful for my own aeroplane.

On the 22nd April, 1937, we left Manchester in a state of bliss and a car so completely loaded with gear that we had to open the sunshine roof and let bits protrude. We were, of course, bound for Bangor and the launching, but a sad disappointment awaited us. The car, possibly with feelings of its own, broke down and altogether four policemen pushed us. It had, of course, chosen to break down in a place where the road was up and one-way traffic in operation. Even this condescension on the part of the law did not appease it, and we spent the day in a garage sending frantic telegrams to Mr. Dickie. The first ran: "Delayed," and the second:

"Load gear yourself." I said before he was an understanding gentleman, and when we arrived late that night *Perula's* gear was not only loaded, but she was afloat.

Of course, for some time we could not find where anything was and we would hunt for days, then discover the teapot in the sail locker. We did not care, we had our boat again and we were happy.

CHAPTER IV

VISITORS ABOARD

No sooner had we launched *Perula* for the season of 1937 than Adams's father was rushed to hospital for a serious operation and I was left alone in charge of the boat and the rest of the fitting out.

Even with the Gazelle to go to at night, the friendly sympathy of Dai, it is not very pleasant for a woman to be left alone on a yacht. Many necessary jobs, especially in rough weather, are quite beyond her physical strength. For hours I would struggle, trying to pull the dinghy up the jetty; I had learned this was by far the safest thing to do, even if only ashore for an hour or two. Getting aboard on a rough night was not easy. I used to discard all heavy clothing such as oilskins and sea boots, in case of accident. The treacherous tides in the Straits have accounted for more than one life.

Most of the men I mixed with were friendly and courteous, but some, naturally, misunderstood a woman who could walk into a bar, tell a doubtful story and stand a round of drinks. When I first joined the Lancashire Aero Club in 1926 I was told: "This is a man's game, Win, we don't want women. You can come, but you will have to be 'one of the blokes'." So "one of the blokes" I became, mixing with men, talking like men, and trying to take my drinks like a man. At a hot-pot supper I was completely at home; in a room full of women I was completely lost.

Nobody actually broke into *Perula* when I was aboard but there was an attempt one night. Although I had no fears on my own account, it would have made a frightful mess on the saloon carpet if I had used the axe with which I had armed myself.

I therefore indulged in an orgy of visitors and made the following discovery—visitors can usually be divided into three classes:

A.—Those who know all about the sea and say they don't.
B.—Those who know nothing about the sea but think they do.
C.—Those who know nothing and admit it.

Having sent your invitation and had it accepted you spend Wednesday and Thursday anxiously watching the barometer, and as your ship rolls her ports under, you groan: "Hope to goodness this south-westerly dies before the so-and-so's arrive."

In the meantime, of course, you are cleaning ship and hoping they won't notice that the sleeping bags have been slept in before.

Friday dawns—bright and sunny—thank Heaven! You clean the brasses and put out the companion ladder (you never use it yourself), take a hasty look at the "wine" cellar and decide if you had better buy a bottle—or if they might bring one. You then row ashore to meet your guests.

A yacht owner should immediately endeavour to classify the visitors. This may often be done when they drive up in their cars.

If Type A (those who know all about the sea and say they don't): They will have on old clothes and mackintoshes, their luggage will consist of a small case or parcel and include deck shoes and a bottle of whisky. They will get out, shake you quietly by the hand and say: "What about 'one for the dinghy' before we go aboard?"

If Type B (those who think they know all about the sea and don't): The man will probably leap from the car, wearing a brand new yachting cap and blazer with brass buttons (especially if he has come straight from the office). His wife will be clad in beach pyjamas embroidered with anchors and wearing high-heeled shoes. They will slap you vigorously on the back, inhale deeply and say: "Life on the ocean wave—what!—That's the stuff to give 'em."

If Type C (those who know nothing and admit it): A car will drive up, apparently unoccupied, then from beneath about fourteen rugs and twelve coats, several suitcases and four hot water bottles, your guests emerge. "We're terribly sorry," they say, "we didn't know what to bring, so we brought everything. We can, of course (this very apologetically) leave anything in the car that is not wanted." You take a hasty look and tell them to leave the lot!

If you have still failed to classify your visitors, the dinghy will provide the next opportunity. Type A will probably have walked ahead, unfastened the painter and have everything ready for you. Type B on the other hand, will exclaim: "The jolly old dinghy, what!" And with suitcase in either hand, take a flying leap into it. If he does not go through the bottom and sink it, his wife will step neatly on the gunwale and upset it. If by some means both these disasters are averted, the male guest will insist on taking the oars. You will spend the next half-hour doing a grand Indian paddling act, in pursuit of the oar he has dropped.

If the visitors are of type C, they will take a nervous look at the dinghy and say: "Have we really got to get into that little boat; are you sure it is quite safe?" "Yes," you reply, for you know they will do as you tell them.

Once aboard your yacht, A and C give no trouble. A knows what to do in any case, and C usually asks. Type B are "the thorns in the side."

When you have finished tea, Mrs. B insists on helping you to wash up, so you quickly rush away with the teapot before she can empty the leaves down the sink. On your return you find the sink overflowing with your precious fresh water. Meanwhile, Mr. B has seized the golden opportunity to put the lavatory completely out of action, in spite of the instructions you pinned to the door. When you decide to go ashore you find the dinghy has gone, Mr. B "having tied 'em up all his life."

Next day it is blowing fairly hard, the glass is falling and you decide to stay at moorings. Mr. B, however, "can't do with these fair weather sailors." He likes a bit of a chop: "Exhilarating, you know, Win, exhilarating!" He pesters you to death until you evilly agree to go out "just to show him."

He insists on helping with the sails, but whatever you do, this is important: Tell him the mainsail is torn and produce only your smallest canvas. I gave Mr. B a mizzen and staysail to play with, and when, in my best nautical language, I sang out: "Let go the sheets," Mr. B did! I spent the rest of the day, drenched with spray, trying to bring the flapping staysail inboard again, after which I returned to our moorings with Mr. and Mrs. B prostrate and rather a "messy" deck.

These are just general cases; there are, of course, special ones. The visitors, for example, who will bring small boys and girls. This usually occurs at springs when the tide is running at its strongest.

On asking your guests if they have seen anything of the dinghy, the wife smilingly informs you: "It's quite safe; little Albert wanted to play with it, he always has loved rowing boats." Two hours later, little Albert and the dinghy are brought back by the ferryman and it costs you at least five shillings. Meanwhile, little Gwendoline has been playing with the electric starter and flattened your batteries.

At last the week-end is over, and your visitors are leaving. This is a most dangerous moment, for in your relief you are apt to be off your guard. You and Mr. B are having a friendly last drink in the saloon while, quite unknown to you, Gwendoline and Albert are assisting their mother into the dinghy. Suddenly there is a piercing scream—you rush on deck to discover Mrs. B suspended in mid-air—her hands on the taffrail, her feet in a rapidly receding dinghy.

"Hang on, love! I'm coming," roars Mr. B.

He leaps to the rescue, catches his foot on the taffrail, turns a double somersault and arrives in the dinghy on the back of his neck. Fortunately, he takes Mrs. B with him but, unfortunately, he lands somewhat heavily upon Gwen and Albert. When the howling has subsided and it is found that no bones are broken, you carefully row your visitors ashore and thankfully congratulate yourself upon getting them safely on dry land. But while you are stowing the luggage into the car, little Gwendoline and Albert, who have, of course, been dressed in their best shore clothes, decide to indulge in a sliding match on the slimy jetty, with results that cause a large splash, followed by a faint on the part of Mrs. B, after which Gwen and Albert are driven away in tears and rugs, and their parents never speak to you again because, "of course, it was all your fault!" Instead of children, some visitors bring dogs. They arrive with profuse apologies and say: "We are terribly sorry, but there was really nowhere we could leave poor Fido; of course, Win, if you object to dogs, Fido could stay in the car, but the poor dear feels the cold so much, don't you, Fido, darling!" You take a hurried glance at Fido: he might be anything from an alsatian to a pomeranian, but whatever decision you come to, Fido will undoubtedly make himself felt. Suppose you say, as I did: "Why, certainly Fido must come aboard, I adore dogs." Then Fido, especially if large and possessing white hairs, will immediately reciprocate the devotion. As soon as you are comfortably seated in the saloon he will leap upon your knee, leaving hairs all over your best navy slacks and lick all the powder from your face.

When you are comfortably in your bunk that night, a timid knock will be heard on your cabin door and a voice will say: "I'm terribly sorry to disturb you, Win, but you know we can't row and er . . . well . . . er, Fido wants to go ashore for a minute." So you spend the week-end rowing Fido ashore at odd times of the day and night. The remarkable part is that if Fido is a nice dog you still adore him.

Suppose, however, you do not like the look of Fido in the first instance: the correct thing to say then is: "Of course, I'd love to have Fido aboard, but (here you pause and pat him lovingly) I heard only to-day of a dog dying after a night on board a yacht; the motion, you know; they can't stand it." If the proud owner replies: "Oh, but Fido just loves sailing and is quite used to it," then, of course, you have to be rude and Fido is escorted to the car with black looks.

You get your guests into the dinghy and have just got aboard, after a hard pull, when one of them says: " Oh, dear! I've forgotten to feed Fido." So you row back to the shore again. It is then discovered that Fido's food is of the tinned variety, and "How silly of me, Win—I've forgotten the tin opener, you'll just slip back to the yacht for one —won't you, dear?"

Then, of course, there is the visitor who will feed the seagulls; just after you have bought a catapult, an air gun, stuck spikes on the top of the masts, erected scarecrows, wire netting and finally discouraged them.

Normally I avert this catastrophe to some extent by saying: "Sorry this is all the bread we have and we are not allowed to throw bones in the Straits, you know; they choke the fish."

Amongst my visitors was the owner of a bakery and, naturally, he and his wife arrived with large quantities of bread: "Don't feed the seagulls, Margery," I implored, "they make such a mess on the deck". "You are heartless, Winifred," she replied. "Anybody can see the poor things are starving, and as for the mess, it will do you good to get up at 9.30 instead of 10 o'clock and clean it up." So out she would go with loaves under her arms and the seagulls came not only from the Straits but I'm sure from Liverpool and Holyhead as well. The air rang with their nasty shrieks and the skies darkened with flapping wings.

Margery had one pet seagull. She called it "Bold Willie": a great ugly brute with malevolent eye and enormous beak. "Bold Willie" had two parlour tricks; he would feed out of her hand, and he could hover above and catch about half a loaf in mid-air, swallowing it in one gulp. He was, indeed, a king amongst seagulls; Margery was very attached to him—until the day she left. She had just put on her shore clothes which included a new and very expensive jumper. "Just a minute, dear," she said. "I can't possibly go until I've said good-bye to 'Bold Willie'," and, with the remaining bread in her hand she went on deck. "Bold Willie" was there and, with a piercing shriek, he swooped down, snatching the bread from her hand and hovered greedily above waiting for more. There was no more, but "Bold Willie" was not to be trifled with. As she gazed tenderly up at him, his bloodshot eyes filled with hate and he brought forth a third "parlour trick."

"You know, Margery," I said consolingly as we tried to sponge the ruined jumper, "they do say that it's awfully lucky." She gave me a look not unlike that of "Bold Willie."

Two visitors came to spend Coronation Week with me; they were of type C and we got on very well. On the morning of the 12th May we dressed ship. We commenced a good two hours before anyone else because, of course, I had never dressed ship before, and I meant to make a good job of it.

"Well, Win," said Don, "where do we start?"

"Hush," I said. "The base, that's the deck, over the perpendicular, that's the mast, equals the co-tangent of the course."

"Good Heavens!" he exclaimed, "What are you doing?"

"Finding the hypotenuse," I replied darkly.

"What for?" he asked.

"To know how many flags to hang between the mast head and the stem," I replied.

"Well, I always thought," he said, entering into the spirit of the thing, "that the square of the hypotenuse..."

By the time we had finished discussing trigonometry, Len, the third member of the party, had put the flags up. "Oh, well," we said, "you haven't done it correctly, but they don't look so bad."

Then we turned our attention to the space between the two masts. This presented difficulties as Len had already used the flag halliards to put up the first lot. "It's no good," I said, "we'll have to start again and put them up all in a piece." Eventually the "chain" was completed; it was not as long as we had hoped, several of the flags having blown overboard. We fastened one end to the stem, the other to the stern, and the main and mizzen mast flag halliards were attached to appropriate points on the "chain." "Hoist away," I cried, and up went the flags. They only got about half-way when there was a horrible "ping" and down came the lot.

Some hours later *Perula* was still "undressed" so we just hung up the flags haphazard and sought consolation at the Gazelle.

We had missed the broadcast of the Coronation ceremony, but arrived in time to assist in the crowning of one of the fishermen, with the verge ring of a compass.

The party waxed lively and long, until Don said: "Don't know how you feel, Win, but I suggest a quiet evening aboard." So we obtained some "Nelson's Blood" and two lemons, and returned to *Perula.*

Shortly after midnight we were playing cards in the saloon, port curtains drawn and wireless playing, when I had a strange feeling that something was wrong. Without a word I got up in the middle of a game and rushed to the cockpit. "Don, Len," I called, "Come up. I think we are moving."

"Rubbish," said Don. "It's that boat there."

"Well," said Len, "if that boat is moving, so are two over here."

We were adrift and to make matters worse I did not know where we had got to. It took a little time to get my eyes accustomed to the darkness. One minute I would think we were going up the Straits and the next I was sure we were going down. "More boats," called Don, "masses of 'em, coming at us from astern."

"Don't be silly," I said, "they can't be," but they were. *Perula* was drifting, stern first and that explained why my landmarks were appearing wrong way round.

Next moment white shapes loomed up on all sides, I rushed into the wheelhouse, pressed the starter button and turned *Perula* for what I thought would be mid-stream. "An island ahead," yelled Len. I put the wheel hard over and shortly after Menai Bridge pier flashed by; in a few more seconds we would have been under the bridge and in the Swellies.

Somewhat shaken, but with our position ascertained, I turned back towards Glyn Garth, and also turned on the water for the engine, which had been forgotten in the heat of the moment, and tried to think. Don lit a cigarette and thrust it in my mouth; we had flown together in the old days and he was always calm and understanding.

I asked him if he could get the anchor ready. He said he would try but had no experience of such things. I then asked if he could take the wheel while I went to the anchor. He thought not: it was very dark and he did not know the Straits. I said: "If I go alongside Bangor pier, could you jump ashore and tie us up?" "Sure," he said, "I'll make a death-defying leap." He did; rather sooner than he expected. There were no lights on the pontoon at the end of the pier and we were towing a good portion of our mooring, making steering very difficult. It never occurred to me to haul it aboard. I arrived practically head on, with a crash that shook the pier and *Perula* to their very foundations.

Don shot through the air like a cannon ball and landed in a heap on the pontoon. Fortunately, most air pilots are experienced in descending violently to earth, so he got up, swore fluently, and made us fast.

My next visitor is deserving of the utmost sympathy. Never, under any circumstances, invite a real pukka sailor aboard a small yacht with a crew consisting of two women. It will simply drive him to suicide or a luny asylum.

Captain "Dash" had his Extra Master's Ticket and had commanded anything from 10,000 tons upward. He and his wife kindly arrived in response to a hectic message from my mother to take care of "poor dear defenceless Winifred."

The first snag was the dinghy. The Captain had always stepped ashore on to a quay, or at least from the gang plank of a tug or launch.

When he found he could not row the dinghy, he was exceedingly annoyed. He felt very keenly the indignity of what he called "being rowed by a damn woman" and used to practise every night when it was dark. Unfortunately, I had usually been out first and attached the bucket, so when he returned to give me my navigation lesson he was not feeling too pleased.

Since the days I had attended the Nautical Academy, I had become "all Admiralty". There is, of course, quite a difference between the Admiralty and Board of Trade text books, and a still greater difference between either of them and the practical navigation of a man who has spent some twenty years at sea.

"Referring to the equinoctial . . ." began the Captain.

"The celestial equator," I said with dignity.

"Equinoctial" roared the Captain, banging his fist on the table.

"Celestial equator," I yelled back. So it went on. He said "rational horizon"—I called it the "celestial hor-i-zon." He used the equation of time—I used "E." The only thing we really agreed upon was that the star Betelgeux was best pronounced "Bettle Juice."

I stuck firmly to the St. Hilaire or intercept method, as laid down in the Admiralty Manual and would have none of the frills or pieces taken away. That the Captain could work out a sight in a quarter the time I did, did not worry me. I knew the natural haversign formula by heart; it made me feel clever and I liked it. I also resorted to pieces of poetry, such as "longitude west, Greenwich time best," and stated that the intercept was "foggy" and therefore "from" if the observed zenith distance was greater than the calculated. All of which was a sheer abhorrence to a man who knew the whys and wherefores of such matters.

So we argued, quarrelled, cursed and swore, until the Captain said, in fury: "You go to one end of the blasted ship and I'll go to the other."

The close proximity of the water also worried him a good deal; he had never been quite so near it before. When he discovered there was only planking 1½ inches thick between him and the water, he liked it none the better.

During the day we did the fitting out work; renewing the running rigging, painting, varnishing, and so on. I had never expected the Captain to be a proficient bo'sun, it must have been years since he had done such work, yet he had forgotten nothing of his early training. He tried to teach me to splice, and he tried to teach me to paint correctly. Give a woman a paint brush and she promptly puts paint all over herself and perhaps a little on the thing she is painting. When she gets tired of a difficult part, she calmly leaves it and starts somewhere else. The Captain, used to smart workmanship and strict obedience, got more and more infuriated as *Perula* began to resemble a patchwork quilt.

Then came the day when we took her into Dickie's Dock. The Captain, used to standing on a bridge and giving orders, found he was merely talking to himself. "A fender to starboard," he called. No response. "Put out a fender on the starboard side," he said quietly and in an ominous tone.

"What is a fender, darling," asked his wife sweetly.

"Oh! One of those things," as he put it out himself "Hard astern," he ordered, but I couldn't hear him, being in the wheelhouse, and went gaily ahead. After the crash, the worst of it having been averted by prompt action on the part of the Captain, he called together his crew.

"Do you know what I am aboard this boat," he roared, "I'm a blasted one man band." Fortunately, his reason was saved by the arrival of a telegram recalling him to his ship.

Visitors in the shape of the Press are, of course, a sheer peril. News of our impending cruise to Norway leaked out and hordes of cheerful gentlemen, armed with note books and cameras descended upon *Perula.*

"Oh, good morning, Miss Brown, now about this cruise of yours, you'll let us have a few pictures for the 'Daily Shockem'. Now, let me see, Bill, what would be appropriate . . . . just stand over there, Miss Brown . . . no, that won't do, more action is what we want, eh, Bill. Just put the mainsail up, will you, Miss Brown? That's fine! Now just stand on that—boom, do you call it—leaning back against the sail. What do you say, Miss Brown? It wouldn't be done; we don't mind that, we want pictures. Hand her that telescope, Bill. Say, that looks fine! We'll have another of that. Now, what can you suggest, Miss Brown? Washing the deck? That would be swell, just slip below and put some shorts on. No, don't really spill the water on deck; might wet my feet. Now we'll have a storm picture; go and dress again, Miss Brown; you know; oilskins and sea-boots, and say, bring that sextant thing you look at the sun through. What? You would hardly be using it a hundred yards from shore? Don't you bother about that, it looks grand. Now for something really good. just climb up the mast, will you, Miss Brown? Sure, I'll pull you up on a bo'sun's chair. No, I won't let go the rope while you fetch it . . . . Sorry, Miss Brown, it just slipped out of my hand. Here, Bill, just shin up that mast and bring that rope down. That's fine. No, Miss Brown, I won't drop you . . . that's it . . . smile and wave . . . splendid! Now we'll have you working on the boat . . . some painting . . . that would be swell. No, varnishing the wheelhouse is far too tame, action is what we want. Bill, bring that bo'sun's chair, we'll hang it over the side of the yacht. Now, Miss Brown, on you get, I'll take it from the row boat. Pass her the paint and a brush, Bill. What? You paint that part on land? Forget it, Miss Brown, forget it. Looks swell, but just lean a little this way . . . a bit more . . . bit more. . . . Really, Miss Brown, you need not swear like that: how was I to know you'd fall in! What did you say, Miss Brown? Oh! . . . Well, come on, Bill, never inconvenience anybody. Good evening, Miss Brown."

CHAPTER V

COMPASSES TO OYSTERS

The Press reports caused some consternation at the Straits. To sail a 45-foot yawl to Norway was considered a handful for two experienced men: for a man and a woman who knew nothing, well! "Surely," people said, "you will take a skipper or at least experienced amateurs?"

I remained adamant. Adams and I were going to do it, and were going to do it alone; at least we would try. "Well, good-bye," they remarked sarcastically, "in case we don't see you again!"

By this time Adams's father was well on the road to recovery, so my "Chief Engineer," as I now called him, was able to slip down for odd days to help me. We seized on one of these occasions to indulge in a spot of compass adjusting. This added still further to the general opinion that "the woman was mad, quite mad."

Perula's compass is a joy to me, but a "blasted contraption" to many seafaring men. It is like my aircraft compass and has a movable verge ring, graduated in degrees, 0 to 360. There is no card, and only the cardinal points, north, south, east and west are indicated. To set a course you merely move the verge ring until the required number of degrees are opposite the lubber line; then turn your ship until the compass needle is between two grid lines which stretch across the verge ring and which are parallel with and on either side of its north and south markings. You have, of course, in the first instance to be careful that the red end of the needle corresponds with the north marking on the verge ring, otherwise you go in entirely the opposite direction.

To me it is much easier to steer by just having to keep a needle between and approximately parallel with two lines, and it saves having to write down the course in case you forget it. I think, especially at night, there is much less eye strain. In the air we always worked in degrees, and from true and not magnetic north, as so many yachtsmen do. We had to make large allowances for wind, the direction of which was given to us by the Meteorological Office as so many degrees true. Until we had estimated the effect of this we could not apply magnetic variation.

My compass, however, has three snags. Anybody accustomed to working in points does not understand it. To enter the tables you have to convert the circular notation to quadrantal. Lastly, the binnacle has no places to insert corrector magnets.

The previous season a compass adjustor had come down from Liverpool; he screwed three permanent magnets to various parts of the wheelhouse shelf and left it at that. In any case, I do not think the poor man liked me, for I had spent the days preceding his visit reading up magnetism in my Admiralty Manual, and was fairly bristling with coefficients A, B, C, D and E, components P, Q, R, and sundry "rods" from "a" to "k".

Of course, I knew very little about them, but to show my knowledge I recited whole passages from the Manual and leaped about *Perula*, indicating various parts of her anatomy as causing such and such a magnetism.

All this, coupled with my odd looking compass, was enough to put the most capable adjustor "off his stroke," and wonder why, if he was not aboard with a raving lunatic, he had been sent for in the first place.

This season, instead of paying five pounds for an adjustor, I rashly decided to expend the money on a pelorus and do the job myself. I had never adjusted a ship's compass before, and a nasty shock awaited me.

Adjusting an aircraft compass is simply child's play compared to a ship's compass. To start with, in the case of a light aeroplane you usually only correct for coefficients A, B and C. You fly, possibly to Croydon Aerodrome, and notify the Traffic Office you wish to adjust compass; you then sit in the machine in lordly state while several porters wheel it to the compass base and line it up, whereupon a mechanical contrivance arises from the ground and puts it in flying position.

"North," you call, in a superior tone.

"North, 'Erbert," yells one of the porters to his mate, who has disappeared into the bowels of the earth, and the entire base swings round to the required direction. You look at your compass, note the reading and call, this time in a slightly bored voice: "North-east, please." So it goes on. When you have obtained all the readings and worked out the coefficients you insert the necessary magnets into a nice little perforated box situated beneath the compass for that purpose. If you have not got a magnet that is fine enough, you cast one of the larger ones to earth with abandon, request the porter to pick it up, and hope the shock has caused it to lose some of its magnetism. If this fails, you break a bit off the magnet, nonchalantly throwing the unwanted part over your shoulder, and stick two bits of matchstalk on either end of the remaining piece. You must, however, do this with complete indifference, for the application of matchstalks is, strictly speaking, "not done," but it saves you hunting round for a suitable magnet.

Now, compare this highly dignified procedure with that of adjusting compass on a small yacht.

To start with, we could not find the fore and aft line, and wasted the first afternoon crawling about with tape measures and hanging up plumb bobs; which, of course, never stayed "plumb" owing to the motion of the boat. Finally, the pelorus was placed in a box on the wheelhouse roof and the box fixed in place by a bottle opener.

I had considered working from the sun, but by the time I had read up how to do it, the sun had sunk. I therefore decided to take eight bearings of Great Ormes Head, add them up, divide by eight and use the mean as the magnetic bearing from which to obtain my deviations. It was rather a blow to my dignity to resort to such a method, but I gathered from the book that it was near enough for practical purposes.

We were off Puffin Island, and *Perula* rolled about in a nasty swell. "North," I called with as much superiority as I could muster in my perilous and recumbent position on the wheelhouse roof I waited patiently for the ship to swing round and stay "put" like the aeroplane. Meanwhile Ormes Head danced about in a most disconcerting fashion. After a bit Adams put his head and shoulders out of the wheelhouse. "Haven't you got it yet?"

"Got it?" I replied with some indignation. "You haven't been on it yet."

He said he had; I said he hadn't, so we decided that he would call out when he was on, but I could not hear him call when he was at the wheel and by the time he had come to the cockpit to tell me, the compass was probably pointing in a totally different direction. If, by some miracle, she was still on the course, then some part of the boat completely obstructed my view.

We went back down the Straits at dark, not on speaking terms. The deck was littered with life belts, light screens, and various parts of the rigging which I had torn down in endeavours to sight my elusive distant object; and I was black and blue through rolling on or off the wheelhouse roof, nearly falling overboard and receiving several cracks on the head from the boom. Needless to say, the compass was not adjusted.

Next day we tried again, this time in the Straits, a perilous procedure for other yachts, as well as for the ferry and Bangor Pier. Ormes Head was again used, and as the water was still and *Perula* had been stripped of encumbrances, the first lot of readings were eventually obtained and the coefficients worked out, The magnets caused some difficulty; I only had the three left by the adjustor, big rods you could not possibly break bits off. Having spent some time boring various holes in the best teak, they were finally screwed home, and the deviations taken. They were not good: I had a maximum of 4½°, but blamed the magnetism of the ship and the lack of soft iron correctors, and Adams looked duly impressed.

The following week a visitor arrived and unscrewed the magnets to clean them, and as I now had so many screw holes in the wheelhouse shelf, the job of putting them back was fraught with complications. Strange though it may seem, this compass, without further adjustment, took us across the North Sea to Norway and back.

The question of charts had been worrying me for some weeks as I had never ordered charts extensively before. The usual paraphernalia from which one does order them had been sent to me. I sat in the saloon night after night, studying the lists and the various small maps, with their maze of lines and numbers. I tried to follow the lines, without much success; if I found a square I liked, the number did not appear to be on the list. After considerable difficulty I managed to order the charts I should want for Scotland and the North Sea, but Norway with its foreign names was completely beyond me, for I had not the slightest idea if I wanted to go from Batalden to Vaagsö, including Fröjsjöen, or not. In desperation I finally penned a letter to J. D. Potter. The first few pages concerned my life history, and somewhere towards the end, a brief announcement that I wished to sail to Norway, and as I did not know what charts I wanted, would they please send what they thought I ought to have? My "business" letters are always a sore point with Adams.

If by any chance a letter-head bears the instructions: "Communications must be addressed to the firm and not individual employees," I always begin my reply: "Dear Mr. So-and-So," and end up with "With very best wishes, yours sincerely," etc. I feel it gives a personal touch, and I really get very much better attention, especially with larger firms, for my reply (devoid, of course, of reference number) causes such consternation amongst the staff that it is finally taken to the managing director. Man has long been chivalrous to helpless women. Even the income tax inspector responded last year.

Two days after my epistle to J. D. Potter a very large parcel arrived. Stuck all over it were large red notices: "Urgent. Ship about to sail." I carried it proudly about the Gazelle for some time, so that everybody could see it, then took it aboard and opened it. I was still no wiser about the mass of charts it revealed, but extracted those of England and Scotland and put the rest away. Never trouble trouble until trouble troubles you.

We sailed on the evening of July 9th. Most of the day I had sat in the saloon drawing pictures of deep depressions. I started at 9.45 a.m. with the Air Ministry forecast: "Weather London calling" boomed out from the wireless receiver as I listened, pencil in hand, ready to take down the coming information. At 10.30 a.m. came the familiar "Good morning, everybody—here is the weather forecast for farmers and shipping . . . ." At 3.45 p.m., Weather London was again calling with a forecast for the next eight hours, and at 4.45 p.m. a further forecast for the next day.

If possible I always use these aviation forecasts in preference to the shipping, for they contain much more detail. They come through on 1,224 metres and, in addition to the three forecasts already mentioned, there are others at 7.45, 12.45 and 20.45 B.S.T. Reports of conditions at various stations, including a few continental, come through at 15 minutes past every hour from 8.15 until 00.15, but the last four reports are not issued on Saturdays or Sundays.

The weather was not good, and as each forecast came I added a warm or cold front or a couple of occlusions, until the saloon table was piled high with pieces of foolscap, and the two yachtsmen who had come to have tea with me were extremely impressed.

Meanwhile, Adams was in Manchester without the least idea he was sailing that night. I had decided to rush him off as soon as he arrived at the Straits, before he had time to think better of it. The plan worked splendidly. As he walked into the Gazelle and people started to bring him farewell drinks, I remarked casually: "We're sailing in half an hour," and he was led in a complete state of bewilderment like a lamb to the slaughter.

It was very definitely a dirty night. We should never have started, and as we walked down the jetty a friendly Scotch skipper said imploringly: "Girrlie, at least wait for the morning." But I was full of enthusiasm, very pigheaded, and would heed no one.

We left the Straits under power, and headed out to sea in the teeth of a strong north-westerly. We had foolishly decided to run on engine alone, and although our R.N. diesel carried us along admirably, sail would have steadied us. As it was, *Perula* was decidedly uncomfortable, and neither of us had the sense to rectify the matter.

At 23 hours, Adams turned in and I took my first four-hour watch. It was a new experience for me to be alone with the wind and sea at night. Ghostly white crests swept towards me, and spray beat on the wheelhouse like the crack of a whip. I was thoroughly frightened; once I thought of turning back, but it meant going down the Straits in the dark; everybody would say: "I told you so," and it takes a brave man to admit he is afraid.

From below came a succession of crashes as crockery flew from the rack and danced wildly about the saloon floor. My legs ached with bracing to the motion, my eyes ached with peering into the darkness and my head ached in sympathy.

On approaching Lynas I met all the Liverpool shipping. Green, red and white lights danced before my eyes. "Green to green, red to red, perfect safety, go ahead." But, at the critical moment, I got the poem mixed up and a huge black hull bore down on me. I turned the wheel frantically and shut my eyes. When I opened them again the danger had passed.

Large steamers always scare me at night. They sweep along ablaze with lights like great "road hogs" and apparently caring naught for a tiny yacht, even if it should have the right of way. Of course, you cannot really blame them; small yacht lights nearly on sea level are often difficult to spot from the bridge of a steamer, and anyway they have a schedule to keep and even a few minutes' delay might cause them to miss a tide and cost their owners a considerable amount of money.

My first watch dragged on miserably, and at times I was quite sure the clock had stopped. At last the sky started to turn a dull grey, and Adams appeared, a lump like a duck's egg on his temple. He had been thrown out of his bunk. Profiting by his misfortunes, I left my spring mattress severely alone, and with one of the root bunks sloping up to its topmost storm notch, I threw myself in it and slept solidly for four hours.

It was a gorgeous awakening. Overcast skies, dark heaving waters, and a wireless aerial that had decided to assist the log line. "Happened an hour ago," explained Adams, "but I didn't want to wake you." I thanked Heaven for an understanding partner.

At 9.45 a.m., temporary repairs having been effected, we tuned in to "Weather London." The forecast was not particularly cheering and I began to wonder what to do. Never sail with a woman in command, she is always changing her mind. I decided to put into Douglas. I decided not to put into Douglas. I decided to carry on to Scotland. I decided not to carry on to Scotland. I decided to make for Lough Strangford and the lee of the Irish Coast.

On arrival at the Lough entrance, however (with nothing but an Irish Sea general chart) the tide took matters out of my hands and decided for me. For a few minutes our boat remained stationary, then gently proceeded backwards. Cheered by this guiding hand on the part of Goddess Perula, I started to sing: "Where the Mountains of Mourne go down to the Sea." Adams just glared.

We changed course for Belfast; it meant going in at dark with only the aforesaid general chart, but we had now been 30 hours at sea.

It was pleasant in the lee of the Irish coast, calm water, blue skies tinged with pink and gold. "Red sails in the sunset," only ours were dirty white and they were not up yet, anyway. I sat in the cockpit eating new potatoes and peas out of a green enamel dish with a spoon, at peace with the world.

If at night you have not got a proper chart, always be bold and make for the largest port; it is sure to be lighted up like Piccadilly. Belfast was no exception, and all the way down the Lough lights winked at us and everything went splendidly until we came to anchor in Whitehouse Roads. The Sailing Directions mentioned oyster beds. Now Adams knew a man who had once anchored on an oyster bed and been heavily fined. It must have preyed on his mind, for every time I said we would drop anchor, he said: "Oysters." It was then 3 a.m., and after spending another hour going round in circles and arguing, I got fed up.

"You'll drop that blasted anchor," yelled the captain, all ladylike, "oysters or no bloody oysters." He did.

The battle was over.

Perula from mizzen (top) and masthead

CHAPTER VI

WRECKING THE CALEDONIAN CANAL

We left Belfast at 7.30 p.m. on the Sunday, in a series of zig-zags. The main halyard, which had been unshackled during the repairs to the wireless aerial, slipped from our grasp and Adams has to go aloft and rescue it. We must have presented an amusing spectacle as I alternately dashed from mast winch to wheel-house, trying to get him up and down and steer at the same time. (Yes, I know we should have shackled the halyard back hours before.)

With Black Head abeam it became obvious we were in for bad visibility, and in a flat calm we once again chugged along under power. "Maidens" refused to show up, and I had begun to doubt my ability as a compass adjustor, when the light appeared through the mist about half a mile on the port bow.

We had both decided to remain on watch, but the mist lifted slightly, so we decided to have two hours sleep each. I got mine but Adams was less fortunate. I had not been on watch long when, standing at the wheel, looking idly into the darkness, I suddenly blinked, stiffened, and looked again. Yes, there it was again, a red glow, that rose up and died out, a flare, out there in the mist. It could only mean one thing, a ship in distress. Poor devils, what had happened? Thank heavens I had seen them. I must tell Adams; we must hurry.

As I tore through the night in a frenzy of anxiety, the flares became brighter and more frequent. "They have seen us," I cried. "They have seen us; oh! how glad they'll be." It was while Adams, still half asleep, was below putting on the kettle and preparing blankets for my shipwrecked mariners, that I noticed a strange coincidence. Each appearance of the "flare" corresponded with a puff of my cigarette. "S.O.S.; save our souls," I groaned. "Nothing short of a miracle is going to save me when Adams finds out I've got him up to rescue a reflection on the wheelhouse window."

Everybody had done their best to cheer us up about the Mull of Kintyre. Just mention the Mull and immediately half a dozen people recall being almost wrecked—"laid flat by a terrific squall," "shipping it green," etc., etc. Perhaps we were fortunate; anyway, we rounded the Mull without knowing it. I chanced to look back. The clouds had lifted and there were two flashes on the starboard quarter and not a ripple on the water.

Scotland in a real Scotch mist. Still under power, we took the flood up to Oban. We were not drawn into the Corryvreckan, nor did the seven-knot tide at Fladda trouble us. Having so lightly disposed of three large bogeys, I became blasé and promptly got lost. (Moral: do not write letters at the wheel.) I had gone up the wrong side of Kerrera and had to approach Oban from the north instead of the south. It looked so bad when people asked us where we had come from.

The Sailing Directions spoke of red mooring buoys in Ardantrive Bay. We spotted a nice pillar-box red affair, and picked it up to find masses of wire, loops and strange rings. We wrestled with it, puzzled. Meanwhile the locals turned out to see the fun. "Are you sure it is all right?" I questioned. "People do seem to be staring at us." Adams admitted he had never seen anything quite like it before, but thought that perhaps Scotch buoys were like that.

To make sure, we launched the dinghy, and I rowed across to another yacht to consult the skipper. The conversation was not very successful; I could not understand his Scotch accent any more than he could understand my Lancashire one. I gathered that the moorings belonged to the *Sea Belle*, and she was not coming back that night, but all the same we were not to use the buoy. This rather annoyed me. I said rude things about Scotch hospitality, consigned the *Sea Belle* to a certain hot region and declared I intended to stay where I was. It was not until some time later that an enraged gentleman arrived and informed us we were on the Admiralty's best seaplane mooring and liable to a fine not exceeding one pound.

The next day was foggy. We hung about until 5 p.m., then got fed up and left for Fort William. At Corran Point the tide swept us into Loch Aber like an express train, and *Perula* turned and twisted in the whirlpools. As we sailed along in the half light, mountains rose up on either side of us in dark and rugged grandeur.

We did not know where to anchor at Fort William and had the usual argument. I always want to follow the Sailing Directions to the letter and anchor at least a mile from the town, in depths of some 20 fathoms. Adams makes rude remarks about me thinking I am the commander of the *Queen Mary* and we get very bad tempered with each other. When at last the spot is decided on, I either put *Perula* astern so violently that we are back in 20 fathoms before Adams can let go the anchor; or else I fail to go astern at all and the chain gets wound all round the anchor stock. So in either case we have to start all over again.

While we were still arguing where to drop, a large steam yacht came in and solved the problem for us. Even I agreed there would be enough water for us just inside her berth. Of course the first attempt was not successful, and while we were hauling up the anchor again, we drifted back and nearly hit the steam yacht, which caused some very superior-looking gentlemen to come out and glare at us. I gave them a disdainful glance as, of course, ships larger than your own are always to be looked down on.

On the whole, I was quite satisfied with our final anchorage; it was opposite a pillar box and a pub.

We liked Fort William; a friendly little town with good shops. I wished we could have stayed longer; climbed Ben Nevis, explored the Fort, the remains of Inverlochy Castle and the Nevis Distilleries. Time was short, though, and next morning we set off for the Caledonian Canal. Adams's foot looked as though he had gout; but the anchor chain had slipped off the winch and I had said "Tread on it." The canal forms a navigable channel between the western and eastern coasts of Scotland, and the route by it is some 350 miles shorter than that round the north coast, where navigation is intricate and weather often stormy.

I was scared stiff at the thought of the canal and when I saw it I was scared stiffer. We arrived at Corpach without the slightest idea of what one should do. Finally we dropped anchor while I went to enquire; for as Adams put it: "You are a woman and once they see how helpless you are they will do more to help us."

I found a door that said "Canal Office," but no one was in. Presently I unearthed a gentleman with long white whiskers, but every time I asked him anything he put his hand to his ear, and said, "Eh?" At last the lock keeper arrived and said he would wave when we might enter the sea lock, "But come in with plenty of way on" he advised, "the tide runs strongly across the entrance."

I returned aboard and waited for the agreed signal. When it came it was with a decided sinking feeling that I headed *Perula* for the narrow lock entrance. It was a horrible sight; two black gates, only about half open, and some 60 yards beyond them two more that were, of course, shut. It was the sight of these second gates that caused me to hesitate, and he who hesitates is lost. "Hell!" I thought, "I'll never stop," and I pulled back the throttle. The tide swung us round; I opened up again too late and charged the first gate with a resounding crash.

"Told you to come in with plenty of way on," said the aggrieved lock keeper, after it was discovered that neither the gate nor *Perula* were badly damaged.

It was a grand beginning and I was exceedingly shaken. The next few hours were sheer misery.

A narrow "pathway" of water with green fields on either side. It seemed all wrong for a boat to be in such a place, and if, as in my case, you could not control the boat properly to start with, it was terrifying beyond description. If I took my eyes off the water for one second, I ran into the bank. Every time I saw a lock or swing bridge I had a fresh fit. As in the 50 mile stretch from Corpach to Clachnaharry there are 29 locks and 10 swing bridges, I had 39 fits; not to mention those experienced on the approach of another vessel.

It was no joke, especially with a following wind, trying to keep *Perula* stationary in mid canal while a lock was being emptied or filled. I have since spoken to a yachtsman who told me he had a light kedge anchor which he threw out astern on these occasions. Of course, there are often stages or mooring posts on the bank, but if you value your paintwork, the kedge seems a better idea.

At Banavie came the second disaster. A swing bridge that didn't—at least not when I expected it was going to. With her engine roaring hard astern, and with considerable cursing from the bank, *Perula* came to a triumphant stand-still, broadside across the canal and, of course, I could not get her back. After I had hit everything there was to hit, the bridge opened. A train was due, but they apparently deemed it safer for the canal to keep the train waiting and let me through; and we proceeded into the eight consecutive locks. These locks are generally referred to as "Neptune's staircase." Before we were through, I had quite a different name for them.

The locks themselves are about 13 yards wide, but the entrance is considerably less. The lock keepers, on seeing a small yacht, either only opened one gate or half opened the two, leaving a clearance that seemed to me like the decimal point of an inch. You could not blame them; they were not to know my capabilities, and all the gates and sluices have to be operated by man power, assisted by the small children of the neighbourhood.

The question of warps had worried us. We had been advised to take four 15-fathom, three-inch warps, complete with heaving lines. Actually we used only two, and the heaving lines not at all. Unless you have paid hands, the lock keepers will not be bothered with more. Sometimes we found there was only one man waiting at the lock entrance. He would catch our after warp, make it fast, then come on for the for'ard one. I had to dash out of the wheelhouse to adjust the after warp, while Adams tended the other.

It is hard work going through the canal with a crew of two. During the 14 minutes you are in each lock, the warps must be constantly attended to, as the water bubbles and swirls about you. Just to make things really enjoyable, it usually rains. Although the regulations (of which there are at least 86) state that vessels "shall STOP their engines at the distance of a full 150 yards from the nearest lock gate," this apparently is not intended to be taken literally. We found we were far more popular with the lock keepers if we kept our engine running and did not ask to be warped through the locks. Fenders must be really strong, and a good siren is essential. We obtained a couple of old electric motor horns, mounted them in series on a loose block of wood, with a lead through the wheelhouse window. The noise they made was enough to waken the dead, yet the contraption was easily removed when not in use.

The canal twists and turns a good deal, and on approaching a dangerous bend, a "whistle board" will be seen on the bank. This was quite homelike and made me think I was back on a road as our motor horns shrieked forth in warning of our coming. In places there is one way traffic, and at every moment I expected to encounter a Belisha beacon, for the canal is, of course, controlled by the Ministry of Transport.

As the evening drew on, we began to wonder where we should spend the night, for navigation is not permitted after dark. In any case I thought it was quite bad enough in daylight. When the lock keeper at Gairlochy said he would find us a comfortable berth, I felt like kissing him, for by this time I was not only cold and wet through, but a nervous wreck. I should have remembered it was the thirteenth lock. He tied us up just outside. *Perula*'s bows were well and truly aground, and in order to go ashore we had to climb down a ladder into about two feet of water. However, as I pointed out to Adams, we were both so wet already that a bit more water didn't matter.

It was still pouring with rain when, with thoughts of a warm fire and cheery evening, we set off in search of the "loca1." Apparently there wasn't one, for all we found was a graveyard and Adams would insist on reading the inscriptions on all the graves.

Next morning we were told that another yacht was expected and we were to wait for it, making the rest of the passage together. This completely destroyed any scrap of confidence I had mustered during the night. "Heavens!" I groaned, "two of us in those awful locks, and its sure to be the steam yacht with the glaring gentlemen."

It proved to be a small motor boat, but my new found relief quickly vanished. It tore through the canal with an abandon that shook me to the core, arrived at the next lock about half an hour before we did, and looked extremely annoyed at being kept waiting. I tried to follow at the same speed, but we rounded a bend at about 7 knots to find a swing bridge closed against us. The motor boat simply ran into the bank without the slightest concern, one of the crew leaping ashore with a warp. "Beastly little thing," I muttered, having eventually extracted *Perula* from a most frightful mess. "It can wait for us after this, I shall deliberately dawdle."

We were now at the highest level of the canal. To quote the Sailing Directions, "about 100 feet above high water ordinary neap tides." I prayed that going "down hill" would not be worse.

Loch Oich, with its maze of islands and shoals, certainly caused me to dawdle, and I went into the next lock prepared to glare at the waiting motor boat more fiercely than before, if only in self defence. The unexpected happened. One of the crew walked across and bade me a polite good morning. "I'd ha spoken afore th' noo," he remarked, "but fa your blue ensign." I felt rather flattered at what I took to be such nice respect, but apparently owners that fly the red ensign do not think much of those that fly the blue. He eventually forgave me that fact, however, and suggested a "wee drappie," producing a bottle from one of his pockets. Before the day was out we discovered that he and his friend had a bottle in every conceivable pocket.

We were now firm friends, so we, too, tore through the canal with reckless abandon. Apparently the idea was to reach Inverness in a day. In spite of the "wee drappies". we did not see the Loch Ness monster, but the Ness Weir caused me some nasty moments. I had not had time to read the directions, that "a vessel after passing Dochfour Lodge pier should keep towards the north-western bank, so as to avoid being drawn into the Ness Weir." That night *Perula* and the motor boat were safely tied up together in Muirtown Basin, and a supper was held to celebrate.

While in Muirtown the authorities like owners to walk down to Clachnaharry and pay the canal dues, as this saves congestion in the sea lock. The dues in our case were five pounds (no charge being made for damage to the canal). Adams was delighted to be in Inverness, as it is his birth-place. The town is only a short bus drive from Muirtown Basin, and we spent the following morning stocking ship for the North Sea crossing. The shopkeepers were very charming and obliging, and altogether I thoroughly enjoyed the atmosphere of this friendly old Scottish town.

In the afternoon we called at the Customs House and, I fear, caused rather an upset. I had not realised I could have cleared outwards at the Straits, nor had I any idea what papers I should or should not have. Fortunately, I had paid my light dues, as the receipt seems to be the first thing a British Customs Officer asks for. If you can produce this and have no bonded stores, he will probably lose interest and tell you that they "don't bother much with small yachts clearing outwards." In fact, I gathered I could proceed to Norway, or anywhere else I liked, without any further trouble.

This was a great disappointment; the procedure lacked dignity, and besides I knew the value placed in foreign countries on a lot of official documents. "Of course, you can clear correctly if you want to," said the official. It is always best to be correct; so I was duly handed over some forms and told to fill them in.

The first I came to was No. 7 (Sale), Master's Declaration, outwards in ballast, so I went back to the counter to enquire who the master was. After some debate, I was promoted to this high office. I was also puzzled who my broker was and how many passengers and crew I had; poor Adams could not be everything. Always resist the temptation to make facetious answers; the forms cost sixpence per quire of 48. Finally, my efforts were torn up and the official behind the counter filled up No. 7 (Sale) for me.

Next I came to No. 35 (Sale), Victualling Bill; it must be produced at the time of clearance outwards, in duplicate. It starts with spirits, skips through beverages, alcoholic and otherwise; delves deeply in tobacco (Negro Head and other sorts); groceries in general; paints, varnish and dutiable oils. The official said I must fill it up in detail, so after some deep study, I tapped politely on the counter and enquired: "Can you please inform me what percentage of a hundredweight half a pound of coffee is?"

Put as half a pound," said the official, with a nasty look.

The paint caused considerable argument, as I put down all the different colours we had, and they only required a rough statement of total quantities. The form was torn up and I had to pay another penny.

The question of oil annoyed me intensely. I had been told I could get rebate on any we took out, but apparently *Perula* was under a certain tonnage and this did not apply, although we should have to pay duty on any we brought in. This I thought was very unfair, and told the official so, at great length. I believe I could have put in a special claim, but it would probably have meant filling up more forms, and I had quite enough forms already, for the thoughtful official had provided me with those we should require for "clearing inwards" as well, doubtless hoping I might have achieved the feat by the time I returned, two months later.

Of course, this visit to the Custom House did not end matters. A Customs Officer also visited us aboard. Finally, a clearance card and label were attached to the afore-mentioned Victualling Bill, signed by the oflicer, and we were apparently ready to depart "correctly."

Next, I sat down deep in thought, trying to word a suitable telegram to "Weather, London," and the following was finally decided upon: "Desire to cross North Sea small yacht kindly wire forecast when weather favourable." What "Weather London" thought about this enlightening request, I don't know; but the reply arrived that evening, much to the excitement of the kind postmistress at Muirtown, who had spent the entire day taking in parcels for us and bringing us letters. I think the forecast was: "Southerly winds moderate sea."

I remember feeling rather grieved they had used so little of the pre-paid reply. Anyway it sounded all right, so we made a large stew and prepared to sail at dawn. The stew was, of course, to be warmed up on the passage, and we carefully skimmed off the grease, in case we should feel sea-sick.

There is something awe-inspiring about waiting to start one's first long sea passage; especially when the cabin light has been turned out and you lie in the darkness and think. I thought of a good many things that night in Muirtown. Next morning we would sail out of Moray Firth, bound for a destination over 300 miles away. At the best it would take three or four days; yet my aeroplane would have taken me across in three hours. Still, I thought, it is a hell of a lot of water for an aeroplane. I remembered the time an engine had cut-out on me over the Irish Sea, and decided a yacht was much safer. Yet again, it was also a hell of a lot of water for a small yacht, especially with a crew on the threshold of their second season. I began to wish we had a wireless transmitting set; something that would make us feel a little less alone; some means of asking for help if— "Silly idiot," I said to myself, "what could happen, it is summer, we don't have storms. . . ." Storms! Horrible thought. I remembered crossing the Atlantic; mountainous waves towering above the decks of an ocean liner; passengers battened down below, some wearing life-belts. If the sea could do that to 15,000 tons, what could it do to *Perula*'s meagre 26 tons?

"Oh! Hell," I groaned, "I wish I'd never started."

CHAPTER VII

THE NORTH SEA

The morning of 17th July, 1937 dawned bright and sunny; gone were my fears of the night, replaced by a feeling of adventure. At 8.50 a.m. we proceeded into the sea lock, in a state of great excitement, and were passed out into Beauly basin at the south western end of Inverness Firth.

The passage through the Firth looks rather alarming on the chart, and while you are in the sea lock, local fishermen will probably tell you some harrowing tales of the banks and shoals that await you. We experienced no difficulty; it was round about high-water and we took the south eastern channel, passing between Chanonry Point and Port George, into the north channel and the Moray Firth.

At 10.59 a.m. the lightbuoy marking the north eastern extremity of Riff Bank was abeam. We streamed the log and set course for Utsira; the latter part not being so simple as it seems. I discovered I had ordered charts that did not meet. However, with that time-worn aid to trigonometry "Pat has brought his pigs back," I remembered "pigs back" stood for perpendicular over base and equalled the tangent of the course; which I found from the longitudes, latitudes and the difference of meridional parts.

We made everything fast on deck, rigged up life-lines and promised each other (very solemnly) that no matter how calm it was, neither of us would go out on deck unless the other was at hand. Even with our lack of experience we realised that "man overboard" was a possibility we had to face, and a very unpleasant possibility with a crew of only two.

With Covesea on the starboard bow, I took a four-point bearing and estimated our position when abeam as two miles off. Adams considered this rather a waste of time and accused me of having done it purposely to avoid washing up. Navigators are always so misunderstood.

Shortly after 5 o'clock we hoisted the main and staysail. It meant heading 10° north of our course, for the wind was south-east-by-east and did not veer until later. The sea may have been moderate for an ocean liner, but it soon became obvious we were in for a tossing. Spray flew over *Perula* as we sailed along, averaging, with the help of a spot of engine, some six knots.

That evening, rather to my astonishment, I managed to check the deviation of the compass by the sun, using azimuth tables and my pelorus.

Of course, I did not know how to do it, but the azimuth tables told me. Admittedly, my shadow-pin was a trifle bent, but I was very pleased with the result, as it agreed with the deviation I had obtained in the Straits. As the Scotch coast began to fade into the darkness, I turned round and had a good look at it; not with any pangs of regret, but merely so that I should know what it looked like when we came back. On leaving a port or anchorage I always make copious notes and draw several pretty pictures on the back of my chart, so that I may be able to identify it on return.

At 10 p.m. Adams turned in. Shortly after the wind veered to south-east, about force 6, so I stopped the engine, not, I fear, out of any wish to enjoy the sound of the wind and waves, but to listen to the dance-music on the wireless. We have a special shelf and plug in the wheelhouse that enables the loudspeaker to be brought up there. In spite of *Perula's* small sail area, she knocked up a good 5 knots, and an hour later, the wind having veered to south, I put her back on her course.

It is a queer feeling being alone on a night watch, to all intents and purposes, in the middle of the ocean. The sea looked completely desolate; not a sign of land; not a ship in sight. I began to wonder what I could do to pass the time. I looked at the log for the tenth time, worked out how far we had probably come, and when we would be halfway there. I opened the tin of biscuits we always keep in the wheelhouse, munched a few and washed them down with hot coffee from the thermos. I usually make a point of feeding like this every half-hour, as it gives me something to look forward to.

Adams and I found these long hours at the wheel gave us a fearful pain in the neck, both literally and metaphorically speaking. I have felt it in a car, and think it is through sitting with the arms stretched forward; for we had a small stool fixed at the wheel. I found the last hour particularly irksome, and began to doubt my wisdom in selecting the first watch. At the time it had seemed better to stay up until 2 a.m. instead of having to arise at that hour. I could then sleep until 6 o'clock and get up in daylight.

By the time we had got the shipping-forecast, had supper, washed up, and put out the navigation lights, it was often well after 10 o'clock before Adams turned in. In consequence, I usually had to stay up until 3 o'clock. When I relieved him four hours later, he would nip off for another sleep, while I tried to pull myself together in readiness for the morning sight.

On the Sunday morning we started the engine again. There was still a decidedly fresh breeze, but engine combined with sails gave us an extra knot or two, and as our Diesel only used five-eighths of a gallon per hour, it seemed worth it.

This I know is "not done." One should breathe God's fresh air and be free of noise; but we had a long way to go and there were only two of us. If we could save a third night at sea, so much the better; and as for the noise, well, when you have spent ten years of your life behind an aeroplane engine, you do not notice any noise—unless the note of the engine changes.

Soon after 7 o'c1ock I started thinking about my morning sight and unearthed my books and my sextant. I intended to get the sun on the prime vertical. I had no practical experience with a sextant, although I had previously carried one about for some years. My father bought it for me about fourth-hand, thinking I might experiment with it in the air. There was hardly any silver left on the horizon glass and the microscope was badly cracked. Otherwise, it was a very handsome instrument and quite good enough for me possibly to drop from 10,000 feet. I never took it up with me, for sextants are not much good in a light aeroplane; nor was mine much good to me on this occasion, for, like "Wind-bag the Sailor," I obtained a position line in the vicinity of Birmingham.

Time after time I checked and re-checked my working, only to discover that Adams, still half asleep, had misread our deck watch by a mere ten minutes.

At noon I tried again, and was all set to get the sun on the meridian, when a large wave knocked me for six. Down I went, cutting my ankle on the wheelhouse door. The moment had passed. I sat up and gave way to tears of rage and pain.

"Never mind," said Adams consolingly. "Norway is a big place; we'll hit it somewhere."

I gave him a dirty look and limped below to bind my wound. During the afternoon, much to my delight I managed to obtain our position from a running fix of the sun.

During the day we split the watches into one hour on and one hour off. I soon found out there was no "off." Apart from my navigation difficulties, there was the question of food. We had wisely, I think, decided on at least two hot meals a day. We started with porridge for breakfast; meat for lunch; toast (I would want this) and cakes for tea; hot vegetables and a sweet for supper. Sounds a bit odd, but it is, of course, my "diet."

Adams had gone on it as well, so as to save trouble! As I insist on most of my food being steamed, Adams spent many of his "hours off" holding large tiers of pans on the stove.

That night on watch my ankle pained me a good deal, so I hit on the splendid idea of lying on the wheelhouse settee, an alarm clock under one ear, in case I dozed off. I couldn't see the compass, but by watching the stars I could tell if we were keeping our course.

I shall never forget that night on the North Sea. It was at the time of the anxiety for Amelia Earhart, the American airwoman, and her crew, who were presumed down in the Pacific. For days ships had been searching in response to wireless messages said to have been broadcast from her machine. I was lying there, half asleep, when the news came over the wireless that the search had been abandoned. As I looked out over the lonely stretch of water around me, I wondered if somewhere on the Pacific, another woman was doing the same. If she was, I hoped she had been spared the words that I had just heard.

When, at midnight, Big Ben boomed out, my thoughts turned to the lonely people all over the world, who were listening as I was to this link with home. I looked out to the north-west, to that faint pink glow, still visible on the horizon. "Norway," I thought, "Norway and the land of the midnight sun." So Saturday passed, Sunday passed, and Monday dawned. *Perula*'s saloon was in a decided mess; seas had swept her deck and some of the water had found its way below; bedding, charts, etc., were somewhat damp. At 9 a.m. we sighted land. Of course, we had thought we had seen it hours before; one always does swear these banked up clouds on the horizon are mountains. This time, however, there was no mistake; mountains did loom up from behind a blue haze, and as we got nearer, strange dancing shapes appeared on the water beneath them; the outlying islands and skerries.

Adams was tremendously excited, but I was far too busy wondering if it was Norway, and if so, what part. I am terribly bad at picking up landmarks; to me a coast line looks all the same. For hours I read the descriptions in the Sailing Directions, look for mountains like saddles and hills like haystacks, but my imagination is such that every mountain looks like a saddle and haystacks appear in one continuous chain.

Utsira is, fortunately, easy to pick up, and before long we spotted the island, about 2 miles on the port bow. This was, indeed, an excellent landfall, and although I bragged about it publicly, I had to admit secretly that it was just as well I did forget to allow for our first tack to nor'ard, for I had also forgotten to allow for the decrease in magnetic variation . . . however, all's well that ends well!

I rummaged among my charts and finally discovered one that referred to Haugesund. When I examined it I had a fit; narrow tortuous channels winding between a maze of islands, rocks on every side.

To make matters worse the Norwegian system of buoyage was entirely different to our own. Amongst other things they go in for "staffs"; red ones, black ones, striped ones and green ones (for wrecks). "Black marks," I read, "are used (1) on the north side of a detached shoal; (2) on the east or south side of a channel, according to whether the general direction of the channel is nearest north-south or east-west respectively. Red marks are used (1) on the south side of a detached shoal, (2) on the west or north side of a channel, according to whether the general direction of the channel is nearest north-south or east-west respectively. A black mark with a white band is used on the west side of a detached shoal. A red mark with a white band is used on the east side of a detached shoal. A red and black horizontally striped mark, is used to mark a shoal which has a channel on both sides of it. Staffs are usually short and thick, red staffs having a blunt top and black staffs having a a pointed; in certain places, however, especially inner harbour areas, long thin staffs are used, and in such cases the blunt and the pointed tops cannot be distinguished."

Thank you very much, I thought; that is all very helpful!

Actually when you get down to the fact that anything red is kept to the north and west and anything black to the south and east, no matter whether you are arriving, departing, or going around in circles, the Norwegian system becomes simplicity itself and is, I think, preferable to our own. It would not do, however, for our Sailing Directions to speak such direct language; we might begrudge paying ten shillings for them.

With all the staffs dancing before my eyes like a nightmare, and various diagrams on the wheelhouse shelf, showing their relative positions in regard to shoals and channel, I, fearfully, headed *Perula* in towards Haugesund.

Adams, who had decided to lower the sails in good time and give us one thing less to worry about, made the horrible discovery that the staysail had jammed and would not come down. "Oh! dear, what shall we do?" I groaned, on being informed of this calamity. There was no time to do anything; we were not only in the thick of staffs, but other ships as well.

At the sight of our British flag they bore down on us with cheers of welcome. "Tell them to go away," I shrieked in panic, but the Norwegians are nothing if not hospitable. Haugesund was not a yachting centre, like Bergen and fjords further up the coast. Our arrival was in the nature of a sensation, both to us and to them as well.

I made a triumphant entry, swept round the right-angle bend into the narrow Smedsund, took one horrified look at all the shipping, and charged the quayside, complete with flapping staysail and devoid, of course, of quarantine flag.

The Norwegians did not mind a bit; crowds rushed to the quayside, seized our warps and tied us up. When they discovered the two of us had brought *Perula* from Scotland in 56 hours I was hailed "Dame Captain."

In the midst of all this excitement the Harbour Master pushed his way through the crowd.

"You can't have that up here," he remarked in English, as he indicated the still-flapping staysail with some annoyance.

I apologised profusely, explaining that it was jammed and that Adams would go aloft immediately to free it. "Don't you want to see my papers?" I added, in some disappointment, with memories of my battle with the Customs at Inverness.

"No," he replied; then as an afterthought, "Where are you from?"

"Scotland," I said, innocently, with visions of the "Q" flag that should have been flying. He gave me one long and reproachful look.

"You have even come foreign," he groaned, and departed hastily in the direction of the Customs House.

I was busy hauling Adams up the mast in the bo'sun's chair, when a nice Norwegian gentleman, evidently thinking it all wrong for a woman to do such work, leaped aboard, pushed me aside and seized the winch handle. Adams shot aloft like a rocket and there remained, amidst the cheers and applause of the whole town, for he was quite unable to make the kind Norwegian gentleman understand when he wanted to come down.

Meanwhile, I had gone below to interview the Customs; one after another they arrived until our tiny saloon was packed. They were all very charming and polite; rather too polite for my shattered nerves. There is not head-room in the saloon, and like all foreigners they would keep clicking their heels together and bowing, and, of course, at the beginning and end of each bow, they bumped their heads.

The Harbour Master finally realised that we needed rest, and having rescued Adams, suggested we should move to the other side of the Channel. "But," he added, severely, "I warn you there will be charges."

With the aid of some small children, *Perula* was moored between two of the immense red buoys that line the western side of Smedsund. The small children, unlike our own, would not accept any payment for their services. All they wanted was to sit on our boat and dangle their feet over the side. They came at any hour of the day or night they felt inclined; climbed aboard and made themselves at home; sometimes men came too, they never bothered us, just had a good look round and departed. To them it was quite a natural thing to do.

It was very peaceful moored there in Smedsund, after the battering of the North Sea. I suddenly discovered my cut ankle was the size of a balloon, so, being a woman, I spent a most enjoyable couple of hours, reclining on the saloon settee, while poor Adams alternately applied cold water bandages and brought me cups of tea. At length I decided I was well enough to go ashore and telegraph our safe arrival to my mother. This matter, however, was full of complications. As soon as I stepped ashore the ground rose up to meet me and continued to rock more violently than the North Sea. As Adams had not got his "landlegs" either, we proceeded to the Telegraph Office like two drunken people.

We had, of course, omitted to bring any Norwegian money, and by this time the banks were shut. At great length and with many gesticulations, we managed to make clear the message we wished to send. Then came an awkward moment; at the sight of our English money, the lady behind the counter shook her head. I drew harrowing pictures of my heartbroken parents awaiting news of their beloved daughter, until at last her heart softened and she sent the telegram "on tick." Adams, who is very strict in these matters, insisted on leaving a deposit of a ten-shilling note in an envelope, so I had to call next day to pay for my telegram and retrieve the note.

That night as I lay in my bunk, enjoying the comfort of my spring mattress without the fear of being thrown violently out of it, I kept drawing the port-hole curtain and looking out at the lights of the town, just to make sure it was Norway and we had really got there. It did seem rather difficult to believe.

"North Wales to Norway," I thought, "in just under ten days, and now I can go to sleep, not just for four miserable hours:

I can go to sleep for as long as I like." I did, for twelve solid hours.

CHAPTER VIII

THE "ENGINEERS"

A famous traveller once said that no matter what part of the world you visit, there is always its counterpart in the British Isles. When I woke in Haugesund next morning I thought I was back in Manchester. It rained, rained, then rained some more. All the same it was very attractive, as we stood in the wheelhouse and took our first real look at our surroundings. We were in a narrow "avenue" of water, bounded on one side by Risöy, along the shores of which rose up quaint wooden buildings. Red, blue, green and yellow warehouses, so dilapidated that at any moment I expected them to collapse and topple like a house of cards on the many small boats moored beneath. They had gabled roofs from which large pulleys hoisted anything from a cask to a boat into the top storey, which tilted further and further over the water as the load went up. On the other side of Smedsund was the town, rising up from the quayside, with the usual shops and hotels. Cafés lined the waterfront. In the channel itself, one way traffic was compulsory for vessels above a certain tonnage. With the deep boom of sirens, steamers of all nationalities would sweep round the bend, pausing at the quay to unload cargoes of coal, coke or salt, and reload casks of herring, herring oil and flour.

We went ashore with the intention of doing some shopping. The thought of this caused me no particular apprehension. We had been in a good many foreign countries and it never occurred to me that this occasion would be any different. I forgot that before there had always been somebody, an hotel proprietor, a ship's purser, or even the proverbial gentleman from Cook's, to aid British travellers; also that we had never had to buy all our own food before. The shopkeepers could not understand what we wanted. In the grocery store I was compelled to go behind the counter and help myself. Feeling a perfect fool, I weighed potatoes, butter, biscuits, etc., while crowds gathered watching me, with a strange but polite interest.

My goods piled on the counter, I trustingly put down all my money (one can safely do things like that in Norway), and the shop assistant helped herself to the correct amount. Then came a real set-back. As I tried to pick up my parcels, she snatched them from me. I put the money down again, but she shook her head. "Perhaps," said Adams, after deep contemplation, "she wants to send them." Here was another problem. I seized a paper bag, drew a picture of *Perula*, and pointed to the water; errand boys were called and we set off in a grand procession, joined by a policeman.

Shortly before 1 o'clock, completely exhausted, we sought lunch in one of the hotels. As we seated ourselves in the dining-room, I thought the waitresses looked rather astonished, but put it down to my navy trousers and cigarette; they were causing something of a stir in Haugesund, where women are still rather old-fashioned.

After we had waited patiently for some time the manageress arrived and explained with difficulty that 2 o'clock was the earliest time we could obtain food. The Norwegians have their largest meal of the day at this hour. "Never mind," I said cheerfully, "we'll go into the lounge and have a few cocktails while we are waiting." But cocktails were a new one on the lady. "Gin and things," I explained; but ginger beer was the nearest she got. It was some days before we discovered that spirits cannot be bought in Norway, except in two or three of the larger towns; even then they usually have to be obtained by the bottle from special shops.

We wandered wearily back to the quayside, where we drank some very weak beer in one of the cafés and ate the usual continental snacks; slices of bread with smoked salmon or eggs and anchovy on top. Later we found an attractive cake shop. Both Adams and I have a weakness for cream cakes, so after much pointing and holding up of fingers, we returned in triumph to *Perula* to have tea. Adams bit small pieces out of five cakes and remarked mournfully: "Slice of bread and jam, please!" We were not to know the Norwegians consider sour cream a great delicacy.

That night we returned to our café. The whole water-front was ablaze with coloured lights that reflected gaily in the waters of Smedsund. We expected to find the usual things one finds in cafés that line busy waterfronts. Crowds of cheery people, music, a cabaret perhaps. We found a few men sitting quietly drinking cups of coffee or glasses of milk, then back to work they would go. A clean-living, hard-working people. The women, I thought, had a particularly thin time. They rarely seemed to accompany their menfolk, being content to remain in the background and tend their wants. In Haugesund I never saw a woman who used powder or lipstick, nor did I see one that smoked. Needless to say, I was regarded with a mixture of awe, wonder and horror, and my title of "Dame Captain" became more firmly established.

One evening we attached the outboard motor to the dinghy, loaded a can of petrol, and set off to explore the waters in the vicinity. We had thought of taking *Perula*, but in view of our limited experience we considered it would be safer for her if we took the dinghy. At the south end of Smedsund we came across a thing I have never seen before; a house built entirely of packing cases. They were piled, one on top of the other, even to a gable shaped roof. It was a most extraordinary sight and I was dying to go inside, but Adams would not go and ask permission, which I thought was very stupid, although, of course, I would not go myself.

Every time we saw the harbour master he reminded us severely of the charges we owed, but when finally an official arrived to collect them, they only amounted to one kroner; the equivalent of one shilling. In spite of our misdoings, I think the harbour master liked us; for every time we suggested leaving, he pointed to the sky and shook his head. Admittedly, the barometer was low, but after three days had passed and still the gale had not arrived, we became I suspicious and left anyway.

We proceeded northward through the Indreled; the channels twist and turn between the mainland and the many islands and skerries that practically line the west coast. It was not so disconcerting as I had expected from the chart, for I was getting the hang of the staffs, perches and beacons, many of which were even provided with arms, showing you on which side to pass.

For a few miles, whilst traversing Sletta, we were exposed to the open sea, but the weather was good and we turned into Bömmelfjord, the entrance to Hardangerfjord, without experiencing any difficulties. This was our first real glimpse of Norway. A sky, blue beyond description, white fleecy clouds mingling with snow-capped mountains, a sun so hot that it was almost painful to walk the deck in bare feet. I lay aft on a cushion, my feet up against the mizzen mast, and marvelled at the beauty of the Norwegian scenery, as *Perula* threaded her way between grey rocky islands, patched with the dull green of pine trees.

As the afternoon got warmer and warmer, Adams, in desperation, shed everything but shorts and vest; he then went below to oil the engine and put his bare shoulder on the exhaust pipe, whereupon there followed a series of ejaculations even warmer than the weather.

As we turned out of Kvindherredsfjord and proceeded down the bottle-neck entrance of Storsund, sheer walls of rock towered up. It takes a bit of getting used to, sailing so close to mountains that you can lean over the side of your ship and touch their rocky sides. In Norway this is often possible, for the more precipitous the mountain the more perpendicular it will descend deep down beneath the water.

Often waterfalls tumbled down a mountain side, almost on top of us. They were indescribably lovely; some, the crashing roaring variety, racing down amid clouds of spray; others mere films of water that fell slowly from rock to rock, giving the impression of a gauzy veil. Engineers estimate that thirteen million horse power could be obtained from Norway's waterfalls, but so far only about three million horse power has been piped and harnessed for use.

The evening was even more perfect than the day had been. The colourings of a Norwegian sunset are, I think, the most beautiful I have seen. I was just about to wax poetic, when a series of metallic sounds rent the air. "Hell!" I said, "it's the engine." We looked at each other in dismay. We were in a foreign country, seemingly miles from anywhere, and something had gone wrong with the engine. "Better anchor and stop it," I said. "Anchor in 90 fathoms?" groaned Adams. "We've only got 30 fathoms of chain."

Most of the fjords are, of course, deeper than the open sea outside them, and 90 fathoms was comparatively shallow. The Sognefjord reaches a depth of 680 fathoms.

Fortunately we discovered we were not far from the small village of Rosendal, situated in the eastern part of Storsund, and one of the few places where the green fields slope, between walls of rock, to a sandy or pebbly beach. In such places a river often flows into the fjord and although the holding ground is usually none too good, the anchorages are shallow.

The engine took us to Rosendal nobly, for were the truth known, we were cheerfully using an unsuitable lubricating oil, but we did not discover this until we got back to England.

Having dropped anchor, north-west of the jetty in 8 fathoms, we reviewed the situation. "It's a piston," I said, although I had not the slightest knowledge of a Diesel engine, so we promptly got out the handbook and started to pull the engine to pieces. The dance music came and went. Big Ben boomed out, the saloon carpet was covered with pieces of engine and still we had not discovered the cause of the trouble.

"We'll put it together again," said Adams. "You never know—it might go."

It did go, it also made the most horrible sounds and dense clouds of smoke poured out. The chief engineer looked a bit disconcerted and I, womanlike, remarked: "You've made it worse."

"Give it a burst of throttle," he said. "That will clear it."

I went obediently to the throttle and pulled it down. Nothing happened. "Fuel!" I exclaimed in triumph. "I've found the trouble."

While we were checking the fuel system we found a rather extraordinary thing. A brass nut on a T piece of the main feed pipe had sheered clean in two. As this portion of the pipe was beneath the floor boards, we were quite lucky to find it, for as yet the resulting leak had not reached serious proportions. This, however, did not solve our problem, and the only thing left that we had not taken to pieces was the fuel pump.

"The book says we are not to touch it," I announced. Adams gave me a superior look and proceeded to unscrew a nut, whereupon a spring leaped out, like a jack-in-the-box, straight into the wheelhouse.

"I told you the book said . . ." I began.

"Shut up," he snarled. "Can't you see I've enough on my hands?"

I returned with dignity to the saloon, and switched on the wireless; it was playing "Rhapsody in blue."

Next morning Adams said to me: "I've been thinking about that engine, Win. Do you remember when we took the inlet valve cages out and I told you we must be very careful to put them back the same way?"

"Yes," I said.

"Well," he continued, "it was awfully late when we put them back and we were very tired . . . . "

"Hell's Bells," I ejaculated. "We've put them back wrong way up." We had, and incidentally closed the ports.

It was whilst we were rectifying this "little oversight" that we found the bent push rod. I had overlooked it before in my hunt for something deeper. A valve had gummed up, due to the oil, the push rod had jumped its socket, causing the metallic cracks, and then, somewhat bent, had slipped back into place.

Of course we had omitted to bring a spare push rod, and as it would take some time for spares to be sent out to us, we decided to telegraph the engine makers, asking them to forward these to Bergen, and in the meantime, get the damaged parts patched up.

The patching being beyond our capabilities, we sought help ashore.

This proved a very undignified procedure. We spent most of the morning walking miserably around the village, brandishing the push rod and fuel pipe, and periodically shouting, "Anybody speak English?" Apparently nobody did. We eventually found a blacksmith's shop, a gloomy looking shed with a smouldering charcoal fire. Two men were at work and looked up as we entered. "Speak English?" asked Adams. The smith shook his head and burst forth in his own language. "Push rod," said Adams, bobbing it up and down, whilst I went "Chug, chug, chug," in what I thought was a very realistic impression of a Diesel engine in action. "Bent," said Adams, pointing to the rod, then doubling himself up in illustration. The Smith smiled sympathetically; possibly thinking Adams had tummy ache. "You," said Adams, pointing to him, "Straighten," the latter remark being accompanied by the action of standing stiffly to attention.

The blacksmith gave a cry of triumph, seized the push rod and cast it into the fire. I was quite sure he did not realise what it was, and the sight of it sizzling in the flames was too much for me. I was about to leap to the rescue when Adams gave me a restraining kick.

The little blacksmith certainly knew his job; he pulled the rod out of the fire, with his bare fingers, hammered it into shape and gave it back to us as good as new.

The fuel pipe was more difficult, but after the smith had given a masterful performance, depicting the passage of a steamer to Bergen and back, we gathered that this part would have to be sent away to be repaired.

We could have been stuck in far worse places, for Rosendal was a very picturesque little village and popular with the Norwegians as a holiday resort. Sun-bronzed boys and girls paddled brightly coloured canoes over the smooth blue waters, beneath the shadow of purple mountains. Others swam out to *Perula*, looking in at us through the portholes, with smiling wet faces. Ashore it might have been England in spring, green meadows, lanes, overshadowed by leafy trees, buttercups, and meadowsweet in the hedgerows.

Amongst other things we received a free and very enlightening education by the courtesy of Herr Hitler. Norway is a popular cruising ground for German liners. As they swept into Storsund, a system of loud speakers called the passengers on deck. Up they would flock in such numbers that the ship seemed to take a perceptible list to the side on which they thronged. When they were all assembled a guttural voice boomed out, describing the beauties of the fjord and the places of interest. So loud was the voice that aboard *Perula* we could hear every word. When the lesson was finished the passengers dispersed again. I suppose it is a very good idea, but to us somewhat disconcerting to have the peace and quiet rudely shattered in this manner.

I was told later that the German government organise these cruises at a very cheap rate on account of their educational and health value, but the German ships did not seem to be very popular with the Norwegians. The passengers are apparently only allowed to spend about ten marks ashore during the entire cruise, which is rather hard on the shop and hotel keepers, who often have a very short season in which to make their profits. Still, I believe that at one time the Germans were not allowed to spend anything ashore, and if they wished to send home a picture postcard of Norway, they had to buy one from their ship that had been printed in Germany.

One day a French yacht came in and anchored beside us, a ketch of some 40 tons. One of her crew of four dived overboard and swam across to have a word with me. "North sea, it is terrible," he said in broken English. "Our sail it is torn and we is all sick." Apparently they had reached Norway about the same time as we had, so the weather must have been worse further south.

When we went to collect our engine parts we were embarrassed to find the blacksmith would accept no payment. Adams held out a handful of money, but the man waved it aside good naturedly and shook his head. If it had been the push rod alone, it would not have been so bad, but the fuel pipe had been sent specially to Bergen and we felt we must give something. There was an awkward pause; then Adams, with sudden inspiration, drank an imaginary glass of beer. A light gleamed in the smith's eye: "Whisky?" he whispered rather like a naughty schoolboy. We nodded. He pointed to *Perula*, held up eight fingers and gave way to gleeful chuckles.

At 8 p.m. Adams and I stood in the cockpit awaiting our guest. There had been some heavy rain storms and a magnificent rainbow joined the mountain peaks. We watched a small boat put off from the jetty and make, with some hesitation, towards us. In it were three Norwegians attired in their Sunday best; the smith had brought his two mates to support him.

It was the funniest party I have ever given. Neither Adams nor I could say a word to our guests, but I think they enjoyed themselves, for some hours later three Norwegians were seen rowing a very zig-zag course for the shore, the remains of our whisky in their pockets.

At Sundal

CHAPTER IX

FJORDS AND INDRELED

On July 28th we left for Sundal in Maurangerfjord. The crew of the French boat had told us there was a fine glacier, and as it was only 15 miles to the north-east, we decided to risk our lack of engine spares for the additional distance, before proceeding to Bergen.

We left Rosendal at 9.10 a.m. and I notice from my log book that we arrived shortly after midnight, but I think I must have meant noon!

We went on deck with the glasses and they revealed a hotel (thank goodness), a shop (that will be useful), and some black and white circles, painted on the rocks (oh! heck). I knew such circles existed, but had been dreading the day I should find them. Situated at the water's edge to the west of the village, they looked rather like targets, and had been painted there, in accordance with the Norwegian custom, to mark a mooring post or ring and a safe anchorage.

To me, anchoring was quite bad enough by itself without having to perform the manoeuvre so that a stern warp could be made fast ashore. Not having much idea of the correct procedure, we paused some distance off one of the targets to take soundings. This was quite unsuccessful, as until you get right inshore the depths to this inlet exceeded 100 fathoms. I took *Perula* a little nearer with no better result. "You'll have to go closer," said Adams; but I looked at the evil looking rocks and floating weed, and flatly refused.

It would not have been so bad if I had had a decent chart. Potters had sent me the best available Admiralty charts, but they appeared to cater for large vessels. In the Indreled, British charts were quite all right, being of a larger scale, but in the fjords themselves I often found myself, as on this occasion, with little better than a general chart from which to work. Certainly many of these small scale charts had insets of the anchorages at the main tourist centres, but these were often at the fjord head, over 100 miles inland. For the cruising steamers that went there direct, up the wide and usually easy navigable waters of the main fjord, the charts were sufficient. For a small yacht that wished to linger by the wayside, they were not so good. I wanted to know what the bottom was like beforehand; not having yet reached the blissful state when I could go charging up to rocks, sounding my way, until our ship was almost touching the beastly things.

So we drifted up and down Maurangerfjord wondering what to do and looking like a couple of fools. The latter fact must have been observed by the Norwegian owner of a small motor boat, for he very kindly hastened to our rescue. Under his guidance we dropped anchor about 30 yards from the rocks. A stern warp was then taken ashore to the mooring post near the target and hauled on until the anchor gripped on the steeply shelving bottom and the stern was only a few feet from the rocks.

Considerably relieved that the anchoring problem had been settled, we invited our new friend below, quite forgetting that our wine cellar was by now sadly depleted. However, I mixed a cocktail with the dregs of several bottles, some apricot juice and a dash of Eno's to "give it life" and counteract the effects.

The Norwegian was greatly impressed with this "English" drink, and insisted on our visiting his boat to sample Norwegian hospitality.

The motor boat had a large saloon (practically the full length of the boat) and the stability of a rowing skiff, yet he and his girl friend had brought it all the way from Bergen. They are great sailors, the Norwegians, and I really think they would go to sea in anything. Hanging in the saloon were pieces of what looked to me like mouldy hams. They were, in fact, bits of sun-dried lamb. You just hack lumps off as you feel inclined and eat them with your fingers. The meat had a pleasant taste, not unlike smoked ham, and was accompanied by freshly boiled salmon, straight from the river, and sundry beverages, including the Norwegian spirit; Aquavit, and the many sweet liqueurs they indulge in.

Back aboard *Perula*, we decided a swim would revive us. We had noticed the water was a most extraordinary colour; a kind of milky blue-green, but without giving it a second thought we dived in. We were certainly "revived"; the milky-green colour denoted glacier water.

That afternoon we set off along the glacier trail; a narrow pathway, winding between birch trees, along the banks of a small stream. In the valley were immense boulders of rock; very nice and picturesque until you realise they have crashed down from the mountains so close above you. You then seek consolation in the fact that it is summer, for most of them came down during the avalanches of the spring thaw. Small cream-coloured ponies trotted up to inspect us. These stocky little animals are typical of West Norway and quite unlike the larger horses of the eastern areas.

All around us we could hear the tinkle of bells tied to the necks of cattle grazing on the grassy slopes. It was very hot walking in the sun and we stopped to rest and inspect some odd looking wires that led up the mountain side. I thought they were telegraph cables and Adams said they were not. The argument was settled when great bundles of wood came shooting down them. They were transport lines, and later we saw many more of them being put to various uses.

We rounded a bend to find our way blocked by four mountain goats. They tossed their heads in rage and glared at us. The goats may have been small, but their horns were not, so we stopped and eyed them with some respect. "When in doubt, feed the brutes," I said, taking some chocolate from the pocket of my shorts. Next moment I was a mass of smelly goats. Then started a grand procession, myself, Adams and four goats. Every few minutes the head goat made a bleating sound, and if I did not stop and give it more chocolate, it butted Adams in the seat of his pants.

Icy blasts of wind now chilled us, in spite of the heat from the sun. Suddenly we stopped, spellbound. Ahead was a small lake, set like a jewel in the surrounding mountains, and at the far side a gigantic mass of blue ice. Cleft and rugged, it swept 5,000 feet down the mountain side from the icefields above. We climbed down to the shores of the lake, to find the water a mass of dead flies. This was annoying, for it had been a stiff walk and I would have liked to bathe my aching feet. Still, as Adams said, Bondhusbreen was a magnificent sight and well worth the journey we had made to reach it.

On July 29th we stood in the wheelhouse and took our first look at Bergen. A city bathed in golden sunshine, situated along the shores of two bays, and encompassed by seven lofty hills. Founded by King Olav in the year 1070, it is to-day the second city in Norway. An important commercial and shipping centre, essentially modern, yet still retaining much of its ancient charm.

All this we knew from the Guide Book, but where to anchor we did not know. We studied the Sailing Directions. We could go into Florvaag, but this was the quarantine anchorage. We could go into Puddefjord, but this was generally used by men-of-war ("the Harbour Master will himself attend on board the flagship"). Small vessels not exceeding a draught of 5½ feet could warp into Store Lungegaardsvand and the Harbour Master (who must be an exceedingly busy man) would open the swing bridge; but I had had quite enough of swing bridges.

Of course there were such places as Vaagen where "the frequent movements of the merchant shipping and crowded state of the harbour, render it inconvenient for vessels to berth there, unless they require to work cargo, or land and embark passengers." If we went there I presume the Harbour Master would inform us to "get to Hell out of it," but the book, of course, did not say this.

Meanwhile a constant stream of shipping wound its way in and out, and around us. Finally, we made a wild dash into Puddefjord, it being the nearest. There were no men-of-war at the top end, but this did not stop us getting into a frightful mess with various steamers, sundry ferries, a number of fishing craft and a few dozen rowing boats.

"Yachts," said Adams suddenly, "moored on the port side". This was good news, until I saw the yachts. There were dozens of them, moored in neat rows, with not the space "to swing a cat" between, and any buoys that were vacant appeared to be in the very centre.

Fortunately the boatman of the Bergen Yacht Club spotted our ensign, rowed out to our assistance and moored *Perula* in the midst of her Norwegian cousins. He spoke splendid English and conveyed to us the welcome of the Club and an invitation to make free use of the club house. We congratulated ourselves on the lucky chance that had brought us down Puddefjord. After interviewing the customs, who had called to inspect the usual sealed envelope yacht owners must carry about in Norway, we hastened to take advantage of our invitation to visit the Yacht Club. "Better posh ourselves up," I said to Adams. "There may be a bit of a party."

Seated on the charming club house balcony we watched the sunset; in solitary state. "Where are the members?" I asked the boatman-cum-steward as he brought our beer. Apparently they preferred to be in their boats, often sailing far into the morning; then home they would go, without even "one for the road." Rather different from our English clubs, where it is usually the discussion of the day's sail that goes far into the morning! Can it be that the Norwegians "do" while we just "talk"? They are certainly an outdoor people, with a deep and simple love for the sea; but half the knowledge in life comes from listening to the experiences of others, and half the fun from recounting your own.

It was strange to wear city clothes again, especially when they had gone somewhat mouldy. I felt thoroughly awkward and uncomfortable, and Adams looked no better, when next morning, armed with shopping list, we set off for the town. There were cosmopolitan crowds; smart women, fine hotels, boulevard cafés, gay with wicker chairs and sun umbrellas. Parks abounded with roses, the streets had "Belisha beacons", but no traffic lights. The shops delighted me; seal-skin slippers, magnificent furs. The bank cashed my cheque without reference (awfully trusting, they had not done it in Scotland).

My arithmetic is always bad, but it could hardly account for the fact that in every shop I gave too little money in payment for my goods. We discovered that almost every article is taxed, and this is automatically added to the bill by the shop assistant.

Food was cheap for, owing to the extensive daylight in summer, fruit and vegetables grow with incredible rapidity. Even in latitude 70° North, hay is made one month after the snow leaves the ground. A three pound salmon cost me 1s. 6d., but don't order peas in a restaurant, not unless you are prepared to eat "pods an' all."

Collecting the engine spares proved a difficult matter. On visiting the Harbour Master to obtain our mail (another job for the poor man), we found the usual "slip" that means a visit to the Post Office. I have had a lot of these official- looking slips. I never know what they say, but they usually mean trouble. We took this one to the Post Office, after the usual difficulty in finding the place, and having shown it to various people and been sent to various departments, which we also could not find, the parcel of spares was produced. I picked it up and walked out.

I was hastily brought back and taken before the Customs, (who looked at me with great suspicion, and waited to pounce as I opened the parcel beneath their eagle eyes. The result was rather a blow to them.

"What are they?" an officer asked, holding up four rather rusty push rods.

"No duty," said another in disgust.

So I picked up my parcel and walked out. Once again I was hastily brought back and for a long time I could not make out why. Apparently a new employee at the engine works had, by mistake, sent the parcel "cash on delivery"; not having any idea of the value of the contents, he had made a rough guess of about £2. Hence the disappointment of the Customs Officers.

"Two pounds for four miserable push rods?" I stormed. "I refuse to pay." And there I stood like the Rock of Gibraltar, whilst the harassed officials held consultations. At length, the Post Office, having been completely disorganised and various forms filled in, I walked out in triumph, complete with the rods, and having paid nothing. In the afternoon we went up Flöien to recover. In the space of a few minutes the funicular whisked us up 1,000 feet, during which time we caused considerable alarm and broke all the regulations, in attempts to get spectacular photographs of the ascent. I had previously received a telegram asking me to write for an English newpaper, so poor Adams was appointed my chief camera man, and as such, I ordered him into the most perilous positions in the name of the Press.

Having reached the top safely, we were more or less thrown off the funicular and stood admiring the view before us. It certainly was grand. Crystal clear air, tinged with the scent of pine, soft springy turf, ablaze with purple heather. We looked down on the town, the blue water and, "Oo look—that white speck is *Perula*." Mile after mile there stretched before us a panorama of fjords, islands and mountains. Many Norwegian towns have these mountain retreats, where the people may escape from the heat and rush of the busy streets and offices.

In the cool of the evening scores of people came up; some to wander between the pine trees and watch the sun set, others to patronise the restaurant, where dancing was usually in progress. We chose the restaurant. Girls in national costume served us, and it was all very attractive until I suddenly started to shiver; a dampness seemed to penetrate my bones. I knew what it was, for I had felt it hundreds of times when flying; the clouds had descended on Flöien. We might have been in a London "pea souper" as we groped our way back to the funicular.

While in Bergen we took the opportunity of visiting one of the "special shops" and restocking *Perula*'s wine cellar. We had to queue up in line, give the order at one counter, pay at the next, and finally obtain our parcel at a third. We were horrified to discover that genuine "Scotch" cost about 15 kroner (over 15s. per bottle). Local whisky could, however, be obtained cheaper. Well known brands of gin also worked out expensive, but my "mother's ruin" problem was solved by an understanding gentleman who winked and whispered "Golden Cock," which was about 6 kroner a bottle.

At 9.55 a.m. on August 1st, we sailed for Aalesund, a passage of about 170 miles, through to Indreled. We had decided to push on to our most northerly point and linger on the way back; as in this way we thought we would be better rested for the return North Sea crossing.

We had looked forward to some sailing, for in the fjords themselves there was little point in using sail, owing to the squally and uncertain winds from the mountains. As usual we fell back on power. Strong head winds cut down our speed. It was quite rough and as spray flew over us, the strong sunlight turned it into dancing rainbows.

By 8.25 p.m. we had only covered 41 miles and were both fed up, so we sought anchorage in Napsvaag. It was a small creek off Undelandsund, and we might have been the only people in the world; not a sign of human habitation. "Gosh!" I remarked, "what an August Bank Holiday." Rather different to the crowds at Brighton or Blackpool. We anchored at the lower end of the creek.

There were targets, but we did not bother with a shore warp as the bottom did not appear to shelve. It would have meant lowering the dinghy, and the smell of roast chicken from the galley claimed our full attention.

We left next morning at 7.15 and by noon we were in Krakhelle sound. I had feared the worst when I saw the name on the chart, and we had not proceeded far before there was a crack; exactly like the last syllable minus the "e." The engine was again rebelling about the oil, but we did not put the valve cage back upside down and were soon on our way again. By 9.10 p.m. we had covered 75 miles and decided to anchor at Skavöy. There were mooring rings on the north side of the island, and as the channel seemed fairly busy, Adams thought we had better put out a shore warp. It took him at least an hour to persuade me to go sufficiently near, so that all our warps joined together would eventually reach to the target.

It really needs considerable judgment to drop anchor so that your ship will be the right distance from the mooring post. I was usually either too far away, and the knots joining our warps gave way, or else too near and the stern of the boat nearly hit the rocks. I have not decided yet if it is best to charge the target stern first, or whether to go up with it on your beam. A lot, of course, depends on the wind and tide. We adopted the first method and forgot the tide was running fairly strongly. In consequence the anchor did not go down in the right place, and before we could lower the dinghy, the stern had swung round at right angles to the target. We lowered the dingy and endeavoured to pull the stern back towards the shore. I took the oars while Adams sat aft, letting out the warp. We had almost reached the target when we came to the end of the warp. I pulled until my hands were blistered, but *Perula* flatly refused to be dragged round against the tide. So in the end we said, "Blow the shore warp," and left her as she was, riding to anchor alone. Nothing is more annoying than to have pulled your boat round, after much sweating and straining, only to discover you have misjudged the distance and the warp is about a fathom too short. You claw frantically at the rocks, knowing that if you can only get on them, you will be able to pull the boat round more easily; but if you don't fall in, and the warp does not slip from your grasp, a gust of wind will probably carry the stern back to where you started and you and the dinghy will go back with it.

We were under way again by 7.20 next morning. It looked like being a glorious day; then quite suddenly, a wall of fog appeared ahead.

"Ron," I called, "come up."

"Can't," replied a voice from the galley, "my porridge will burn."

By the time I had explained the situation and told him what I thought about him and his porridge, the fog had closed in on us.

At first I thought it was early morning mist, that would clear in a few minutes, but it grew steadily worse and I became more and more agitated. Fog is bad enough in open water, but in a passage from Ulvesund to Aalesund it is perfectly b—. Fortunately, I had worked out my compass courses the previous night, but the look of the chart had been so hair-raising that I had worked out three different routes before I was satisfied.

We had to pick up a channel barely a hundred yards wide, marked by two poles, and on either side a mass of submerged rocks. It was now Adams's turn at the wheel, so I sat for'ard in oilskins, straining my eyes into the fog, until I imagined I saw rods, poles and perches on all sides. At last I really did spot a pole, and spent some hectic moments wondering if it was red or black, for if we went on the wrong side we should be on the rocks. My problem was solved by the appearance of the second pole; we were dead between them, right on our course. Thoroughly cheered, I returned to the wheelhouse and started to sing the popular song of the moment, "I lost my dog in a thick, thick fog"; but Adams never appreciates my musical efforts.

We were now heading for Stadtlandet, exposed to the open sea. Even so, the wretched place was lousy with rocks and white breaking water would suddenly loom up through the fog. We duly picked up a whistle buoy that didn't, and continued round the headland. Here I had intended to take the fjord passage, but deemed it safer to keep to the open water, in spite of the rocks that still haunted us. I started to sing about the dog again and had just reached the part: "and at half-past two when the moon broke through," when it did; or rather, in our case, it was the sun.

Washing day at Romsdalfjord and *Perula* under Seven Sisters, Geiranger

Gudvangen, Naeröfjord (top) and Florö

CHAPTER X

MAINLY ABOUT ANCHORAGES

Aalesund is the centre of the western bank cod fisheries, and we arrived with the fleet: sturdy little boats, slightly larger than *Perula*, with wheelhouse a good 8 feet high, situated aft. They reminded me of Paris taxis, for their diesel engines, often single cylinder, all chugged in exactly the same manner and clouds of smoke puffed from funnel exhausts of the stovepipe variety. They charged at us from every side, cutting across our bows and making me a nervous wreck.

We tried the little harbour on the north side of the town, to find codfish everywhere. We got out, after much shouting and some very nasty moments, and beat a hasty retreat to Aspevaag on the south side. This was very much bigger and far more reassuring, and we eventually tied up to a nice red buoy, N.N.E. of the beacon situated in the centre of this natural haven. The buoy was littered with fishbones, but was large enough to hold a liner. "At last!" we said, "a night's sleep free from worry."

At 1.30 a.m. we woke to hear the noise of an engine, followed by a bump. We dashed out with fenders. At 2.45 a.m. came another engine and another bump. The fishing fleet evidently shared our idea of a comfortable place to tie up, and before dawn poor little *Perula* looked like the ham in a railway sandwich.

On August 5th we went on to Molde, a distance of some 35 miles, anchoring east of the town in 10 fathoms. The Norwegians speak very highly of the beauties of Molde, which is often called "Town of Roses." It is pleasantly situated on a wooded hillside, overlooking Moldefjord, and commands a magnificent view of the mountain ranges—Dovrefjellene and Langfjellene, or long mountains. Perhaps we ourselves were feeling mouldy (pardon the pun!) but we left next afternoon for Aandalsnes.

I must have had mixed experiences there for my log book states: "Good anchorage east of town, 5 fathoms, don't go too close to shore, it dries, take bus up Trollstig, worth seeing; don't go mountaineering."

We had not been at Aandalsnes long before the Arandora Star arrived and all the prices in the shops were doubled. "Look here," Adams would exclaim, in some heat, "we aren't off that big boat, we're off that little one," and the prices, as if by magic, returned to normal.

I do not blame the Norwegians for trying to make on cruise ships. I fear at times I felt heartily ashamed of my fellow countrymen and women.

Many seemed to think they had "bought the town" and acted accordingly. We spent a miserable day being mistaken for "loca1 sights" by the Arandoraites, and for "Pleasure Cruisers" by the Norwegians.

It was while we were ashore that we saw attractive postcards of mountain peaks, abounding with glaciers. Next day, when the "big boat" had gone, we bought one of the postcards and walked around the town showing it to people and looking enquiring. After several people had tried to hire us cars that were beyond our means, we found a bus. It was the new mountain transport from Aandalsnes to Valldal, but we only knew that the bus driver had nodded his head at the sight of our postcard.

It was all delightfully uncertain, riding on that Norwegian bus, without the slightest idea where we were going, or if we would ever get back. We set off along a pleasant valley, then started to climb. The wooded country was replaced by stark jagged rock, and something rather like a piece of tape appeared to zig-zag up the face of a sheer precipice. It was, of course, the road we were going up. This road, winding in twelve hair-raising curves up the side of Bishop Mountain, was completed in 1936, and is considered one of the marvels of modern engineering. The hairpin bends turned me hot and cold. Could we get round? No. The bus driver was naturally taking the climb with as much speed as possible, and with shrieking brakes the bus would skid to a standstill on the brink of a precipice, to reverse and try again. I tried to console myself by thinking that the driver possibly had a wife and family and wanted to live. At one point, near the top, the road crossed a raging waterfall, which sent showers of spray through the sunshine roof and caused an American lady to put up an umbrella, which she poked in everybody's eye.

Having paused to allow the American gentleman to take a photograph of the "cute little Fall," the bus at length came to a standstill at the top of a marvellous plateau. Adams and I got out. The American was very envious and said he would give a thousand dollars to do likewise. I, with an eye on the main chance, was all for accepting and sailing him round to Valldal next day in *Perula*. Adams, possibly with memories of our last American visitors, dragged me from temptation.

We decided to climb the "King," a majestic peak, rising behind the weather-beaten face of the Bishop. We were wearing rubber deck shoes and had none of the ropes, ice pick, etc., that one takes mountaineering.

As we got higher, the wind became stronger, and the ascent more difficult. Sheer walls of rock—I don't know how I got up them. But all went well until I looked back. The road seemed miles below; I lost my nerve completely and stopped. Adams swore at me and I swore at myself, but I could neither go on nor back.

"You blithering idiot," he groaned. "What good is it doing you, hanging there to a wretched bit of fern?"

I had to admit it was doing me no good at all, but I clutched my fern with renewed vigour, as the wind howled and shrieked about me.

I have often been 10,000 feet in the air and thought nothing of it, yet here I was not half that height and in a sheer panic. They say it is contact with the earth that makes the difference. I know famous pilots who dare not look down from Blackpool Tower.

Adams gave me a cigarette and did all he could to make me move. Then it began to rain, beastly driving stuff that cut our hands and faces and soaked us to the skin. I saw a huge blanket of grey rolling towards us, blotting everything out. If the clouds reached us, we should never get down. Spurred to action, I started the descent sitting down. Inch by inch I lowered myself. Adams was furious; said I would break my neck, but I dared not stand up and turn round. The clouds got nearer, and in desperation I endeavoured to take a short cut over some ice. I remember letting out a frightful howl . . . but everything happens for the best; if my foot had not slipped, I might still be up the mountain.

As Adams escorted a very tearful and bedraggled yachts-woman (with perceptibly less seat to her pants) back along the road, the clouds enveloped us completely. Fortunately, we found a tourist hut, where we drank hot coffee, until the bus came, on its return journey. After a nightmare descent, with visibility only a few yards, we eventually reached *Perula*, where the log book entry, "Don't go mountaineering" was made with much fervour.

From Aandalsnes we went back to Aalesund, and then left for Geiranger, the fjord famous for its waterfalls. The "Seven Sisters" or "Bridal Veil." We left Aalesund via Borgundfjord, Humlesund and Vegsund. The Sailing Directions referred to it as "a channel available for small vessels with local knowledge," and added that "Steamers must sound their whistle or syrens in good time before entering Vegsund, as only one vessel can pass through the channel at a time." Vegsund certainly was narrow, so much so that there appeared hardly room for *Perula* between the light posts that rose up on either side. It was well marked, however; in fact, at the far end there were so many marks that we did not quite know where to go. As we passed through, we noticed a bridge in the course of construction. It has now been finished and allows a clearance of some 54 feet.

We spent a night anchored at Stordal, tied up between a buoy and a mooring post, north-east of the village.

We continued our passage at 8.10 a.m. and opposite the entry in my log book for 1 p.m. is the brief announcement, "Stopped to photograph falls." This process was actually anything but brief, and completely disorganised the shipping in the fjord. To start with we lowered the dinghy. For this purpose we have a derrick. It had been designed for us that winter by Mr. Campbell of Dickie's, and very excellent it was proving. With the help of the mast winch the dinghy could be raised or lowered single-handed; although in high winds it was safer for the wheelhouse to have two people on the job. The derrick could also be used for hauling aboard heavy stores, or visitors who fell in. It also proved a good means of keeping a bumping dinghy at bay in moderately calm weather. We dropped the dinghy into Geirangerfjord with some violence, and I was leaning over the side of *Perula* in an endeavour to unhook the derrick without getting into the dinghy, when Adams seized this golden opportunity to drop the derrick boom on my head.

After I had been brought round, it was decided he should row about the fjord, taking photographs, whilst I alternately manoeuvred *Perula* underneath the falls and posed on deck. Of course, when I was in the right place he was not, or if we did both happen to be right, a steamer charged across the picture at the critical moment, and the wash nearly wrecked the dinghy.

After Adams had rowed about 10 miles and I had nearly hit the falls several times, we gave it up in disgust. As I said to Adams "the damn things aren't worth taking anywayay," for I had been very disappointed at the sight of the "Seven Sisters." Perhaps it had not rained lately, for all I could see was a few miserable trickles of water.

It was not until we were under way again and I chanced to look back, that the real beauty was apparent. Seen from this angle the falls merged into a magnificent filmy veil, that appeared to widen and become more fairylike as the water fell, some 4,000 feet to the fjord below. Ablaze with enthusiasm I promptly stopped *Perula* and we started the photography all over again.

At length we arrived at Maraak, the village at the fjord head. A French cruise ship was already there and, much to our disgust, we became another "sight" for the sight-seers. We were having some difficulty in anchoring. We had found a target north of a stone jetty and dropped anchor in 8 fathoms, but the depth at the stern decreased to 4 fathoms, and it was, in fact, one of those places where, just when you have got nicely settled, rocks start bobbing up on either side of you.

We were in the midst of all these difficulties when the cruise ship sent out a launch, full of passengers, for a free entertainment. As it swept about us, the French people bowed, cheered, or otherwise applauded our efforts. At last, to our relief, it went away, but no sooner had it done so, than another one arrived. Finally this also headed back to the cruise ship, the passengers still bowing and waving, no one, not even the crew, facing the way they were going.

Meanwhile, a seaplane was landing, right across the path of the launch. Adams and I took one horrified glance. "Look out," I yelled frantically, "for Heavens sake look!" The more Adams and I shouted and pointed, the more those delighted French people bowed and waved, at what they doubtless took to be a charming demonstration of "entente cordiale."

Strange how the most dramatic moments are often humorous. I could tell the seaplane pilot was nearly frantic, yet there was something intensely amusing about the occupants of the launch, so totally oblivious of the danger. At last our warning struck home, a sailor turned round and saw the whirling propellor, bearing down on them at 50 m.p.h. He leaped about 4 feet into the air and nearly fell over backwards. The launch swerved violently, the seaplane passed safely by and Adams and I collapsed on deck in a fit of helpless laughter.

On August 13th, I read from the Sailing Directions: "Vessels navigating these waters are strongly advised to keep in mid channel, owing to landslides." We had left Geiranger, and as we sailed down Tafjord I found it hard to believe such peaceful waters could have brought wide-spread death and destruction. The evidence remains; a clean indentation in the precipitous side of a mountain, that towered above the fjord.

Many will tell you of the tragedy of Tafjord; of the tidal wave that swept all before it, when several million tons of mountain came crashing down. They heard it in Aalesund, 60 miles away. Villages and farms that once lined the banks disappeared; a small boat, peacefully at anchor, was eventually found in a green field. "Yes," sadly continued a man who had witnessed the calamity, "a little boat, so like, it might have been yours."

"Come on, Ron," I said, "let's get out of this. It's Friday, the 13th;"

Strangely enough, the following year, I saw this very boat in Aalesund. I was rowing the Harbour Master aboard *Perula* when I noticed it moored near to us.

"Hallo," I said, "that boat wasn't there before."

"No," he replied, "it has just come from Tafjord." He then told me the same story of the adventures that had befallen it.

At Tafjord we, unknowingly, collected Percy. One often reads of ships being haunted, and Percy was the ghost of *Perula.* He was not a respectable ghost; he neither clanked chains, nor walked about with his head tucked underneath his arm. He merely whistled and, what is more, whistled in exactly the same way as Adams and I did, when we wanted to call each other.

I was sitting peacefully at the wheel when Adams, who had gone below for a nap, suddenly dashed up.

"What is it?" he asked.

"What's what?" from me.

"What do you want?"

"I don't want anything."

"Then why the Hell did you whistle?"

"I didn't."

"You did."

"I did NOT."

So it went on.

Having spent most of the day dashing up to see what the other wanted, we anchored that night in Honningdalsvaag, the mystery of Percy still unsolved. I had picked this anchorage because I felt it would sooth my nerves. I had now learned a little Norwegian; for example, I knew tomater were tomatoes; poteter, potatoes, and appelsin, orange (which I kept buying in mistake for an apple). I also knew that honning was Norwegian for honey. "Honningdal," I said. "The dale of honey; oh! Ron, we simply must go there, it will be such a sweet place."

Things aren't always what they seem. If the Tafjord wave had hit Honningdal the day before it would not have looked any worse to us. Still, I should not be rude, it gave us a good sandy anchorage in 8 fathoms, and the one shop, opened specially for the sudden custom, provided Teddy cigarettes—you ought to try them some time.

We left next morning at 7.05, ran into fog, had more trouble with Percy, and some anxious moments with the overhead power cables that stretch across Nordfjord. Overhead cable can be very disconcerting. You are going along, probably half asleep, when you suddenly see a great wire, that appears to be on the point of dismasting you. Having put everything hard astern, you hastily consult your chart. Probably the cables have been erected recently (well, within the last five years) and are not marked. For example, those in Tafjord.

Of course, there has probably been a Notice to Mariners and, being a conscientious mariner, you always pay Potters to send these to you, but if you are like me, you toss them into a drawer, unopened, in the hope they will eventually cancel each other out. Next, you turn to the Sailing Directions, but there appears to be no mention of the cables. You then proceed towards the shore to see if the height might be written on the pylon. It is, but in Norwegian, and you cannot read it. You hang about for some time, in the hope that a ship with a taller mast than your own will come along. If it does not, you sneak very gingerly beneath the cables, as close to the shore as you dare, because they "do sag so frightfully in the middle." Having got safely under, you enquire their height at the next village and are probably informed, 50 metres!

The next village in our case was Davik, and according to my log book: "Good anchorage, 8 fathoms; another cock-eyed place."

Next day at 11.10 a.m. we continued up Nordfjord and anchored at Loen. We went to look at Olden first, but our chart had a plan of Loen and a hotel was marked. My log book reads: "Bad anchorage, strong currents and whirl-pools from river, very shallow towards hotel jetty; grounded dinghy. Finally changed anchorage to off first jetty, north side, not much better." It will be gathered that we did not enjoy Loen. We had come some 60 miles inland; it had rained all day and when we dropped the hook, *Perula* gave a pretty demonstration of the waltz. We tried to get out of the whirlpools by going closer inshore, Adams sounding. He signalled 10 fathoms, cast the lead again and nearly had a fit. It stuck in mud at less than one fathom; so did *Perula*. We got her off without much difficulty and spent the next hour deep in the study of whirlpools. This process consisted of sitting on deck in the rain and darkness, casting pieces of white paper overboard; but they all went round in circles. We then departed to the second mentioned anchorage, off the first jetty. Adams, with memories of Alfred, suggested keeping an anchor watch. "All right," I said, "but I'm going to the hotel." It looked very swell, with dancing and things, so we poshed ourselves up, lowered the dinghy, and set off. I took the oars, for I was beginning to fancy myself as an oarswoman, but after a few pretty pulls the dinghy stopped suddenly and I shot backwards over the thwart. We decided to walk.

Next day we went back some 40 miles down the fjord and finally anchored at Eid; north of steamer jetty, between red and black poles, 8 fathoms. I strongly recommend Eid if you wish to water your ship; working the village pump is excellent for the figure.

CHAPTER XI

A SAGA AND THE SOGN

On August 16th we started southwards again. We intended to go through Rugsund, but one look was sufficient for me so we went round by the main channel instead.

That night, having covered about 50 miles, we arrived at Florö, on the northern side of Brandsöy. I had wanted to visit this island on the way up, as to me the letters F L O R O indicated flowers; actually it is pronounced more like "floo-rer." I surveyed the crowded harbour with apprehension. The usual coloured warehouses jutted out into the water, leaving little nooks and corners, into which ships had tucked themselves. The Norwegian idea of a comfortable berth is to be as near the main street as possible; if they can tie up to a lamp-post, so much the better. They also like to assemble in great numbers, packing their boats like sardines.

There was a buoy; one of the big variety for which I was developing such a love, but it was only a few yards from the end of a street and other vessels had already pounced upon it. There was still room for us, but I could not see myself turning *Perula* round in that maze of shipping. I therefore turned her round in mid fjord and made a triumphant entry into Floröhavn backwards. This somewhat shook the locals and annoyed Adams for, of course, the stern kept swinging and I had to keep going forward again.

We liked Florö. It is at first sight a rather dilapidated little town, with semi-paved streets, but the surroundings are beautiful and the people charming. Mr. Olsen, the Lloyds agent, invited us to his home, and he and his wife visited us aboard. When the harbour master brought our mail, I made a bad faux pas. I gave him a cocktail glass of "Golden Cock" and a jug of water, thinking he might possibly like to add a few drops. Norwegians always take their drinks long; to one small whisky, they will add a large-sized bottle of soda. The poor harbour master viewed the small glass, wondering where he was going to put the water. He solved the problem by downing the gin, in one, followed by the entire contents of the jug, which I had intended for the three of us.

Owners of British yachts should always remember to keep a good supply of soda water for Norwegian guests. If you have not got an ice box, the bottles can be attached to a 10 fathom line, put overboard, and hauled up from the depths when required. If kept in the saloon, on a rough day the bottles are apt to explode.

From Florö we went to Kinn. I am not the kind of person who normally visits old churches, but the legend connected with Kinn church had intrigued us. We arrived to find a wild-looking island, formed of a mountain that had the apperance of being cleft in two. It loomed darkly up, washed by the open sea and surrounded by rocks. We sounded our way in, looking down at the rocks beneath us, the seaweed that swirled about in the swell, and began to wish we had not come. We risked dropping anchor on the west side of Kinnesund, feeling quite convinced it would get caught in the rocks and never come up again.

The next half-hour was spent in the dinghy, sounding with an oar, as *Perula* showed a tendency to swing. Back aboard a frightful smell greeted us. "Good Heavens! I put a stew on three hours ago." We turned despondently from the galley and got the shock of our lives. Framed in the wheelhouse door was a most odd-looking child. For a moment he looked at us, lips trembling, eyes full of tears, then vanished as quickly as he had come.

"Great Scot!" I said. "Did you see what I saw?"

"Yes," said Adams. "But do you see what I see now?"

Our second visitor proved to be an alarming sandy-haired gentleman, unshaven, naked save for brief trunks and a large knife. "Good morning," he said. This was reassuring; the apparition had at least not been the effects of "Golden Cock."

He proved to be a student from Oslo University. Each summer he goes to Kinn; to be alone with "the ocean, the vind and his books." Climbing the rocky crags, he hunts the sea eagle, swimming like a fish, he dives down midst the brown seaweed, exploring the ocean bed. Each year the little house he is building nears completion and already his bed of potatoes yields a fine crop. I had often read of such people, but never before met one. His joy in the things nature gives was something rather fine.

As we wandered along the sea-washed shore, I found myself catching his enthusiasm for this wild rugged place. A mournful wail rather changed my ideas. Ahead of us was the church that, for some 1,200 years, has stood, a monument in Norwegian history. Roaming the few untended graves was the unkempt figure of an old man clad in a red woollen cap. The student laughed and tapped his head. "Take no notice, the silly man calls for his wife; she is dead." Somewhat shaken, I watched him unearth a large rusty key; the old church door groaned and creaked and we walked into the past.

It was all there. The Princess and her two ladies; the crouching form at the foot of the Princess, the thumb of one hand missing. In paintings and plaster figures we saw depicted the legend told to us at Florö the story of Princess Sunniva who, with her ladies in waiting, fled from her country to escape a marriage against her religion. Sailing from Ireland, on separate ships, the three ladies vowed that wherever they landed each would build a church. One lady landed at Kinn, and the Princess at Selje. From this point the legend deals chiefly with Sunniva, possibly on account of her unfortunate end. Apparently the building of the church was not going too well, until she obtained an unexpected helper. At that time the fjords were supposed to be haunted by trolls, evil beings not human, yet in the form of man. Even to-day many of the Norwegian peasants believe in the existence of such creatures. One of these trolls, hearing of the beauty of the Princess, went (with bad intentions, I fear) to Selje; but when he saw her, cross in hand, he is said to have fallen at her feet and become her slave. He was returning from a nearby island where he had gone to collect stones for the church, when a sudden storm blew up. The boat was badly damaged and, with the wooden prop for his oar broken, the troll used one of his thumbs instead; hence the lack of the thumb on the hand of the crouching figure in the church.

One day the Princess beheld Viking ships approaching the island. Knowing what her fate would be she prayed to be saved. As she did so, the rocks above crashed down, and the Vikings found her dead.

Some years later, Sunniva became the first Saint of Norway. Of the three churches, only one remains, that on the island of Kinn, into which have been put all the relics relating to the legend. So it stands to-day, on that sea-washed shore, partially rebuilt but seldom entered.

Before leaving Kinn we invited the student to have "coffee" aboard. In Norway they seldom take afternoon tea as we do. As he entered the saloon and saw the lace tablecloth (reserved for visitors), the bowl of roses (given to us at Florö), and the plates of sandwiches and cakes, he paused in the doorway, lifted his arms, and cried: "It is not a boat. No! It is a magnificent hotel." Perhaps, after Kinn, it was!

That night we anchored in Skivenœsvaag, north of Aafjord. The Sailing Directions say it "provides anchorage for small vessels with local knowledge", my log book says: "Foul place; rocks all around; had to come out astern." We went in at dark so failed to observe the rocks.

Next morning Adams said: "Have you seen it?"

"Seen what?" I asked.

"Our anchorage," he replied.

It certainly was a sight for the gods, by whose grace *Perula* was eventually extracted, stern first.

We were now in the Sognefjord. We had saved it for the last and were not disappointed. If I had only a week or two to spend in Norway, I should make for the Sogn and stay there. In a way it is a tourist centre, with palatial hotels, etc.; but in most places quite unspoiled and the scenery magnificent. By the time you have penetrated its entire length—136 miles—and visited the many branch fjords, you will have seen almost all there is to see in this part of Norway, for the fjords are all much alike.

Percy had been with us again, all up the Sogn. It really was annoying, for although we suspected whistles were due to him, we dared not ignore them, in case they were genuine. It proved, however, to be his last day. That night Adams gave the engine a top overhaul, and although I hate to disappoint lovers of the supernatural, I fear Percy's decease was connected with a drop of oil.

We were anchored at Balholmen, in a small inlet named Esefjord. It was an excellent anchorage, in depths of about 7 fathoms and no bother of mooring posts. Ashore the shops were good and we spent some enjoyable hours in the hotel as guests of a member of a Lancashire yacht club, who had introduced himself on the quay while we were alongside for water.

It was our first experience of a Norwegian evening meal. We found an immense table, piled up with every possible food; hors d'oeuvres, shell fish, salmon, chickens, cold meats, vegetables, salads, sweets, ices, cakes, etc. You took a plate and the necessary implements, then walked round, helping yourself. Of course, I went "off my diet," and my plate contained a bit of everything. I also returned for further helpings, washed down by the usual accompaniments to a cheery evening; after which I danced. Next day, astonished fishermen beheld an English yachtswoman apparently being violently seasick in a flat calm fjord.

While we were anchored in Esefjord, some Englishmen rowed by on their return from a fishing expedition. English fishermen are usually very "posh" in Norway; they arrive with about 15 rods and 50 different flies and get annoyed when the local small boys arrive with a bamboo pole and a jar of worms and hook all the best salmon. I fear these gentlemen had been similarly thwarted, for one cast a sneering eye on *Perula* and remarked, very much old school tie, "Good God! Fancy crossing the North Sea in THAT." Whereupon I thrust an enraged face through the porthole and yelled: "Fancy crossing the North Sea without! you B. F." Weak, rude, but justifiable.

From Balholmen we went to Fjaerland; we liked it best of all the places we had visited. We anchored close inshore, opposite the Mundal Hotel, in 10 fathoms. As we rowed up to the little jetty, a voice exclaimed: "Hello, Miss Brown, how are you enjoying North Wales to Norway?" I was sure I had never met him, yet he obviously knew all about us. It turned out he had been to Manchester on business and had read my newspaper articles.

Fjaerland is noted for its glaciers, for situated in the neighbourhood of the fjord is Jostedalsbreen, the largest glacier in continental Europe, with an area of 580 sq. miles and elevation of 6,795 feet. Several branches of this glacier sweep down almost to sea level, so that afternoon we hired a car and set off.

For some people, blue ice holds an irresistible fascination and at that time I was one. My blood tingled with anticipation as our "chariot" bumped and rattled over an apology for a road. Every few minutes we came to an abrupt stop, while our assistant chauffeur (small boy wearing large goggles) climbed from his perilous perch on the mudguard to open rickety, wooden gates or shoo cattle from our path. An hour's drive and a short walk brought us to Suphellerbreen; two huge masses of ice, one above the other, joined by crashing waterfalls and set in the midst of amazing vegetation. The lower half, or secondary glacier, had been caused by the fall, and subsequent freezing together, year after year, of pieces of ice from the upper. The formation had been such as to leave a cave, composed of ice, at the foot. It was one of the most beautiful things I have ever seen. Through a thin curtain of falling water were revealed the ice—blue depths of the cave. Obeying the impulse that many feel at this sight, I started off towards the cave.

"Come back, you idiot," called Adams, but on I went, my one idea to stand in the chilly depths, behind the curtain of water.

"You'll start an avalanche," he yelled.

"It's quite safe," I said. "I won't be a second." Adams bounded over the loose stones through the water, seized me by the scruff of the neck, and dragged me away. I was most indignant at the time, but thankful later.

The previous year another Englishwoman had used the same words as I

—before guides dug out her body.

We spent the evening ashore at the small hotel. Walls hung with home-made tapestry; blazing pine logs in the cheery hand-painted fireplace. A man came in wearing an enormous top-hat and carrying a crooked stick. He was followed by girls in national costume; black skirts, dainty aprons, embroidered bodices of scarlet, blue or green, depending on the district they came from. Someone seized my hand and I found myself in a circle doing weird steps. Adams had been roped in too and was looking the complete picture of an embarrassed Englishman.

Round and round we went, to the low chanting of Norwegian voices, which became faster and faster as the man in the top-hat led us in a wild "caterpillar" in and out of the rooms. This was followed by a kind of "Oranges and lemons-cum-Irish-jig." Then the men formed one circle and the women another. The singing was mournful and slow, as the circles alternately passed beneath each other's outstretched arms.

"We are looking into the grave," cheerfully whispered the girl next to me. "Our arms represent overhanging branches."

I never gathered whose funeral it was, but it was a real good "do." Apparently each dance represented a Norwegian legend, which we were acting to music.

As we went back aboard the fjord looked indescribably beautiful. It was full moon, the mountains towered up on either side and, in the distance, the glint of Jostedalsbrae could be clearly seen against the starry sky.

Next day was Sunday. From miles around the peasants came to the little wooden church; old women with picturesque shawls on their heads, children in national dress. Some had left their mountain homes at 3 and 4 a.m. On foot, in carts, or small boats, they came.

Many of the Norwegian women spend the summer high up in the mountains; for as soon as the snow clears, it is usually the lot of the eldest daughter to take the cattle to the Saeter or upland farm. Here she lives milking the cows and goats, making cheese and butter. Sometimes other women climb up, taking her food and bringing back the things she has made; but some Saeter women have to deliver the produce themselves, either on foot or by transport lines. It is a hard and lonely life, yet most of the women love it and look forward to the time when they can go to the Saeter.

Besides the ordinary farms there are many silver fox farms. All over Norway you see them, for the people seem to keep silver foxes as we keep hens and chickens. Long low rows of wooden cages, screened with wire netting; but if you have a sensitive nose do not go too near. On the west coast the foxes are fed on the coarser types of fish, so it costs little to keep them. Thirty to forty million kroners' worth of skins are exported yearly; no mean achievement on the part of the original Mr. and Mrs. Fox on their importation from Canada.

After a good-bye party aboard *Perula* (Oh! dear, where shall we put fifteen people?) we returned to Balholmen and then set out for Naeröfjord. This fjord, also a branch of Songefjord has the reputation of being the grandest and gloomiest in all Norway. In places perpendicular walls of rock rise 3,000 feet on either side of a passage barely two cables wide. A 5½ hours' sail brought us to Gudvangen at the fjord head, where we anchored in 12 fathoms, opposite one of the targets on the east side. If we had proceeded a little further round a bend we could have obtained a better anchorage, but the sight of some sandbanks and memories of Loen caused me to err on the deep side.

Ashore next morning we found the village a mass of "stolkjerrer," small traps pulled by the cream coloured ponies. There were hundreds of them, awaiting the arrival of a German cruise ship.

It used to amuse me intensely to watch some tiny village preparing for the arrival of a big ship. First, boatloads of cars would arrive from the neighbouring fjords on what we called "Adams's ice breaker", for at the first sight of this car transport, which was blunt at both ends, Adams had spent a considerable time getting agitated about the "proximity of ice." All available means of transport having been unearthed and dusted, stuffed polar bears, reindeers and such like, were carefully placed outside the shops, and the more picturesque inhabitants dressed up for the occasion. The ship would then arrive and the peaceful village became an uproar. The roads were impossible; if you were not run over, you were blinded with dust. Motor horns shrieked out and the pony traps swept by with the tinkle of bells. Everybody was arguing, bargaining and taking each others' photographs. As soon as the big ship left everything was whisked away to the next village. Orange peel and chocolate paper still floated about the fjord, but otherwise all was peace again.

CHAPTER XII

HOMEWARD BOUND

It was now August 24th and high time we were thinking of home. In fact, I advise yacht owners, especially if inexperienced like Adams and myself, to start thinking of their homeward passage by the middle of August. In Norway the autumn comes early and the nights become dark again. At North Cape the end of July sees the end of the midnight sun, and by about November 18th there is only twilight at mid-day. Further south, in the vicinity of the Sognefjord, complete midnight sun is, of course, never experienced, although from May until about the first week in August there is little actual darkness.

After a third and farewell visit to Balholmen we left for Bergen, breaking the passage for a night's sleep at Sildevaag, Feje. It was tender memories of the Fiji Isles in the South Seas that took us to this anchorage and, although there were no palm trees or hula girls, we quite liked it. The depth is 4 to 5 fathoms; mooring posts are provided and as the anchorage is fairly close to Hellisöy light, it makes a good haven for a boat en route to or from the Shetlands.

Next afternoon we were back in Puddefjord, moored off the Bergen Sailing Club. The club boatman again proved a real friend in need, setting up *Perula's* rigging and doing all he could to help us. We went along to the Weather Office, situated in a kind of institute in a park. I think now that we must have seen Hr. Sverre Petterssen, Chief of "Vervarslingi paa Vestlandet." He spoke excellent English and was very charming. When we told him we wanted to cross the North Sea in a 45 foot boat, he told us frankly we had left it too late. Gales were raging and a whole succession of depressions would be sweeping across the North Sea. Forecasting for three days ahead, especially from east to west against the general direction of the weather, was almost impossible. We might wait a week and then find it no better. Anyway, he promised to do what he could, asked a great many questions about our boat and suggested we should call next day.

We returned to *Perula* decidedly down in the dumps. We tuned into the British shipping forecast and listened to gale warnings. It was not pleasant, sitting there on the wrong side of the North Sea.

Next morning we went back to the Weather Office. Our cruising speed had been carefully gone into, and they thought we might just sneak across. We should have to pass through the outskirts of the disturbance which was causing gales in Scotland, but they expected it would turn north and be dying out by the time we reached it. South westerly winds would be replaced by strong northerly, and these should carry us across in time to escape the next depression.

"What do you think, Miss Brown?" asked Hr. Petterssen. "There may be a gale, but I am inclined to think the wind will not exceed force 6 or 7." As I was pausing, somewhat horror-stricken, he continued: "If you do not take this risk, this map will show you the weather which is coming across the Atlantic."

I took one look and said: "Thank you very much. Good-bye." We sailed within half an hour.

A distance of 24 miles brought us to Marsten Light, and some Norwegian fishermen waved a friendly good-bye as we headed out into the open sea. We were taking a slightly longer passage by sailing from Bergen, but it seemed worth it. There was a light breeze from the south-west, so once again we proceeded under power, with mizzen and staysail to steady us. In this way we could keep to our course without tacking, and averaged 4½ knots.

Ahead of us clouds were banking up, and we looked back rather longingly at Norway's blue skies and evening sunshine. Then, being in what I thought was open sea, the navigator departed below to read. Suddenly a voice called: "Should there be any rocks about?"

"Good Lord, no," I replied.

"Well, you'd better look at the chart again," persisted Adams. "There's white breaking water ahead."

"God speed the rooks!" I cried, "I've drawn our course clean through Marstensboe."

This rock, which is usually awash, is situated 8 cables west-south-west of the island on which Marsten Light stands. I had never noticed it, for my large scale chart ended at the light, and on my North Sea general chart the cross denoting the rock was naturally small. This is no excuse, however; I certainly ought to have seen it.

We had sailed at 12.55 p.m. on the Saturday, and by Sunday the wind veered and freshened. Up went the mainsail and an inspection of the log showed we were doing 8 knots. That night we passed through the fishing fleet, always to me a hair-raising experience. On Monday morning the sun came out and I obtained two sights which gave a position 10 miles south of our course. They had been the first sights I had obtained, for although stars had appeared during the night, I had considered them rather beyond me. Shortly afterwards the wind died completely. At 11.05 we sighted Kinnaird Head and by 1.30 we were abeam, having covered the 240 miles from Marsten in 44½ hours.

As *Perula* sailed down Moray Firth, I called to Adams— "Ron, do you think you have had plague, cholera, yellow fever, typhus or smallpox; and if so have you recovered, are you still ill, or buried at sea?" "Have you gone barmy?" came back a startled voice. "No," I replied. "I'm filling up the declaration of health for clearance inwards."

Having put a large "No" to questions 1 and 2, I turned to question 3. "Are you aware of sickness or deaths amongst the rats and mice aboard, other than is attributed to poison or any other method employed for killing them?" I thought how nice it was of the port sanitary authorities to be so concerned about dumb animals. Having no rats or mice I put another "no" with a clear conscience. Questions 4, and 5 were eventually disposed of in the negative, although the latter caused me to feel my neck for "glandular swellings."

The "Diseases of Animals Act" is very instructive. The ordinary person has no idea of the complications involving the importation of such things as ruminating animals, swine, cow-tail hair (if not attached to the tail), sausage casings, pickled pelts, pigs' feet, cheeks and offals. Dogs, etc., go into quarantine for six months, or are "secured to some part of the vessel by a collar and chain and muzzled with a wire cage muzzle so constructed as to render it impossible for such dog while wearing same to bite any person or animal, but not so as to prevent such dog from breathing freely or lapping water." If you bring a musk rat or grey squirrel, then you are "for it"—they are absolutely prohibited. Let a policeman see you landing a cat (without licence) and you will be landed in quod.

Then, of course, you must fill up forms C No. 142 and 142A, declaring any of the usual dutiable goods and having been given notice No. 8 (to owners and masters of British yachts and other persons concerned), you will not be able to evade anything by looking innocent and saying you didn't know.

Having eventually filled up the forms we arrived at the sea lock to the canal, having actually remembered to hoist the "Q" flag. Unfortunately, I thought the lock gates were open when they were not, but various people rushed about seizing warps and once again the canal was saved. Our friend the Customs Officer came aboard and gave us our "Pratique," and we spent an enjoyable time at Muirtown before proceeding.

On September 2nd we again set forth to wreck the remainder of the canal. It was blowing hard and *Perula* was shipping water in Loch Ness. By the time we reached Fort Augustus we were both fed up and tied up for the night.

When you are in the canal all kinds of people will chat to you as you are waiting to be passed through the locks. Many will come aboard and even sail with you to another lock. Some are very nice and, being duly impressed by your owning a yacht, may even invite you to lunch or dinner. At one place Adams came below saying: "Win, I've been talking to an awfully decent bloke, he knows all about boats, is staying at the local and its nearly dinner time."

"Invite him for a drink," I said approvingly, forgetting the "gipsy's warning".

We got our invite to dinner, after which our host returned aboard with us for a "hasty nightcap."

"My dear," he remarked, taking a photograph from his pocket, "I have a gift for you—the main street at Bilbao—observe; a cross marks the spot where the first bomb fell." By 4 a.m. I was beginning to wish the gentleman from Bilbao had been standing on the same spot. I yawned, very deliberately, four times.

"My dear child," he remarked, "you are weary—we will all have another drink."

At 5 a.m. I said: "Don't you think it is getting late?"

"Late, my dear," he replied, "I am quite comfortable where I am." He was; at 9 o'clock he was still there, I having been to bed in the meantime.

That evening a large steam yacht arrived. "Hallo, old boy," exclaimed the gent from Bilbao to the owner. "Back from Norway? So are we; come aboard for a drink, old man." The owner gave him one of those looks that only owners of large steam yachts can give to presumptuous persons on small craft. Two of his party, however, came aboard and later we were invited back for cocktails—but we had to leave rather hastily.

Midnight came, and our "lodger" was still with us.

"Are you going or have I to throw you out?" I said crossly. In the early hours we got him out. "Quick," said Adams, "batten down the hatches, lock all the doors and put out the lights."

We were only just in time.

"Winifred, my child," called a voice, "let me in. I have been locked out of my hotel." There followed a fearful banging and bumping, then silence.

"Has he gone," I asked.

"Has he Hell," said Adams, who had crept to the wheelhouse. "He's knocking up the steam yacht now."

After a bit footsteps were again heard on *Perula's* deck and the banging began again. Then there was a fearful crash, a muttered curse, a splash, and silence.

I leapt up. "Where are you going?" asked Adams.

"To save him," I cried.

"Save him be damned," growled Adams. "If you open that door I'll throw you in the blasted canal."

I spent an awful night, with visions of a white face floating in the water. As soon as it was light I wakened Adams. "Let's go," I said, "before they start dragging the canal." . All morning the vision haunted me. "Poor man," I said, "even if he did stamp his cheroots out on the saloon carpet; he was very nice."

"If I'm any judge," said Adams, "he threw a brick and not himself into the canal."

"Oh! Ron," I cried in horror, "how can you speak like that? If he is not dead, he's probably got pneumonia."

We were in open water, going through a loch, when there was an insistent blowing of a motor horn on the bank.

"The police! " I gasped.

"Police, my eye," said Adams, handing me the glasses. It was the gentleman from Bilbao.

That night, instead of anchoring at Fort William, we sought cover behind a small island and sailed at dawn for Oban.

"Let that be a lesson to you," I said to Adams. "Never speak to strangers on the canal banks." But I quite liked the gentleman from Bilbao. I still have the photograph pinned to the mainmast.

We were stuck at Oban for five days waiting for weather. I did not exactly enjoy my stay there. To add insult to injury, I was walking along the promenade in my best yachting kit and feeling mighty superior at having "been foreign," when a seafaring gent with a rowing boat called out to me, "Take you for a nice day's sail, lady?"

The late shipping-forecast on September 9th announced, "Winds moderating," and we decided to sail the following dawn. All I can say is that the wind took a long time about moderating, for we made the passage from Oban to the Straits in 32 hours. The wind was north and it was our first experience of a really bad following sea.

Once Adams said to me, "Have you looked astern?"

"Yes," I replied, "but I'm not doing so again."

A great mass of water would tower up behind us and start to break. Just when it seemed nothing could prevent it crashing down on us, *Perula* shot forward. As she lost speed another great wave would come racing and curling up behind us, and we would go through the surf-riding act all over again. It was almost impossible to steer, and of course we gybed more than once. I think we were both rather scared, for neither of us suggested turning in and we carried on with hourly watches through the night.

Having rounded Chicken, the weather improved slightly, and on September 11th we arrived at the Straits. It felt good to be back. One or two of the boats sounded their sirens as we passed, and the Beaumaris ferry "dipped" to us.

Of course, somebody was on our moorings. I had written Dai asking him to have them clear for us, but he had been overruled by the popular opinion that "indeed to goodness, *Perula* will not come back in this; mad though the woman is." I must say I have never seen a mooring vacated more quickly; we had barely circled round before the other ship was off; and at 3.15 p.m. the little white buoy bearing *Perula's* name was hoisted aboard, and she was home.

She had sailed approximately 2,500 miles in two months and never given us a moment's anxiety. Our R.N. diesel had run almost solidly for 450 hours. Harbour dues in Norway amounted to the equivalent of 1s., and we paid some 2s. for water. Fuel and lubricating oil for the cruise cost approximately £8. Norway is an ideal cruising ground; we both felt we had enjoyed a good and cheap holiday.

"Of course," I said, "it was hard work at times, but you know, Ron, given a sound ship, a faith in weather reports, the odd spot of common sense and a large sense of humour—well, if you ask me, this cruising business is not so difficult as it seems."

Perula was laid up on October 6th. We had been more than satisfied with her and for once there seemed little work to be done on her.

"We'll have the topsides burnt off and repainted," I said.

"What about a horse for the staysail?" asked Adams: and this was agreed on.

The bilges were to be thoroughly cleaned out and the ballast refastened; for we both had a feeling we had heard it bumping about on occasions. As I said to Mr. Dickie: "It would be very unpleasant if it went through the bottom." Last but not least was the question of a wheelhouse chair; the stool was not satisfactory.

"What sort of a chair do you want?" asked Bill Campbell in some horror.

"You are a naval architect," I replied. "Design me a nice one, so that I sit at the wheel in comfort."

After a bit he returned with a sketch and the words, "Will this do?" The proposed chair had a comfortable back, could be slid into position on a mast-track inserted in the floor of the wheelhouse, and a foot-rest was provided beneath the wheel.

"Fine," I said. "You are a genius, Bill."

With all these details decided on, we sadly made our way homewards.

"You are driving too fast, Ron," I remarked, severely, as the Welsh scenery flashed past.

"We're hardly doing 30," he replied.

"Seems like 70," I replied.

"Must be after travelling at 5 knots . . . . Where shall we go next year?"

CHAPTER XIII

"WHERE ANGELS FEAR TO TREAD"

It was Christmas Day; not in the workhouse, but in my Lancashire home. I was sitting in front of the fire, having dined well if not wisely. Perhaps it was the Christmas cards on the mantelpiece that gave me the idea—the reindeer and robins rampant on glistening snow. Perhaps, again, it was merely the effects of the festive season, but in the middle of extracting a chestnut from the fire, I remarked:

"We'll sail to Spitsbergen."

"What!" said Adams.

"Don't be a fool," said my mother, and went on reading her book.

I was full of enthusiasm. The atlas had to be brought and I pondered deeply on the Arctic Regions.

"It's a cinch," I said. "We will sail to the north of Norway, hop across to Bear Island, only 220 miles of open sea; then after a night's rest we can carry on to Spitsbergen. The South Cape is only 122 miles from Bear Island, so we'd do this last part in 24 hours." In that cosy warm room it appeared a brilliant idea. When I got some reports on Arctic conditions, I began to doubt my brilliance.

I wrote first to the Norwegian State Railways, London. What they had done to deserve this infliction, I do not know. It was one of my usual letters, lengthy life history, followed by a string of questions regarding temperature, ice, what clothes I should need, and finally, did they consider such a cruise practical? This, having caused some stir in Cockspur Street, was sent to the National Travel Association of Norway, from whence, having caused more consternation, it was sent to Tromsö.

At length a report came from Hr. Winther-Hansen. I had to pay £1 for it, but there were five typewritten pages and Hr. Hansen was the Meteorological Expert of "Vaervarslingen for Nord-Norge" (which I think means weather-forecasting for North Norway).

The report began by describing the state of water in regard to ice, and read as follows: "The west coast of Spitsbergen is normally free from ice at Prince Carl's Foreland and northwards, to the mouth of the Icefjord. South of Prince Carl's Foreland there is some ice." This was rather disconcerting for my quick dash to the South Cape, as Prince Carl's Foreland is well up the coast. But, the report continued, "Normally this ice disappears at the beginning of the summer. Some years, however, the ice drifts in summer from the east coast round the south cape and northwards along the west coast and makes navigation difficult, may even block the Icefjord completely." (Definitely not so good.) "This, for instance, happened in 1915. Then the ships had great difficulties in forcing the ice and penetrating into the Icefjord. Some of them had to give it up, and a couple of them stuck in the ice and must be left by the crew." This cheering remark was followed by: "We deal here with ships specially built for going in the ice." I tried very hard to forget *Perula's* 1 1/2-inch pitch-pine planking and read on. "The north coast of Spitsbergen is normally free from ice in summer. The east coast of Spitsbergen (Storfjord) is often blocked by ice all the summer. When it happens that the north-east winds force the ice towards the South Cape, the Storfjord becomes free from ice. The fjords are normally frozen every winter, but this fjord-ice breaks up and disappears in the spring; but it may happen that the drifting ice drifts into the fjords and fills them up, after the firm fjord-ice has disappeared."

All this was very difficult. I gathered that the safest part of Spitsbergen was the north coast, "normally free from ice in summer," but it was a hell of a long way. If we went to the west coast we might get into Icefjord all right, but if strong north-easterlies blew, the ice might drift up and we might not get out. The east coast had to be ruled out; we might wait all the summer for favourable winds to clear, Storfjord. In any case, wherever we went, it seemed that ice would be waiting to pounce and block us in some fjord even if it did not crush us to bits.

Next we turned to Bear Island. The report stated: "Easterly winds are most frequent and force the Polar ice towards the island, so that it becomes blocked for periods of variable duration." (Oh! dear, dear, I said to myself; I am enjoying this.) "Under normal conditions the waters are free from ice at the end of May. In bad years the ice may lie round the island until July. But under favourable conditions the sea may be free from ice even all winter, or ice and open water may alternate."

Regarding the best time of the year to make the crossing, Hr. Hansen stated: "It is considered most important to choose a time when the risk to meet ice is small, and in that respect the months of July and August are recommended. July is also the month when heavy storms are rarest." (We'll go in July.) "On the other hand" (I feared this) "the months of July and August are very foggy, but I think one must consider the ice to be considerably more dangerous than the fog." I turned up his statistics for fog. The mean I number of days with fog were 18.7 at Bear Island in July and 15.3 in August.

There were also tables giving the mean number of days with "Strong gale or more (9 Beaufort or more, 18.3 metres per second or more.)" I must say that the "or mores" were rather upsetting; as far as I was concerned 9 Beaufort was a calamity. I was cheered to find that under Bear Island for July these gales were marked as 0. The next page disillusioned me. Under a heading of: "Particularly we will emphasise the following facts," was the happy announcement: "Though the mean number of days with strong gale at Bear Island is 0 in the months of May and July, it is not allowed to conclude that strong gales will never occur in these months." (Thank you very much, Hr. Hansen, thank you very much indeed.)

Next I bought the "Arctic Pilot." Amongst other things it contained hints on ice navigation by Lieutenant-Commander Neoupokeff. Apparently if about to hit an iceberg, "every endeavour should be made to receive the blow on the stem, which is the part of the ship best suited to the purpose." If trapped in drifting ice, "it is well to drop an ice anchor on one of the larger floe bergs," and, I presume, go with it. Lastly, "If a vessel is beset (closely surrounded) in ice, boats and provisions should be got clear, as she might be crushed in a moment."

After this I wrote to Professor Rudmose Brown, who had made passages in Norwegian ships. I had never met him, but he very kindly gave me a lot of valuable information and strongly advised me not to attempt the passage without a pilot. He doubted if the Norwegian authorities would allow it in any case.

I also wrote to Major Smales, who has cruised Norway extensively, as far as North Cape. I had never had the pleasure of meeting him either, but last year he gave me the most helpful information regarding the best route, ports of call, etc. He, too, did not advise me to proceed beyond North Cape; he had talked with the fishermen and knew what it could be like.

To me it is rather wonderful that these men should be so kind to an unknown woman, who is nothing but a blasted nuisance. While it may seem that I heeded not their advice, I feel extremely indebted to them for their information.

With all these reports to hand, Adams and I held a "Committee Meeting." Shall we or shan't we?

"Well," I said, "it will be a grand adventure."

"It will," replied Adams, "if you have the sense to turn back in time." So it was decided, "towards" Spitsbergen, and not necessarily "to" Spitsbergen, So that we could not change our minds, I promptly went off and sold the story to the Press. Not many yachtsmen realise that a newspaper will cheerfully pay your expenses if they think you are going to drown yourself. I was guaranteed £70 with a possibility of more.

Charts had to be ordered; about 80 of them. This was left to me as Navigator. Day after day, week after week, I worked on them, often sitting up till 2 a.m. or 3 a.m., only to go to bed and dream of the wretched things. I think it is very wise, especially with a small crew, to do your chart work during the winter and not at the actual time of your cruise. Of course, if you are sailing only, and have to tack, it isn't so good, but in our case, relying mostly on power, courses could be worked out beforehand, the Sailing Directions studied and notes made of tides and dangers.

Last year, after a hard day's passage, I had found myself sitting up most of the night, preparing my charts for next morning.

This year I was using Norwegian charts. They can be obtained from Jacob Dybwad, Oslo, and payment made by cheque for the amount of kroner on receipt of the bill. Major Smales had given me this hint the previous year, but I had feared the language complication. I found Norwegian charts excellent in every way. There are, roughly, three classes of chart. The large-scale (maalestokk 1: 50,000) which cost 2 kroner (two shillings) each. The intermediate (maalestokk 1:100,000) that cost 2-40 kroner, and the "mindre maalestokk", which we would call generals, which, together with those of Svalbard, are slightly more expensive.

On the large-scale charts the light sectors are shown in colour. On the general charts, however, the lighthouses are merely indicated by red and yellow blobs. One night I was working on a general, but no sooner did I find a lighthouse than it disappeared. One minute it was there, the next it was not. Suddenly, one of my lost lighthouses turned up in the middle of the North Sea. I looked at it in amazement. "Gosh!" I said, "I've gone crackers." Then I discovered that the heat of my hands had been melting the "blobs" and I had been busily distributing them elsewhere! This was, however, quite an isolated case, and must not be held against Norwegian charts.

Meanwhile, Adams was equally busy with bo'sun's work. Periodically he had been down to Bangor, returning with car-loads of gear until his house looked like a young shipyard, and his poor mother was nearly frantic with the smell of paint, varnish and tarry ropes. Amongst other things, he decided to bring the sails home and wash them (only about 600 square feet). After some argument the mainsail was sent to the laundry. This will possibly cause the pukka yachtsman considerable horror, but the laundry had promised to treat it with care, doing the job at the week-end when they had room to spread it out flat and scrub it with fresh water only. It came back looking very fine.

With the mainsail at the laundry, Adams got busy scrubbing the mizzen and staysails on the cellar floor, a proceeding that caused much bad language and "house-maid's knee." Then, one beautiful morning, he carried the sails in triumph to the clothes-line, spread them out and stood admiring their spotless whiteness. "Ping" went the clothes-line. "Flop" went the sails onto the dirty soil of a Manchester garden. Better not tell you what he said as he carried them back to the cellar to be washed again.

In the midst of these preparations my mother arrived on the scene, armed with a newspaper and the words, "Winifred! Ronald! You are not to go." She had been reading the case of a seaman who had deserted his ship because it was bound for Bear Island. No wonder poor mother was perturbed, for the judge, after hearing the seamen's description of our Arctic haven, dismissed the case, saying he did not blame the man.

On April 11th we went down to Bangor and put in a week's work at the yard. We had decided to paint *Perula's* interior ourselves. All we succeeded in painting was our own exteriors. Nothing seems more difficult to paint than the inside of a small boat; corners, posts and beams, etc. To make it worse, in our case, we had not even headroom. Never attempt to paint the under-deck, that is, unless you have the patience of Job and the skill of an A.R.A.

To start with I tried to be clever and save labour by mixing flat white with enamel, "because," as I said to Adams, "it requires a coat of each, and by mixing them we'll do it all in one."

We started with the galley. I lay on my back on the upper bunk and endeavoured to paint the planking above me. The paint ran down the brush handle into my eyes and mouth. Adams said I was being wasteful, and when I sat up to remonstrate my hair stuck to the fresh paint. After several more rows I got on my dignity and told him to do the blasted job himself. I wriggled round on to all fours in an effort to get off the bunk and promptly stuck my rear quarters to my latest handiwork.

I next decided to paint the pot-shelf and cupboard doors with teak paint. They were already nice polished wood, but I had the paint fever. When I had finished and saw the result, I could have wept. Adams, who is an understanding soul, took one look at my face and used the rest of our turps washing my efforts off

Then, of course, our friend Bill Campbell, Dickie's designer, would come and give kind advice. Seated at a safe distance, he would light a cigarette and remark: "Women never could paint, they all dab. Look at that bit you've missed: is that part supposed to be finished? I call it a streaky mess. You should have washed it first. Talking of washing, have you seen yourself lately? You do look funny!"

At the end of three days, Adams and I ached all over and *Perula* was a decided mess.

"It looks awful," I said. "Never mind," he replied. "We'll know better another year, and it might not look so bad when the gear is back to distract attention."

Perula was launched on April 27th. It seemed we should never get through the necessary work. There was the rigging to do; compass to adjust; decks to paint, and many other odd jobs. We were now using non-slip deck paint, a mixture of paint and silver sand. It looked well and gave an excellent grip. It is best applied at the last moment, and spare cans should be carried as it tends to wear off in a month or so. We find, in the first instance, a gallon (approximately 25s.) makes a good job of *Perula's* deck. After this, about half-a-gallon (well let down with turpentine) is sufficient to keep the surface and appearance good for a season. Decks, of course, look much nicer unpainted, but we do not have the time to look after them.

About this time I was also kept busy answering what Adams termed my "fan mail." The moment a newspaper announces an impending adventure, no matter if you are going to Borneo, Timbuctoo, or a mere cruise, about a quarter of the population of Great Britain desires to accompany you. Letters start pouring in with the weirdest addresses. I had one addressed to "Winifred Brown of the Waterpool," presumably, because I live in Waterpark Road. Others just put my name and England, Lancashire, Wales or Manchester, and hope for the best. Some go to the newspapers, others to my father's business, and a lot were addressed to *Perula* herself!

The writers can usually be divided into three types: those that want paying for their services; those that do not; and a few who are ready to "sell their motor bike" or such like, · and give you the proceeds for their expenses.

There is the condescending gentleman who tells you he has travelled all over the world and might accompany you as a great favour, if your plans are sufficiently interesting. I am always rude to him.

There is the school marm who is crushed between four walls and must "break free to express herself." But not on us, dear lady!

Some give their family-tree and tell you how "refained" they are. Others assure you they are "cool, courageous and companionable". I tell them I am "cowardly, cantankerous and contaminable."

Then there are little mill girls, who have "treasured your photo above that of any film-star." Not to mention small boys who "can't stand girls wot paint their faces and curl their 'air."

Seafaring men write, too. Some want paying enough to "keep the old girl." One offered to bring a piano-accordion and play to me. There are pitiful cases of old skippers who cannot get work. When you reluctantly have to turn them down, they write again, wish you luck, and very often give excellent information and advice.

Most of the applicants send their photographs, preferably taken on the Norfolk Broads (please be sure to return). For the most part they admit having no knowledge of the sea, but they will "work their fingers to the bone", or "you ought to try my plum pie, come round some time."

It surprised me to find the spirit of adventure that exists; the people ready to "chuck their job" for the "romance of the sea". One day I will hire a larger boat and invite them all for a two-week's cruise of the Irish Sea in November for there ain't much romance in a heaving yacht; working day and night and trying to have a bath in a wash basin. I think many would return to their "four walls" with considerable satisfaction.

At the end of April two friends, Bill and Peggy, came over to wish us God-speed on our journey, only it was Peggy herself who nearly took a "journey." We came out of the Gazelle on a pitch-black night; it was blowing stink and, of course, spring tides. Bill and I took an oar each, but when he pulled I didn't, and after about an hour we were further away from *Perula* than when we started. Meanwhile, Ron was sitting aft with Peggy, who was nursing a hot-water bottle she had borrowed from Dai, and both were passing rude remarks.

"It's the dinghy," I said, "she's too light to carry four in bad weather. We'll go back to the jetty and land Bill; he weighs the most." I thought this was rather crafty of me, for both Bill and I had been secretly thinking we could row much better without the other's assistance.

Bill was eventually landed and Ron took his oar. Ron and I were used to rowing together; we usually sat side by side, and it was known at the Straits as our "brother and sister act."

"We'll be back for you soon, Bill," I called, but although we rowed and rowed, the dinghy hardly moved.

"Hurry up," said Peggy, plaintively, "my bottle is getting cold."

At length, after a fearful struggle, we reached *Perula*, but before we had time to ship our oars and grab, the tide swirled the dinghy round and we were swept away.

"Blast it," I said, and then, "My God!—where is Peggy?"

"Help," came a faint voice over the water.

"Where are you?" yelled Ron.

"Hanging on to *Perula*," came the reply.

"Row, Win, for Heaven's sake, row," said Ron.

"We're coming, Peggy," I cried, straining every muscle. "Hang on, dear, we're coming."

We were. Ron caught a crab and nearly lost his oar. "Poor girl," I wailed, "she will be frightened to death."

Just then her voice was heard again: "Row, you damn fools."

"Coming, Peggy love," I yelled, "coming."

"Well, you'd better hurry," she called, "I can't hold on much longer."

We struggled on, but we were right out in the stream, pulling against the full strength of it, and made little head-way. Peggy's voice came again. "I can't hold . . . I—I'm going."

"She's in," groaned Ron. "Poor Bill, standing helplessly on the jetty—watching his wife drown like this . . . ."

Peggy had no intention of drowning; she could hardly swim, but cool as a cucumber she kept calling as the tide swept her down the Straits. We managed to put the dinghy in her path, I grabbed her by the scruff of the neck and Ron dragged her aboard. "N—now, look what you've d—done," She said, with teeth chattering, "I—I've lost my hot-water b-bottle."

By this time we were about halfway to Menai Bridge and the dinghy was half full of water. Ron sat aft, his arms around Peggy, trying to keep her warm, while I rowed. At length we reached the jetty.

"Where the devil have you been, keeping me waiting like this?" shouted Bill, somewhat annoyed.

"Didn't you see?" I gasped. He knew nothing about it.

We knocked up the Gazelle. Mrs. Owen brought hot blankets and brandy—Ron drank the brandy.

"Well!" I said, "you are a beauty, eating the invalid's grapes."

"If we'd had to tell Bill she'd gone," he groaned.

"Thank Heaven," said Peggy, fervently, from behind a blanket.

"Yes, dear," I said, "thank Heaven you are safe."

"Oh, I wasn't thinking of that," she replied, "I've found my hot-water bottle." The question of food for our trip had to be gone into very carefully. We expected to be able to buy fresh food most of the time, but a good supply of canned and dried goods had to be taken in case of emergency. We took 6 dozen tins of vegetables, 16 tins of meat, 5 tins of soup, 2 dozen tins of milk and cream; the usual cereals, macaroni, dried fruits, tea, coffee, sugar, etc.

At the last moment we decided to take bonded stores. Owing to *Perula*'s small tonnage special permission had to be obtained from the Commissioners, H.M. Customs and Excise, Custom House, Lower Thames Street, E.C.3. This arrived on the Saturday morning, May 7th, and we proposed to sail on the following Tuesday. A telephone message to MacSymon's Stores, Liverpool, worked wonders, and on the Monday the Customs Officers from Bangor were aboard, busily sealing up 3 dozen bottles of spirits, 2,000 cigarettes, and 6 tins of butter. We had ordered the butter as at many of the smaller places in Norway it is only possible to buy margarine. The saving by having bonded stores is enormous. Popular brands of cigarettes worked out about 30s. per 1,000; whisky about 4s. 2d. per bottle; rum 2s. 11d., and gin 2s. 3½d. I strongly advise any yacht owner bound for Norway to take bonded stores. With the country being practically "dry" British yachts are expected to be well supplied! Of course, on arrival in Norway, their Customs impose some restriction on the amount you can have out.

Clearing outward seemed much easier on the second occasion. The bonded goods were aboard before the Customs Officers arrived. I had collected them from the station by car, and with many anxious moments loaded them into the dinghy, which nearly sank beneath their weight. The various cases are naturally sealed, so you are allowed to handle them, providingthe seal is unbroken. Next, I had to decide where they were going to be put. This is very important. Obviously, it has to be some cupboard or locker which can be sealed, and is yet easy of access. I chose the one in the saloon, with the following disadvantages: Holes had to be drilled in the best woodwork to pass the sealing tape through, and the bottles, with their straw packing, made an awful mess on my best fawn carpet.

At the Straits, however, I was fortunate. Mr. Owen and his assistant took compassion on a lone woman, bored the necessary holes themselves, making them as unobtrusive as possible, and having carefully counted the stores, packed them away and then brushed up for me.

The papers did not seem half so difficult. There was the usual Master's Declaration and Victualling Bill, but this time I was allowed to miss out the odd half-pounds of coffee, quarter tins of red paint, and concentrate on the bonded stuff, which was also entered in a Yacht Stores' book. Mr. Owen had also obtained for me a clean Bill of Health, a magnificent document that stated: "I, the undersigned, Officer of His Majesty," etc., "send greeting," continued that "Whereas the vessel called *Perula* was about to sail to Spitsbergen and other places beyond the seas," the said officer "did hereby make it known to all men" (at the time of granting these presents) that neither Adams, Bangor, nor I had "Plague or Epidemic Cholera." Strictly speaking, I do not think it is really necessary to have this, but I was very delighted with it.

Having paid 5s. for shipping bonded goods in an un-approved place, my friends of the Customs departed, and I turned again to my wireless weather-reports and thoughts of the morrow.

Adams had gone home to Manchester to say good-bye to his people, but was coming back that evening. I had not gone because I hate good-byes, they only make everybody miserable and do no good. I much prefer to depart and leave a postcard to say I have gone.

For once there was a singular absence of "deep depressions," and it seemed fairly certain we should get away in the morning.

We spent our last night in the bar-parlour of the Gazelle. I shall never forget it. After all we were setting out on what was, for us, a rather doubtful proposition. Adams had come back looking rather upset. I, on the other hand, was in high humour, having been busily celebrating with the gentlemen of the Press.

So there we sat, just as I had wished it. Tankards in front of us and no very intimate friends or relations to take lingering last looks. I always enjoy being with pressmen. I like the way their calendar is referred to in terms of murders and explosions. "Good Lord, old man, fancy seeing you, haven't met you since so-and-so did in his wife and four kids . . . ." Dai was there, and Mr. McNeil kept looking in. It was a cheery night and we were laughing and talking long after we should have been in our bunks. At last I rose.

"Sorry to break up the party, blokes, but if we are sailing . . . ."

"What time do you expect to leave, Miss Brown?"

"Heavens above! Have a heart."

"You'll come ashore at 9.30? That's better."

They saw us off to the dinghy and watched it thread its way between white shapes towards a light that flickered in the darkness. As they watched, probably they said: "Not a bad day, chaps, must get some good pictures of them in the morning, for the obituary."

PART II: HORRESCO REFERENS

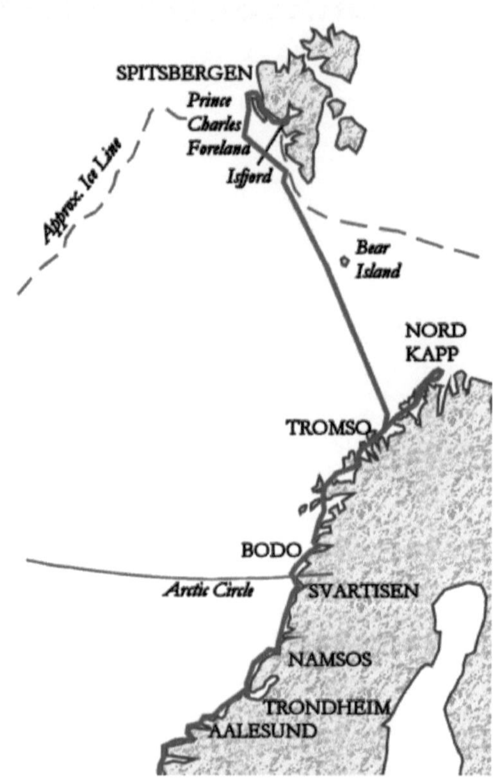

Perula's second voyage to Norway

CIGS
CHOCO
CHOCO
BISCUITS
MILK
WHISKEY
ME ON WATCH!
W.B.

CHAPTER I

OUTWARD BOUND

M.Y. "Perula" from Menai Straits towards Spitzbergen. May 10th, 1938. 12.00. Wind light variable. Barometer 29.99.

We are off! For the last hour the words have kept running through my mind. Off for Svalbard (cold shore), the Norwegian name for the Arctic regions, which include Bear Island and Spitsbergen. It is a bit scaring.

I am sitting at the wheel, trying to write and watch the compass at the same time. As I look back at the Lighthouse and the Perch off Puffin Island, I cannot help wondering . . . shall we ever see them again? On our port bow is another yacht from the Straits; having sailed by to wish us luck, she is heading back. On the starboard bow is a large porpoise, also, I suppose, come to say "Good-bye," in its own fishy fashion.

Shortly before 11 o'clock this morning we hauled the dinghy aboard and started the engine. A small crowd had gathered on the jetty in front of the Gazelle, pressmen and the staff of the hotel. As we sailed by I could see the maids' white caps and aprons, the waiters' white shirt fronts. I went on deck to wave and . . . "Get back to the wheel you B.F., d'you want to sink the Bangor ferry!"

It is a beautiful day, blue skies patched with cumulus clouds. *Perula* sways gently on her way as the Welsh hills fade into a haze. "Gosh! That's a damn good smell from the galley." Adams is cooking lunch. He came up a little while ago and remarked hopefully: "You must be tired; shall I take the wheel for a bit?" Strange how concerned we become for the helmsman's welfare when potatoes have to be peeled. I just looked up, ignoring the potatoes completely: "Can't you see I'm writing?" I can see it will be an invaluable excuse when I want to get out of a job of work.

We are in luck to-day; it is so calm that lunch is to be served on the saloon table. Much better than the usual procedure of eating out of enamel bowls in the wheelhouse. Might as well make the most of the calm while it lasts. The 10.30 weather forecast said, "winds freshening". Sometimes I wish I had not got a wireless aboard, then I could go blissfully on enjoying the sunshine while it lasted, instead of drawing horrible looking sketches of pressure distribution, wind direction, and worrying how it will affect us. I expect by nightfall the seas will be sweeping over us and *Perula* dancing about like a cork. Wonder why we go sailing.

Lunch was a great success. I came back to the wheelhouse half expecting to see the Straits again, but *Perula* must want to go to the Arctic, she has kept her course beautifully and the Isle of Man is in sight. Must be quite 40 miles away; never sighted it so quickly before; this weather is too good to last.

Midnight: Wind south, force 5: Sea moderate: Barometer 29.9. I was right about the weather, it was too good to last. The 3.45 p.m. forecast gave warning of fresh southerlies and the 4.45 p.m. increased them to strong. The usual depression is approaching Ireland, blast its eyes.

Wind came at 5 o'clock and we hoisted the main and staysail. At 8.45 p.m. we rounded Chicken, Isle of Man. The skies had become dull and leaden; black clouds were rolling up from the west. I am very wickedly writing this on my night watch. Needless to say, the wheelhouse light is on, so I ain't exactly watching! Adams, lucky blighter, turned in at 10 p.m. and is now sleeping peacefully below. I've done all the usual things to pass the time. Smoked about 30 cigarettes, eaten two large packets of chocolate, half a tin of biscuits and drunk some whisky and milk. I'll be sick before I've finished.

It is darned cold and I look a picture of elegance in two thick jerseys, a large coat, several mufflers, and a pair of long white bedsocks pulled over my deck shoes and trouser legs. Fortunately, the new wheelhouse chair is very comfortable. It is starting to blow up from the south-east; white crests are appearing and it looks like being a dirty morning.

"Hell! There goes the boom; knew I would gybe if I did not watch!" The wind has veered south again; shall have to go out to the sheets . . . . Back again, somewhat shaken; nearly went overboard, but the life line saved me. Serves me right for "breaking rules," and going on deck by myself. Will have to put this writing away; the wind is all over the shop. I have picked up Copeland Light; we should be abeam about 2 a.m.

May 11th, 8 a.m.: Wind south, force 3: Barometer 29.8. It is calming down, but the glass is falling. All night we have been running up the Irish coast and should round the Mull in about three hours. We cannot be far away but rain is falling and visibility is rotten. I shall be glad when we are round the devil; feel it is the lull before the storm. Ah! Here is Adams with a nice bowl of porridge for me, piled up with brown sugar and half a tin of cream.

Crinan 9 p.m.: Remember that song "The wind is blowing, the snow is snowing?" Well, I am singing it gleefully. The wind is blowing; the glass has fallen 4 points and for all I care the snow can start snowing, for we are safely at anchor in Loch Crinan, having covered 200 miles in 31 hours.

We rounded the Mull at 11.5 a.m. without any trouble and sailed up the west coast of the Kintyre peninsula. The wind had freshened again from the south, throwing up a nasty choppy sea. I spent most of the day with my eyes glued to the wheelhouse clock, wondering if we should lose the flood into Crinan. We did. By the time we arrived the ebb tide was fairly boiling past the loch entrance. *Perula* stood still, spray broke over us, and for a horrible moment I feared we were going to emulate our Strangford episode and go "backwards," but the strong wind, coupled with full engine, won.

We passed into the sheltered waters of the loch and dropped anchor in 3 fathoms, in what they appear to call Crinan harbour, but to me it looks more like a nook in the rocks. I should probably have anchored much further out but for some helpful advice from the crew of a brown ketch.

After we had cleaned up we lowered the dinghy and went ashore. I wanted to let my parents know where we were, for I knew my father would have been following the weather reports. In the "local" we met the crew of the ketch and discovered she was built by Dickie's of Loch Tarbet, a coincidence which called for another pint. Crinan is a pleasant little place and we spent an hour or so watching ships pass through the canal, that narrow waterway that runs between the sound of Jura and Loch Fyne and which is often used by small ships to save rounding the Mull. With memories of our experiences in the Caledonian Canal we felt rather thankful we had not to do any "canalling."

Tobermory. May 12th: We left Crinan at 10.20. Not a bad morning. Glass still low, mainly grey skies, but an occasional burst of sunshine. Had a few anxious moments with Dorus More, that narrow channel where the tide sweeps through at some 6 to 8 knots. I had timed things so that we went with it, and more or less gave *Perula* her head, for I had often heard that a boat left to herself would be swept clear of any dangerous rocks. *Perula* was certainly swept, and for a horrible moment I thought we were going to make a spectacular passage through the Gulf of Corryvreckan as well, and was about to leap to the hatches. I had been reading the Sailing Directions which state: "If, however, a sailing vessel should be near the eastern entrance of the Gulf, during the west going stream at springs, she will be carried through. Then the hatches should be secured and she should endeavour to pass through the middle of the Gulf and will probably be taken by the stream between the most violent breakers, etc." Fortunately, I regained steerage control in time; we caught the northwardflood and charged like a scalded cat between Fladda Lighthouse and Dubh Sgeir; thence up the Firth of Lorn to Mull Sound. We arrived at Tobermory at 4.45 p.m. and are anchored in about 6 fathoms east-south-east of the jetty, close to a wooded shore.

Portree. May 13th: I know we should not have sailed on Friday the 13th. Since leaving the Straits the glass has fallen from 30 ins. to 29.5; something was about to happen. We left Tobermory at 9.15 a.m. I was anxious to cover the stretch of open Atlantic to Sleat Sound and thence to the shelter of Portree. We had not gone far before we knew we were "for it." The wind was south-west, about force 6. We had a terrific struggle to round Ardnamurchan Point. I must have forgotten the tide; we remained practically stationary, while *Perula* rolled her scuppers under. At length we made slow headway. At 10.30 we picked up the unpleasant words, "Warning of southerly gale," and spent a hectic day "racing the gale to shelter." Eventually we arrived at Portree at 8.30 p.m. in a state of great jubilation. "We've done it, Ron," I said, "we've raced the damn thing; and now we'll have a nice long stay in port, while it blows itself out." At 9 o'clock I again remarked: "We will just tune into the shipping forecast and see what we've escaped." There was no mention of the gale—we had had it.

Looking back, I suppose it had been pretty foul and the wind had increased steadily. With Rhum, Eigg and Muck to port, I had to have a rum myself, for to quote my native Lancashire, the weather "were proper mucky." We passed a small coaster heading south; one moment she would shoot up on the crest of a wave, only to disappear completely in the trough. She amused me so much that I called Adams up to look at her. Having just been thrown on the back of his neck in the saloon he remarked peevishly: "Don't know what you are laughing at, have you thought what we must look like?"

Even when we reached the comparative shelter of Sleat Sound it took us all our time to carry our small mainsail. Sudden squalls rushed down the mountain sides; you could see them coming as they tossed the water before them into white-capped heaps of flying spray. Then, with a shriek and howl the wind would come, laying even beamy *Perula* nearly flat and taking all my strength to hold the wheel as she shot forward. Usually the squalls were accompanied by blinding rain which blotted out the land on either side of us. Not too clever in the narrow Kyle Rhea. In Loch Alsh narrows I nearly felled the ferry. I was so busy judging the passage between the lighthouse and the buoys that I never saw it; a low lying contraption that looked as if it was being pulled across on a string. Adams shouted a frantic warning and I, in the midst of having tea, swallowed a shortbread whole, choked, and put *Perula* hard astern (with the sails up, of course). The ferry rolled by quite unperturbed.

Portree is, of course, the capital of the Isle of Skye. We are anchored north-east of the jetty, fairly close in, depth 8 fathoms. From the water it looks rather desolate on this May evening. The town stands in the midst of jagged cliffs patched with dull olive green and almost hidden in low grey clouds. Around us the hardy fishermen are sitting aboard their small boats mending their nets. The boat next to us is called *Brothers' Pride.* She is a neat, well-kept little craft, and the two brothers are solemnly at work, undisturbed by anybody or anything.

Stornoway May 14th: We did not leave Portree until mid-day; spent the morning shopping. Already we are feeling our shortness of supplies; tried all over to buy fresh vegetables without success. At last in desperation I said to one shopkeeper, "What's the matter up here; don't you grow vegetables?"

"Aye, lassie," he replied, "but ye're in the North the noo, they dinna ripen until June."

"Heavens above," I said to Adams, "if they call this the North, what's it going to be like further up?" So we carefully rationed out our tinned goods, dividing them up into four monthly supplies. "Because, Ron," I explained, "it will stop all the favourite kinds being eaten at one fell swoop." I also separated what I called an emergency ration which was not to be touched except in case of starvation. In fact, I have hidden the various portions away so carefully that I am sure we shall never be able to find them!

The passage to Stornoway was uneventful until off the coast of Lewis. I was sitting at the wheel, wondering why the water was so calm and the weather so peaceful when, according to the reports, we should be having strong winds. I decided we must be running up in an occlusion. I did not quite know what an occlusion was, but there was one about, and it sounded well. Then I saw some black pointed shapes dotted about in the water ahead. Thinking they were buoys put out by fishermen to mark their nets, I went on deck to ask Adams if he know of any rule as to which side I should pass. "Hell!" I suddenly exclaimed. One of my "black buoys" had whirled in the water and was charging straight at us. As it got nearer we distinguished the lines of a huge shark. "Quick!" I yelled. "Camera." Nearer and nearer it came; I watched fascinated. I could see its blue-coloured nose, the great body, and remembering the stories I had heard of these Scotch basking sharks, I clutched firmly to the rigging. The previous year several of them had attacked and sunk a small fishing craft, while one, with more ambition, had actually smashed the port holes of an inter-island steamer. As our shark reached us he gave a playful swish of his tail, and some 30 feet of him glided peacefully beneath *Perula's* keel. I mopped my brow in relief. After that we saw quite a lot of them, and even became bold enough to chase one or two, in search of pictures, but I admit the proceeding sent cold shivers down my spine.

We arrived at 8.30 p.m. and had just manoeuvred into the rather crowded little anchorage well up on the port hand opposite the Custom House, when it was suddenly discovered that part of the anchor was missing; the stock pin, to be exact. So the locals, who had watched us go in with such difficulty, had the added pleasure of watching us come out and hover around, disorganising all the shipping, while Adams endeavoured to carve a piece of wood to fill the gap. Finally, I got fed up and retreated to a position south-west of Creed Point, inside a line joining the point and a wreck buoy, where we are now anchored in 6 fathoms. Adams is very cross, because we are, of course, about half a mile from the town. He says it looks so damn silly, but I don't care.

May 15th. 2 pm.: Wind N., force 3. Slight swell. I am worried, more worried than I have been for a long time and I do not know why. We are three hours out from Stornoway and heading for Cape Wrath, the headland that forms the corner of North and West Scotland. I know it has a bad reputation and that when strong winds oppose the tide, a very dangerous sea kicks up, but while Wrath can uphold its name and be "proper wrathful," it can also be like a lamb. To-day it should be lamblike. We are making about 6 knots under power and sail. Long rollers are coming in from the North Atlantic; I have never experienced such big ones before, but there is nothing violent about them. We just climb steadily up them, then slide down the other side with hardly a perceptible roll.

Perhaps our departure from Stornoway has upset my nerves. We had quite a pleasant night ashore, and in one of the hotels we were greeted by a yachtsman from the Hamble River. He appeared to know all our movements for the last day or two; the route we had come and the weather we had experienced. Apparently he had been aboard an inter-island steamer which had kept passing us between its stops at various ports. He told us our adventures with the ferry and the squalls and, lastly, the anchor had provided the passengers and crew with quite a good entertainment. He seemed quite impressed with *Perula*, but not, I am afraid, with her crew. He told us we were the first yacht of the season up North and that everyone was very pleased as we were a "herald of spring." Made me feel quite like a cuckoo!

On asking where we were bound and being told Spitsbergen, the entire smoke room sat up, waved its ears, and collapsed into hoots of mirth. Finally Adams and I departed amid a chorus of: "Why go from one winter to another?"

"Rather it was you than me."

"Well, good-bye and good luck; you'll need it." We intended to leave at 8 a.m. but woke to find thick fog. "It's a good sign," I said, "early morning mist with the sun trying to break through—couldn't have a better day to tackle Wrath." We decided to leave as soon as the fog lifted. It did lift, and we did leave, only to have it descend on us again worse than ever. Stornoway was completely blotted out. We could not return and our route lay round the Eye peninsula, which we could not see either. This was rather a setback, for I had not bothered to lay off any courses for the first few miles, expecting we should be coasting. Of course, the protractor kept rolling off the table; it is one of those handsome brass ones on rollers; I could not find a pencil; the dividers were not in the case, and all those annoying little things happened that make true the saying, "more haste, less speed."

Having narrowly missed Biaston Holm, we set course for the Hen and Chickens. Possibly we would have been wiser to make for open water, but a good deal of traffic comes in and out of Stornoway and I feel it is better to hit a stationary rock than another craft which is moving. In the case of the rock you can get out and walk or at least sit on top of a buoy or beacon. So, with the fog-horn sounding Adams sat for'ard, peering into the blanket of white; sharks circled about us and I tried to produce my best navigation form. Every few minutes I would bob my head out of the wheelhouse and shout: "Have you seen the Hen yet?" "No," replied Adams. "Think the damn thing has gone to lay an egg." Silly name for a rock, anyway. Finally it loomed up on the starboard bow and we nearly felled the Chickens, having intended to leave it on the port hand.

After this the fog lifted and the weather is now quite decent, but I am all on edge and cannot settle to anything. Having smoked cigarette after cigarette I came below to write, thinking it might distract my mind, but it is no use.

4.45 p.m.: I have just changed course for Loch Inchard. We were 15 miles from Wrath and now we are heading back down the west coast for no apparent reason.

Loch Laxford. 10 p.m.: I am either psychic, or the goddess *Perula* whispered to me. We are anchored here in Fanagmore Bay; it's blowing like stink; the wireless is playing "Home Sweet Home," and believe me it feels like it! At 6.30 p.m. we hit the Scottish coast, almost literally. The northerly wind had increased to force 6, and driving rain reduced visibility to about 100 yards. I turned *Perula* somewhat thankfully into what I thought was the entrance to Inchard; then things happened quickly. In the space of a few minutes the wind increased to gale force and we were surrounded by rocks which, according to the chart, should not have been there. It was us, of course, who should not have been there. I looked at the white breaking water. It was chucking itself up some 8 to 10 feet. I did not know where to turn. "Get where it isn't breaking," said Adams, with great logic, "then we'll get the mainsail down before the wind does it for us."

It was bitterly cold on deck. The rain stung our faces and hands, numbing our limbs. With the mainsail safely stowed, we turned to the chart; it was no use, we could not make out where we were.

"We'll have to go back to open water and ride it out," said Adams.

"God forbid!" I murmured and turned with renewed vigour to the chart. At last it dawned on me; we were south of Handa Island and, thank heaven, quite close to Laxford.

We turned *Perula* north, against the wind and sea. At full throttle we barely made headway. I have never known the sea get up so quickly and we were shipping it green.

"We can't go on like this," said Adams. "Can't we?" I said grimly. "I'll get into that blasted loch if it's the last thing I do." The damn place was only just round the corner.

"Are you sure you have the right entrance this time?" he said rudely.

"Yes," I snapped. "The Sailing Directions clearly say you look for a red cliff; there it is."

"Humph," he grunted, "all the cliffs look ruddy to me."

Having taken an hour to cover about 2 miles, we staggered into Laxford. The waves fairly swept down the loch, and after some debate we decided to make for the anchorage in Fanagmore Bay. It is a godforsaken place; just one or two small farms. The inhabitants, hardy Scots, did not even trouble to look at us as we came in. We are tucked away in the west corner, close inshore, and a rock has just bobbed up to the south-east; but it is a comfortable anchorage in about 5 fathoms.

Adams chose this, of all nights, to develop our shark films, and our new and rather complicated developing tank would choose to go wrong in the middle. We had to put all the lights out, and he has spent the evening working in the dark and I've spent it counting 1,320; 720 in developer and 600 in fixing. Naturally, the photographs were a dismal failure.

So ends a "perfect day."

CHAPTER II

NORTH OF SCOTLAND

Abeam Cape Wrath. 5.55 p.m. 16th May.

Left Loch Laxford at 1.55 p.m. Northerly wind, about force 4, and a fairly heavy swell. As we rounded Whale Back and headed north I looked back and made my usual notes on the entrance to the loch. First I noted that when abeam Whale Back, a pointed mountain marks the entrance; but in bad weather this may be obscured in cloud. I also noted that from the north, Handa looks like a headland and not an island. I still think the rocks, south of the entrance, look red. With these facts carefully written on the back of my chart, I feel I can in future find Laxford without difficulty. It is a useful haven on a coast where good anchorages are few and far between.

At 4.15, Bulgie Island was abeam. I had debated whether to go inside or outside it, and decided on out. This is not necessary, but just shows how careful I am—when it does not matter. In fact, it must be my careful day, for having been advised to give Cape Wrath a good berth, I have done so. We are getting a slight tossing, but a tanker, closer inshore, is getting a real ducking and I am pointing it out to Adams in great glee, for about half-an-hour ago he said: "Give it a good berth, certainly; but not five blinking miles."

Duslic, or Stag rock, has been worrying me, but I can see it now. It lies about three-quarters of a mile N.N.E. of the lighthouse. It can be avoided by keeping Bulgie Island in sight until the summit of Faraid Head is open northward of An Garbheilean.

As I look at the North Scottish coast, I begin to realise the majesty of the sea. Sheer walls of rock eaten away by the force of pounding waves; cleft and rugged with great yawning caves. When the caves become too deep, the top of the cliff falls in, leaving gigantic pillars of rock. There is not a single tree in sight, and hardly a blade of grass.

10.p.m.: We are now anchored in Loch Eriboll—have christened it Loch 'Orrible. It is another desolate-looking place and we are not bothering to go ashore. There is a road, however, and we were quite excited at seeing a motor-car going along it. Still, I should not be rude about Loch 'Orrible, it has provided us with a comfortable anchorage in 9 fathoms at the south end of Camas-an-Duin. Up to date we have covered 458 miles. Only about another 2,000 to go.

Orkney Islands. May 19th: We have been at Stromness for the last two days. Had quite a good passage from 'Orrible. The only thing that bothered me was that you see the high land of Hoy first, and in the distance you are apt to think it is the whole of the Orkneys. Don't let this kid you into changing course for the middle of it; you will only have to turn northwards again when the rest appears—as I did.

I had been dreading the 8-knot tide in Hoy Sound, but it did not worry us; there were no overfalls to speak of and we chugged peacefully into Stromness harbour. With the aid of "Jimmy," we dropped anchor at the top end, N.E. of the last pier, in 3 fathoms by lead; 1½ by chart.

Jimmy had boarded us halfway up the harbour and promptly appointed himself our friend, guide and boatman, for which services he would accept no payment. His attitude is typical of these friendly Islanders. Everything they possess belongs to everyone else. No matter what hour of the day or night we wish to go ashore or back aboard, Jimmy is there (with a different boat each time) to row us. He is a real godsend; he takes me shopping, carries my parcels, and saves me from sudden death. The main street in Stromness is exceedingly narrow and paved with flagstones. There is no separate pavement, and the quaint old houses and shops rise up on either side barely four yards across from each other. The first morning I was "jay walking," thinking I was on a pavement, when Jimmy grabbed me by the scruff of the neck and yanked me into a shop. A car shot by, missing the shop door by inches. Apparently it is customary to seek refuge in this manner; a good opportunity to drop in for a chat.

Nearly all the shopkeepers own boats.

"Fine little ship you have," says the butcher.

"Sailing my little craft to Glasgow to see the Exhibition," says the ironmonger, trying not to look horrified at my request for "a hot-water bottle, please." I was finding the weather very cold, probably due to the winds, which were now blowing hard from the north-east.

Jimmy took us to see the Provost, a fine white-haired man, who obligingly supplied the shipping-forecast from the wireless on the counter of his shop. He also provided me with splendid socks of real Orkney wool which, though not perhaps so well known, is equally as good as the more popular Shetland variety.

May 20th. 9p.m.: Bound for the Shetlands. We left Stromness at 11.25. I was very undecided; the forecast was still fresh north-easterlies; head winds. It would be none too pleasant crossing the Röst, that stretch of open water between the Orkneys and Shetlands, where the tide rushes through, from 5 to 7 knots, and when opposed to the seas, makes the waters in the vicinity of Sumburgh Head far worse than Cape Wrath. Also, the Orkneys are an annoying place in that the tides being so strong there is hardly a haven you can enter unless they are with you. Unless you are careful what time you leave you find you cannot get back should you desire to do so, at least not until the tide turns.

The passage of 120 miles would take us a good 24 hours under favourable conditions, and although Fair Island is dotted in the middle, so to speak, it is not much use for an anchorage except in settled weather. I had to make up my mind quickly, for at 3 p.m. we lost the tide through Holm Sound, 18 miles away.

"What shall we do?" I asked, but Adams and Jimmy would not commit themselves, although their expressions looked "stay-in-portish." "Let's have a bang at it," I said, impatiently. "It isn't blowing N.E. here and we can always get back at three o'clock if we want to." I was keen to get off, for anti-cyclones were coming up, and with luck we might get them for the North Sea crossing.

Jimmy accompanied us halfway down the harbour, then seizing my hand he wished me luck, and leaped into his boat. "We must write to him," said Adams. But friendships of the sea are such that we suddenly discovered we knew neither his surname nor address.

Scapa Flow disappointed me; I had expected to see a good deal in the famous war-time naval base. All I saw was part of a gloomy hull or mast of a vessel protruding from the water of a blocked sound. There is something very pathetic about the sight of these old block ships lying there and being broken up by the rushing tide. Rusty old hulls that were once sound; ships that have served their country and now lie rotting.

I was soon to get a much closer view of these ships, for I had decided to leave Scapa by Holm Sound. This Sound is officially closed to navigation on account of the block ships that stretch almost across Kirk Sound, through which you first pass. The passage between the old "Thames" and another old hull is about 200 yards, and the tidal stream attains a strength of about 8 knots.

Several of the local men had advised me not to take this passage, others said there was little to it. I also knew that Major Smales had been through and found no difficulty. The trouble was that once the tide caught us there could be no turning back or stopping to think. I had memorised the chart as best I could, but as we neared this rather doubtful exit, I began to wish very definitely that we had not come.

"Ron," I said, "this is damn silly, we're inexperienced, strangers to the district, and here we are going through a channel many of the locals would think twice about and . . . . Oh! hell, our insurance won't cover us." As we rounded Skaildaquoy Point, I nearly had a fit. The block ships appeared to stretch right across. But it was too late to turn back. I thought of the words of the Stromness blacksmith. When he came to mend our anchor, he had found me poring over the chart. "Don't let the Sound worry you, lass," he said, "make up to the north shore until you are abeam the opening, then let her go through. You'll be all right."

It is sound advice to steer for the north shore, for while you do so the tide carries you crabwise nearer and nearer the block ships, and on the starboard hand there are submerged dangers you might otherwise hit. When abeam the opening I headed *Perula* for it. The water fairly boils past the old wrecks, but we had steerage control and through we went without the slightest trouble.

Next I had been advised to steer fairly close up to the disused lighthouse to miss shoal ground, after which course is altered to starboard, down the widening channel of Holm Sound, and out to sea. Another block ship lies on the port hand shortly after passing the lighthouse; it is submerged, but marked by a green wreck buoy.

I have given these details rather fully because the Sailing Directions naturally refrain from saying much about a channel which is closed. I do not think Kirk Sound is nearly as black as it is painted. You can see the worst of the block ships above water and there is plenty of room between them for a yacht.[1]

Safely through, I heaved a sigh of relief, yet at the same time I felt rather disappointed; it had been almost too easy, like going to the dentist. You get all worked up only to find he does not hurt you at all. Copinsay was abeam by 3.20 p.m. We streamed the log and changed course for Sumburgh Head. The weather is much better than the forecast indicated; a bit of a swell, but easterly winds, force 3, so we are under sail and power, and *Perula* is quite comfortable.

We have just sighted Fair Island and are finding that a larger allowance

1 NOTE.—Since this was written Scapa Flow has been re-fortified and fresh enquiries should be made before attempting Kirk Sound.

should be made for the cross-tide than you would expect. For this tide-work I am finding my old course and distance-calculator useful. C.D.C.'s, as we call them, are much used in aviation to estimate the effect of wind on a course, and obtain the resultant speed over the ground. Mine is composed of two discs, a bottom one marked 0-360, and a top one which rotates over the bottom one, and is transparent and marked with squares. Two revolving arms with sliding pointers are attached in the centre of the top disc. Having set an arrow on the top disc to the true course on the lower disc, one arm is set to the wind direction and its sliding pointer to the wind speed. The second arm is then moved round until its sliding pointer, set at the cruising speed, is on the same line as the other pointer. The number of squares between them represents the ground speed and the direction in which the second arm is pointing is the true course to steer, allowing for the wind. It is, of course, merely a means of solving the triangle of velocities without paper or pencil or messing up your chart. By substituting tide for wind and knocking the o's off the arms (i.e., calling 60 m.p.h. 6 knots, etc.), I find this instrument saves me a lot of time. My C.D.C. is composed of celluloid and apt to warp, but they are also made in brass.

A trawler has just given me rather a shock. It looked as though it was going to charge straight across our bows, but when about 50 yards off, turned and ran parallel with us. I suppose the skipper just wanted to see who we were and if we wanted anything. Greetings having been exchanged, he is now heading off to his fishing. I have a great admiration for trawler skippers: they are grand men, always willing to give small craft a helping hand.

Lerwick. 10 p.m. May 21st: Arrived Lerwick 9 o'clock this morning, Sumburgh Röst having given no trouble. Did not quite know where to anchor, but Captain Harrison, the harbour master, had seen us come in, and signalling us alongside Victoria pier, he told us to drop just outside the motor-lifeboat. This is an excellent anchorage, close E.S.E. of the breakwater; most convenient for the town, yet out of the traffic. Going in we felt rather alarmed, as the bottom can be seen quite clearly, but there is a depth of 2 to 3 fathoms.

We hurried ashore for our mail and sent the usual prepaid wire to "Weather, London." The wind had freshened from the south and Lerwick harbour was quite choppy. It looked as though my anti-cyclone had gone astray, but, just in case, we stocked ship for the North Sea passage.

At the Straits I had talked grandly of sailing direct from Lerwick to the Arctic Circle, but I have now obtained a wholesome respect for these northern waters. It is still early in the year, and the big rolling seas rather scare us. Discretion is the better part of valour, and I have decided to take the shortest possible crossing. Even so we bought sufficient provisions for about two weeks, a lengthy procedure that ended in the usual procession, Adams and I, a string of errand boys, and the local Press.

In the afternoon the Customs came aboard, and in spite of my sweetest smile I had to pay duty on bonded stores consumed, having broken the seal while still in British waters. This, of course, is quite permissible, as long as you report to the Customs at your next calling-place. Entry was duly made in the yacht Stores Book that a certain percentage of whisky and gin had been consumed and I had to pay out about 25s. Considering the initial cost, it worked out about 15s. per bottle, more expensive than if I had bought the bottles in the ordinary way. The only consolation is that the Orkneys and Shetlands are practically dry, and we have got something to drink, whereas otherwise we might not have had any. Also, in a port one is always expected to entertain.

After tea the telegram arrived from "Weather, London": "Winds increasing fresh tonight vicinity Lerwick otherwise settled quiet." It sounds good, but unfortunately the wind had already "increased fresh" and is, in fact, fair howling. It seems silly to set out, yet if we do not we might miss the "settled quiet" beyond.

I think the worst part of this sailing business is making up your mind. Anyway, I have drawn my usual pictures, decided we are in the lower half of a disturbance which is travelling north-east, and have assured Adams (with a conviction I do not feel myself) that as we sail east the barometer will rise. He is very trusting and quite ready to leave tonight, but I did not have much sleep last night. It is nasty, cold and wet; also I am rather scared of tackling the northern part of Bressay Sound in the dark. "On second thoughts," remarks the Meteorologist(?), "having studied the pressure distribution I feel that owing to an 'associated secondary', it would be advisable to wait until dawn."

North Sea. 6 p.m. May 22nd: Dawn, as far as we were concerned, proved to be 7 a.m. In driving rain we hauled the dinghy aboard, and we proceeded out of the northern part of Bressay Sound, under power. Outside the wind was light and variable; we optimistically hoisted the mainsail, but it was no good. The boom crashed from side to side as we rolled in the swell. On those occasions Adams always wants to lash the boom in position, and I do not; so we get rather cross. He says: "It's chafing the gear, why won't you have it lashed?" I frown darkly, and having no reason other than an instinct that may or may not be right, reply: "I don't like it and I don't think it is done."

By 2 p.m. there was not a breath of wind. We had reached the "settled quiet" and with it came fog. A thick belt, with visibility less than 50 yards; as Adams put it, you could just about see "two waves".

Now, thank goodness, the fog has cleared, but I do not like the look of the weather. Still, this beastly oily swell and a horrible grey mass ahead. It is a queer feeling to be in a small boat that appears to get smaller every minute, in the middle of a very large North Sea, that appears to get larger every minute. Sometimes I begin to wonder what would happen if anything went wrong, if one of us was taken ill; if anything happened to *Perula.* Then I stop thinking quickly. We are not on any recognised shipping route; we have no wireless by which we could send an S.O.S., and we have even lost our distress rockets. I think I must have used them last Fifth of November. Sometimes I wonder why we ever cross large expanses of sea in little boats, working and worrying ourselves to death, cooking under difficulties, having to wash-up and generally living in the utmost discomfort. It is far more romantic and exciting to go and see a good film of the sea at the local cinema. I must remember in future.

North Sea. 8 a.m. May: 23rd: I'm so tired. I feel convinced my neck will not support my head any longer. At 10.30 last night the fog came down on us good and proper. Darkness was coming on and we could not see a thing. To make matters worse, I had stepped down the engine-room companion ladder when it was not there, and sat heavily upon our fog-horns with results that caused them to cease "horning." They were the two motor-horns we had used in the Caledonian Canal the previous year, and Adams had just unearthed them because our klaxon appeared to have "fog on its chest."

I think it was the most miserable night I have ever spent; no "off duty" for either of us, of course. We took it in turns one at the wheel, the other sitting for'ard on deck, peering into the fog, listening and periodically smiting the ship's bell with a large hammer. The bell still bore the name *Monavic*, and possibly due to corrosion, it could not be persuaded to ring in any other manner. It was bitterly cold on deck in the dampness, notwithstanding the bonded stores which were rapidly decreasing.

A gipsy once told me my imagination would be the curse of my life. Last night it was. As I peered into "nothing" I saw "everything." Ships charging down on us, really big ones, doing at least 15 knots and never expecting to find a small yacht in such lonely waters. I quite forgot that previously I had bemoaned the fact we were not on any shipping route. *Perula* was "sunk" a thousand times, and Adams repeatedly changed course on my reports of "light on the port bow." In fact, if a vessel had really come, I feel sure we should have hit it; putting its appearance down either to my imagination or rum.

Most things can be got used to, however, and as the night progressed I became quite hardened. "What's a little fog, anyway!" So, with poor Adams smiting the bell on deck, I curled up gracefully on the damp staysail on the wheelhouse floor. Needless to say, the Chief Engineer, eventually returning for "warmth," was horrified to find the Captain fast asleep!

Visibility started to improve about 4.30 a.m., and shortly after it began to rain. It is fairly clear now, and let us hope it stays clear, or we shall simply have to stay outside. There are so many outlying skerries that I dare not even contemplate what it would be like attempting to hit the Norwegian coast in fog—hit would very definitely be the word.

CHAPTER III

BACK IN NORWAY

Noren. 11 p.m. May: 23rd.

I have been called most things, taken for a spy in South America (and damn near shot), but I have never been taken for a smuggler before. I may be a drinker of rum but I am not a "runner" of the same.

We sighted land at 9.45 this morning. I presumed it was Norway, but due to the overcast sky had been unable to get a sight all the way across. I am never particularly sorry when I cannot get a sight; it is a lot of work and my results do not always justify it. The mountains started to show up fairly clearly. They were capped with snow, rising into a sky that was now blue, and on the starboard bow a large mass of white glinted in the sun. I took it to be the Sognefjord with its glaciers. There is something rather fairylike about the Norwegian coast; it looks so unreal. Fantastic peaks of misty blue, purple and white, and beneath them small dark islands that appear to be suspended in mid-air. Mirage effect is very pronounced.

Of course we got lost. On approaching these out-lying islands they all looked the same. We could see ships in the Indreled beyond, but the channels into it seemed a mass of breaking water. So we kept sailing first north then south, as I saw my usual mountains that resembled saddles and hills like haystacks. It was bitterly cold on deck and my eyes were streaming as I tried to pick up landmarks through the glasses. The sight of a lighthouse cheered us up tremendously, for I had originally set course to Hellisöy but it was not it, and having no list of lights, we had to search the charts and Sailing Directions for pictures or descriptions of lighthouses.

It was 3 o'clock before we did find Hellisöy, a red iron tower with two white bands. We had hit the coast slightly south of our course, then turned north too far out and missed it.

We were now on "home ground" so to speak, for we had sailed this part of the Indreled the previous year. We debated about putting into Feje, but we really wanted an anchorage with a telegraph station so that we could cable home. Parents always get worried when small yachts make sea passages. There were no big towns nearer than Bergen, and anyway we did not want to go south. Adams, studying the chart, gave an exclamation of triumph. "Here we are," he said, "Noren, the very place." Sure enough, there on the chart, near the entrance to the Sognefjord, was the familiar picture of our anchor and the letters T.S.

It felt good to be back in Norway. The same old poles, sticking up like broom handles, the same fishing boats chugging along with the same noise, the rocky islands, the fjords and the mountains. The colouring was magnificent, far more beautiful than it had been later in the year. Feeling thoroughly excited I went below and poshed myself up all ready for shore.

We reached our destination at 6.30 p.m. and looked helplessly about. "Where is it?" I said. There was no sign of an anchorage, just a bare mass of rock. Closer inspection revealed a beacon of sorts, making a passage about 20 yards wide between two islands, which earlier had blended in with the high ground. There was a sunken rock in the entrance, but as usual the Norwegians had kindly placed a pole on it, with an arm pointing which side to pass. What lay beyond was veiled in mystery.

"It looks dreadful," I groaned, "even if we get in, it doesn't look as if we shall ever get out; you would pick a place like this." Adams looked disconsolate but dignified. At length, after remarks such as: "You're hitting a rock." "For heaven's sake, mind the pole," we entered, to find ourselves in a delightful little haven. There were only four or five wooden buildings, two of which appeared to be inhabited, but there were plenty of targets painted on the rocks. After some argument as to which one we should use, we dropped anchor and tied up astern.

As usual, the "Q" flag was not flying. As I said to Adams: "It's no use putting it up here, there won't be any Customs Officer in a godforsaken place like this." We decided to nip ashore, send our telegrams, then return straight aboard, and report this unorthodox behaviour at Florö, where they would probably remember us from last year. Feeling rather sorry I had put on my best trousers and jersey, we set off in the dinghy for the building bearing the Norwegian telegraph sign (a tin plate with a kind of horn on it). The "Reception Committee" took the form of a large dog that barked furiously and leaped madly about the small jetty.

"Wonder if it bites?" said Adams doubtfully.

"Leave it to me," I replied. "I'm wonderful with animals."

I was. As I climbed the slippery steps, murmuring, "Good doggie, there's a nice doggie," the "doggie" took one bound at me and with his forepaws firmly planted on my shoulders, nearly sent me flying backwards into the water. It was, however, merely a demonstration of affection.

This disturbance brought forth a portly gentleman, clad in navy trousers and a magnificent pullover. "Speak English?" I asked hopefully. He shook his head and burst forth in his own language. I shook my head. "Umph," he grunted, and that appeared to be the one word we had in common. We pointed to the telegraph sign over the door of his shop (he is shopkeeper as well) and he took us inside.

It took us over an hour with the aid of a dictionary to send our telegram. To start with, he insisted upon understanding the message before he would send it, which I suppose was very wise. The word "Salford" in the address caused a great deal of trouble. He was very suspicious of it and wanted to leave it out. I tried to explain it was an English city by saying, "Bergen, Norway. Salford, England"; whereupon he promptly wanted to send the message to Bergen. He was not to know we had just arrived foreign. Meanwhile, two customers in the shop were becoming impatient, but he just waved them aside and got busy with the procedure of sending telegrams to England. This had to be looked up in various books, after which there followed a fearful battle on the telephone with the Norwegian equivalent of P for Percy, Z for Zebra. The Exchange kept giving him the wrong department and he had to start all over again.

At length the message was sent; we bowed, shook hands and returned aboard for what we thought was a well-earned rest.

An hour later I was dozing peacefully in the saloon, when something leaped on me. It was the postmaster's dog, his owner having arrived aboard, this time in the guise of a Customs Officer, for which purpose he now had on a grey cloth cap. I showed him the ship's papers, but the English words conveyed nothing, so he shook his head and said "Umph." He produced some papers, apparently for me to fill up; the Norwegian words conveyed nothing to me, so I shook my head and said, "Umph." Two hours later we were still "umphing" and had proceeded little further. Adams, resigned, turned out the stove on our supper and produced drinks. This just about finished it. At the sight of our bonded stores our friend nearly had a fit! They were, of course, officially declared in the stores book, but in proof gallons as 1.65 whisky, 1.49 gin, and 1.37 rum. Possibly he thought the figure "one" denoted one bottle of each, and on seeing a whole cupboard full, he was probably justified in thinking we were rum runners. Our arrival direct from Shetlands at so small a place was in itself suspicious. We had not hoisted the "Q" flag, and had tried to send a telegram he did not understand.

He decided to search the ship. Every few minutes he would leap up, gesticulating that some cupboard or locker must be opened for his inspection. He searched the wardrobe, wireless cupboard, the pan lockers. I had been waiting rather gleefully for him to pounce on the largest "cupboard" of all, but he must have guessed what it was. I made a mental note, if smuggling, choose the lavatory.

Finally we all got fed up and filled up papers at random; I think I declared a ton of pickles, but was past caring. He has just departed, after the usual bowing and shaking hands. Adams said, "Thank goodness that's over," and is now trying to resurrect the supper.

Florö. May 25th: Adams was quite wrong, it was not over. Next morning I chanced to look through the porthole. "Heavens," I groaned, "he's coming again." There he was in his rowing boat, complete with dog and black bag. "Have we time to get away?" said Adams. "He's sure to have spent the night reading up the procedure for dealing with English smugglers." Next moment, however, our friend was aboard and we were going through everything all over again.

At last the bottles, having been counted about five times, were all packed away again, and our friend opened his black bag. Alas! he had forgotten his sealing clippers. He looked at the stores, then looked at us, and was torn with conflicting emotions. Dare he trust us not to nip any out in his absence? He was probably as fed up as we were and decided to risk it. On his return with the clippers, the little metal tag was attached and we bowed and shook hands once again.

With one thought in our minds we dashed to the engine, started it up, almost forgetting the anchor in our haste to escape before he changed his mind and came back again.

We arrived at Florö late last night, and this morning three very amused Customs Officers visited the "English Smugglers" and straightened out our papers. Apparently with a crew of two we are allowed three bottles a week out of bond. It only seems like a week or two since we were here before; everybody seems to remember us; handshakes in the shops and reunions with our old friends.

Aalesund. May 31st: We arrived here for one night on May 26th and have been here ever since. If any British yachts are coming to Norway and want a good time, the best advice I can give them is: "Come to Aalesund." I have always thought that North of England hospitality wanted some beating, but the people here simply would not allow us to leave. Our welcome has excelled anything I have ever experienced. From large modern homes to lonely farmsteads, in country houses or log cabins high up in the mountains and on boats large and small, we have seen Norwegian life as few foreigners are able to see it.

Our days have usually started with an invitation to "breakfast"; not breakfast as we know it, but to cocktails, lobster and wine, at 11 a.m. This is followed by dinner at 2 p.m. Plates of freshly caught salmon, salads, sweets thick with cream. After a nap comes "coffee" accompanied by delicious pastries; supper at 8 p.m. is "just a snack", possibly another couple of salmon. That is "town life". Meals are served in beautiful airy homes, on large verandahs over-looking the fjords.

We have learned a good deal of Norwegian manners and customs. To start with, you must never drink at table unless some one says "Skaal" to you, and to you directly. Usually it will be your host and you take a hurried glance to see what he is drinking; for you must respond in the same liquid. After that various people seem to skaal each other, and you end up by having a mass of glasses round you and hastily taking a sip of each, depending on which course the person who addresses you has reached. At one supper I was diving wildly for beer, then back to aquavit, on to port, and back to beer again, with an odd sip of whisky or liqueur thrown in.

The meal ended, you rise from the table, shake your hostess by the hand, and say "Takk for mat." The first time this happened I thought how rude we were, going home as soon as we had finished eating. I was just going to put my hat and coat on when I noticed the guests were assembling in another room. We were merely thanking our hostess for the meal, and when doing this, if you want to be extra polite, you tell her the soup was good, the fish excellent and so on. If next day you meet your host or hostess, you must say "Takk for sist," thanks for yesterday.

In Norway, man is, of course, far the more important of the sexes. Sometimes in a café our host would remain seated while his wife rose to order the food and tend to our wants, for in most Norwegian cafés it is customary to select from a counter the dishes or cakes you require for your party.

One night we had a Norwegian couple aboard to supper. You cannot leave dirty plates about on a small yacht; so after the meal, Adams slipped unobtrusively into the galley and began washing up. I remained seated at table, drinking coffee and entertaining our guests. Suddenly the

Norwegian man became very red, embarrassed and uncomfortable. For some moments I puzzled, wondering what was the matter, then it dawned on me. He had seen Adams washing up while I, a woman, sat at table. To him, it was horrifying; an insult to his sex. His wife, however, sat up, looked in wonder and promptly decided to adopt English habits herself!

On the Wednesday, we had a really good party at the Aalesund "Sailing Hut," as they call it, situated on its own little island, some twenty minutes by ferry from the town. It is an impressive building, standing on top of a hill, surrounded by trees. Snow-clad mountains rise up behind and reflect on the fjords beneath. The club has 240 members and, during the season, Wednesday and Saturday are the "big nights."

When we arrived, most of the members were already seated at small tables on the verandah, which lines the dance floor, and after we had enjoyed a very large and excellent supper, we were officially welcomed to the club.

The President, Hr. Aslak Solbjorg, presented Adams and me with club brooches, after which we commenced to dance the night away, and most of the morning as well. Aalesund may be officially "dry" but the sailing club is far from it.

It was almost midnight sun and there was no appreciable change of light; except perhaps that the great open fire of pine logs burned more brightly between the hours of 11 p.m. and 1 a.m. Outside, the fjords and mountains were bathed in pink and gold; the view from the sailing hut is magnificent.

With the sun high in the sky we all boarded the ferry, which promptly fell into the spirit of the occasion by taking up a list of 45°. Everybody joined in community singing, both English and Norwegian. On approaching the town, however, our President came round restoring order with a series of "shushes," and we trooped off, all looking very sedate and respectable.

With the sun shining it seemed all wrong to go to bed, so we accepted an invitation to visit another boat. The owner was a commercial traveller, and Norway being a place of water, his calls were naturally made by boat. The saloon showroom seemed to house everything from a packet of hairpins to a grand piano. Our host could not speak a word of English, but to show his welcome, insisted on giving us many of his samples and, much to my delight, finished up by kissing Adams. Adams had the laugh, however, when the ship's engineer, mistaking my sex owing to my yachting cap, showed me round the engine room, clad only in his pants and vest.

My yachting cap is an innovation this season. I had not worn one before because I felt that on a woman it looked a bit musical comedy. Also, I was inclined to favour those tough sea dogs who considered a bowler hat (with six coats of varnish) more appropriate for an owner skipper. In short, I thought a yachting cap was pure swank. But going foreign a little swank is often useful. Several times already I have been called "Captain" and treated like the master of at least 10,000 tons.

On the other hand, people are apt to stare at me in the street and say: "What is it?" But I just give them a withering glance and walk on. The engineer was not the first one to mistake my sex owing to the head-gear, coupled as it is with navy trousers and a burberry. The first day I wore it in Bangor, I went into the ladies' department of a shoe shop to buy some deck shoes. The sales-girl gave me a crushing look and said: "It's the gents you want." Knowing sea-faring men, she probably thought I was trying to "get off." Again, in the Orkneys I was peacefully gazing into a shop window when I staggered beneath a vigorous slap on the back and a jovial voice exclaimed: "Well, if it isn't old Jimmy." When I turned and the poor man saw that "Jimmy" was a woman he went crimson with embarrassment and muttering "Sorry," fled as if for his life. For the most part, here in Norway, I am spared experiences such as these, for I cannot understand what the people are saying about me, which is perhaps just as well.

For the week-end, the harbour master, Captain Christiansen and his wife joined the crew of *Perula* and we left Aalesund to visit some of the real Norway; fjords and villages unheard of by the tourist. Our course lay under the new Vegsund bridge, and if the Captain had not been aboard I should never have dared to take *Perula* under it. As it was, a small crowd gathered on top and watched in awe, expecting our mast to go, for by Norwegian standards we have a very tall mast. We sailed down narrow fjords edged with pink and white fruit blossom, under the shadow of snow-capped mountains. A strangely beautiful world, the top half still deep in winter, yet the lower bathed in spring. Rich green grass, wild violets; even apricots, strawberries and tomatoes growing out of doors. *Perula* caused a great sensation at the smaller places, entire villages flocking to the quayside. Many brought presents; chocolate coloured goats' milk cheese, pails of milk or cream, and bottles of home-brewed beer. When we invited them aboard to look round they were delighted. On they came, in an endless procession, until *Perula* sunk at least a foot deeper in the water. All the men came first, being, of course, the most important; when they had finished the women and children arrived. Adams and I sat in the saloon as a couple of exhibits. We could not speak to our guests, but Captain Christiansen told us afterwards that our visit had created such an impression upon these simple country folk that for the next ten years at least all happenings would be referred back to the time when the British yacht came.

In return we were invited to their homes, spotless little wooden farms and houses. Many had picturesque grass-covered roofs, with buttercups and meadowsweet growing round the chimney stack. Often the bed was in the parlour, with beautifully embroidered quilt and cushions. Old-fashioned lace mats draped the furniture, but the floor was usually bare. The women were served with coffee and home baked biscuits; the men with more home-brewed beer, accompanied by the usual "skaals" and "takks."

At 11 p.m., when the sun started to sink, the entire countryside was tinged with gold, the snow turned from deep pink to purple and the fruit blossoms, reflecting the same shades, took on the form of a second layer of snow. May is one of the most delightful months in Norway. Ski-ing parties are still being held in the mountains, the sun shines brightly and the cruise ships have not yet arrived.

Captain Christiansen was delighted to be back aboard a ship; he spent most of his time at the wheel. Adams and I were only too glad of a chance to sit back in lordly state. As the Captain liked to rise early, Adams would get up, start the engine for him, then go back to bed and leave him to it.

We got back to Aalesund on Monday to find great excitement. "Cirkus, cirkus!" joyfully yelled the Norwegian kiddies. I looked round for the conventional caravan of the English travelling circus, having forgotten Norway is a place of water. A sleepy old schooner glided up to the quayside. And talk about Noah's Ark! The animals, people and equipment that came off that old ship would have filled an ocean liner. Instead of looking for a nice green field or space of open land, the entire contraption was erected by the quayside. I looked at Captain Christiansen, rather expecting him to explode at the littering of his domain, but apparently such things are done in Norway. I would give anything to see the circus ship arrive in London or Liverpool; the harbour master's face would be a joy to behold.

That night a friend, Hr. Moa, took us to see the show, and we found an identical turn we had seen at Morecambe last winter; so you now know where circuses go in the summer time.

To-day we have had breakfast with Hr. Stephansen, Vice-President of the Sailing Club and Director of Shell. This was followed by a car drive to Hr. Larsen's cabin in the mountains. To-morrow is Sailing Club night at the "hut" so "you can't possibly leave to-morrow." As about a week has slipped away, at dawn we are planning to do likewise and send our apologies.

CHAPTER IV

SUNDRY BOTHER

Namsenjord. Midnight. June 3rd.

We celebrated our last night in Aalesund by having a fire. We decided to stock the "bunkers" (a locker underneath the wireless cupboard) in readiness for our passage north. I fear we must have mistaken the Norwegian for "Coalite." After consulting the dictionary at great length, we asked for "Firti kilo rögfri kull." What we got I do not quite know. We were sitting in front of the saloon fire when we started to choke and cough. "They have done us," I said, indignantly. "It isn't smokeless coal at all." Suddenly the bulkhead burst into flames. I seized a syphon of soda and Adams dashed to the galley for the kettle (I wonder why we carry three fire-extinguishers?). Fortunately, the flames had not got a hold and the affair was a matter of seconds; but Adams has had to saw away part of the bulkhead and now I shall have to keep an aspidistra or something there, to 'ide the 'ole.

We left Aalesund next morning at 7.20, June 1st, and had a disgusting passage to Kristiansund. The first few miles are described by the Sailing Directions as: "This part of the Indreled is only available for vessels with local knowledge"; the next part as "wide and free from dangers" (thank Heaven!) and the last part as "very foul, one of the most difficult parts of the Norwegian coast to navigate".

It would not have been so bad if it had not been the "day after the week before." The last part was not only a mass of rocks, but exposed to the open sea, and the wind naturally chose this moment to blow hard from the north.

"Where's Kolbeinsflu?" I said, with some annoyance at the non-appearance of the light and whistle buoy by which I had planned to change course.

"I think," said Adams, "we got a notice to mariners about it before we left."

"Well," I replied, crossly, "what did the notice say?"

"Only that it had disappeared," said Adams, mildly. I was saved from an apoplectic fit by the appearance of Kolbeinsflu, which had apparently been captured and brought back.

For five hours the seas swept over us. *Perula* pitched and tossed like a broncho, and all the flowers (that a woman will collect in port) upset. "Confound the blasted wind," I said, throwing the last of the tulips overboard. "Wish to hell it would quieten down." Whereupon the weather obliged, and added a nice thick mist. This was, of course, far worse than the wind, for the channel lay between submerged rocks.

We reached Kristiansund at 9 o'clock, but did not anchor until 9.30, because there were so many buoys that we quarrelled for half-an-hour as to which we should use. In the end we dropped in the worst possible place in Vaagen, and horrified the locals by tying up astern to a black pole marking the channel. When we wanted to leave next morning, the tide had come in and covered most of the pole and our warp!

The next day was spent having a thrilling race up Trondheimsled with a Norwegian fishing boat. They were slightly faster on engine, but with every puff of wind, up went our sails and we would shoot past them. Then, of course, the wind dropped and they would pass us. About 2 p.m. we got a really fresh breeze and led by a mile. Whereupon the fishermen brought out odd bits of canvas, blankets, etc., and before we had finished we both looked like the week's washing out to dry. We won by a short head, however, and feeling rather like Oxford turned off with a cheery wave to spend the night at South Leksen, anchored behind a small rocky island, 4 fathoms, fair bit of tide running—leave it at that. Trondheimsled is very easy to navigate; we came up it with nothing but a general chart.

This morning we left South Leksen at 7.20 and got in a slight mess with Grandevik, which is one of those places where the rods, poles and perches are never the ones you think they are. Abeam the northern end of Valsö we got into a real "muck" which ended by my treating some Norwegian fishermen to an entertainment second only to the Folies Bergère. Adams was nobly doing the week's wash.

"Swop you an extra hour at the wheel if you'll do mine as well." In consequence, I had been at the wheel for some time, and with my usual care had come all round Valsö, instead of taking the inner passage. With Valsööre light on the starboard bow, Adams, having just hung up the last of the "smalls," took over. Without explaining properly where we were, I departed below to have a bath.

I had just started my ablutions when I heard him call: "There's a rock here not marked on the chart."

"Never mind," I replied, cheerfully, "draw it in with a pen and we'll know where it is coming back."

Next moment two huge rocks shot past the porthole, and an agitated voice shouted: "Don't know where the hell we are." Seizing a small hand towel, I rushed on deck, draping it round me as I went. There was a bitter N.E. wind; I was sure I would catch pneumonia, but rocks seemed to be all around and something had to be done quickly. We were right off the main Indreled, completely lost. I was busy with my hand-bearing compass when I saw . a Norwegian fishing boat threading its way between the rocks. "Follow that boat," I cried, but had reckoned without human nature. The sight of an English yachtswoman racing about the deck, clad only in a hand towel and not 200 miles from the Arctic Circle, was too much for the Norwegian skipper. He took one look, stopped his engine, and called up the crew. We glared, pointed, and tried to "shoo" him off. If we moved forward a few yards, he just followed us. There was nothing for it but to keep on taking my bearings with as much dignity as possible. Actually, Adams, possibly thinking I had taken the inside channel, had carried straight on instead of turning N.E.

Having taken the inner passage through Stokksund we eventually arrived at Buholmraasa, a real nasty piece of nature where the swell from the open sea breaks on submerged rocks on either side of you. It is never so bad if it is calm and you cannot see they are there.

Namsos lay over to starboard, and if you want a really nice time you can go there through Flatangerled. I took one look at it and did not. You can also go inside Grundene but I could not read the Norwegian description of the leading lines on my chart, so went round everything. We are now proceeding down Namsenfjord in heavy rain.

It seems pretty queer to be writing in the middle of the night without a light, still it is rather nice. All the lighthouses have been put out for the summer, so you do not get all agitated wondering if you are going to get in before dark. Also, there is no bother of navigation or riding lights, a great boon when they are oil, like ours. Of course, if you are not careful you forget if it is to-day or yesterday, but I like it on the whole. We should reach Namsos in about two hours and I shall not be sorry: I have been up over 18 hours.

Edshaug. June 5th: Arrived Namsos at 3.30 a.m. yesterday and tied up to a mooring buoy off the town. After a few hours sleep we woke to find the rain still pouring down, so we went ashore in oilskins and sou'westers to do the week-end shopping.

Namsos is a timber centre and quite different from the usual Norwegian fishing port. Round the harbour are saw mills, fronted with compounds of floating logs; made me think I was back in Canada. Objects like floating huts proved to be small ships piled high with timber; others staggered along, towing strings of logs that appeared to stretch endlessly behind them.

Rain is always depressing and Namsos is probably very nice on a fine day, but by tea-time I was saying: "Let's get out of this," and we sailed for Rörvik. It was silly, the barometer was low and "after the low comes the blow." It did. We left via Rödsund and Storö and, on reaching the main Indreled at Naerösund, it blew up from dead calm to a violent squall in about two seconds. I have never seen the weather change so quickly; you could actually see the wind coming, furrowing the water before it into white-capped waves. The Vikten Islands are described as "possessing hardly any harbours of refuge and, in addition to being surrounded by outlying rocks and reefs, are rendered still more dangerous by an on shore set into the bays northward and southward of the group". The wind was

S.W. We tore up Naerösund at about 10 knots, almost being "pooped" by the following seas. Rörvik was impossible. A hasty look at the chart revealed Edshaug, a small creek off Nordsalten, some 8 miles northwards. In normal circumstances I might have funked the entrance, but it was our only chance of a night's sleep.

Having drawn diagrams of the various poles, we got there all right about 10.30 p.m. First we tried to anchor by a target in the narrow entrance, but there was not sufficient shelter. In fear and trembling we went on into a very small and practically land-locked bay. It was too small to be given in any detail, even on a large scale chart, and I felt far from happy. A beacon apparently marked shoal ground in the centre, and an odd pole was stuck here and there.

By this time it was blowing really hard and, although the water was fairly calm inside, the wind rushed down from the high ground in fierce squalls. We tried another target on the lee side and after great difficulty managed to get a long warp ashore. Naturally *Perula* desired to head into wind, and as we desired her stern to wind, we ended up broadside. Back aboard we were trying to pull the stern round from there, when the anchor started dragging. "Mind the beacon," shouted Adams; but I was already at the wheel. There was little enough room to manoeuvre in the best of circumstances, but with the stern tied to a rock, the result was a real pantomime. I succeeded in winding the warp all round us, while Adams dashed frantically about with the boat-hook trying to save the propellor from being fouled. In the end we cast the warp off and we were back where we started.

Having eventually tried all the targets we turned to tree trunks. "We'll tie her to anything," I said in desperation, "trees, rocks, poles, only for Heaven's sake let's get her made fast."

It was while we were battling with a tree trunk that we chanced to look up; a Norwegian fishing boat had chosen this happy moment to break her mooring and sit gracefully on the rocks, while our dinghy had chosen the same moment to blow away from the shore. "Good gracious," said Adams, "shouldn't we do something about that fishing boat?" But I had troubles enough of my own and, with a string of choice oaths, was bounding through the water in pursuit of the dinghy.

So on we went, dragging anchor, winding it up again and shedding warps as lizards shed their tails. We were both completely exhausted, quite frightened and thoroughly wet through. We never thought of the obvious course; to take our ship away from this squally haven and ride the blow outside. Decisions like that only come with experience and, in any case, the mere thought of it would have scared us stiff. One hope seemed to remain—a small jetty made of tree trunks, in the lee of a rocky cliff. I had serious doubts if there would be enough water, and the rocks protruded, but I charged it at an angle of 45°, put *Perula* hard astern and Adams jumped ashore. Having made fast with our four remaining warps we spent a dismal hour in the dinghy rowing round to retrieve the others.

It was now about 4.30 a.m. and as we sat in the saloon eating cakes and drinking hot whisky, I suddenly said: "Oh, Ron! How nice, I've just remembered it's Whit Sunday." He gave me a look that said quite clearly where I and Whit Sunday could go.

This morning, having had a sleep, I heard voices. Two men were standing on the jetty and, burning with hospitality, I invited them aboard for a drink—this, of course, consisted of raising my arm, tilting my head, and pointing to the wheelhouse. One accepted the invitation and appeared to desire very urgently to tell us something. He kept saying a word that sounded like "loose." Thinking something had come undone, we looked up the Norwegian for unfastened and showed it to him in the dictionary, but he shook his head. We passed him the dictionary and he produced the word "loads."

"Heavens!" I exclaimed, "a ship is coming to load cargo, we'll have to go and it's still blowing like hell." With great difficulty we wrote down the Norwegian for "Ship come, we leave?" He shook his head again and we had another drink. "Englishman," he said at length and pointed to a house on shore. Off we went in search of the "Englishman", who proved to be a retired Norwegian ship's engineer, who had last spoken English about twenty years ago. While he was trying to remember some, we were invited in, and his wife served coffee and "lefse." Lefse is a typical Norwegian country dish, a kind of doughy substance wrapped round cheese and sprinkled with sugar and spice. The making of the "doughy substance" is a great art; large thin cakes of it being baked, stored, then dipped in water before use.

Our host, Hr. Jacobsen, found his English coming back remarkably quickly, and the mystery of "loose" and "loads" was solved. They were the Norwegian words "Loss" and "Lods," meaning pilot, whose services we were being offered. The pilot, a gentleman named Marius, then invited us to his house, where his daughter played the piano, and "A long way to

Tipperary" was sung, for our benefit, in Norwegian.

Our friends then decided that we had better move *Perula* and, with their assistance, she was tied up alongside an old grey sailing vessel named *Fanny*. Marius departed below and returned in triumph with an ancient bill of sale, showing that *Fanny* had started life on the south coast of England in 1874. So two British built ships ride proudly, side by side, in this rather remote corner of North Norway. Old *Fanny* seems to fuss round *Perula*, sheltering her from every squall, as though she has found a long lost grand-daughter.

This afternoon Edshaug took us for a picnic. Men with fishing rods over their shoulders, women with baskets of food, and children skipping gaily ahead, everybody happy and laughing. "Think of it, Ron," I said. "Here we are in Norway, setting out with a crowd of friends for a Whit Sunday picnic, just like thousands of people are doing at home." Having crossed the peatfields, we pitched camp on the shores of a lake. The men lighted a fire to heat the coffee, while the women beat up the eggs. Eggedosis is a great Norwegian dish, foaming bowls of white and gold that are finally mixed with sugar and some rum, this last brought by us after the hesitating request that, as they could not buy any, a little from our bottle would "make the eggs so good."

I had my first lesson in fishing, with a 15 foot bamboo pole and worm for bait. Neither Adams nor I are fishermen, both of us having an absolute horror of putting a worm on a hook or pulling a fish off one. But in Norway all English people are supposed to be experts in the art. I could see great things were expected of me. I watched the others deftly cast the bait well out into the lake. "Easy," I said to Adams. "Watch me." Having hooked four trees and various members of the party, Marius came to my aid. At last I got it into the water and no sooner had I done so than the little cork float disappeared. I had caught the first fish of the day! It was so small you could hardly see it, but there was great excitement and England's reputation was saved. In all I caught seven fish, including the largest, a 5 lb. salmon trout. Adams said: "Mugs for luck," but it was only jealousy; he had not caught any.

As the sun disappeared behind the trees, we all sat round the fire and the girls sang Norwegian folk songs. I do not profess to be musical, but there was something so sweet and beautiful about the strange mournful half-tones that I felt I could weep.

Brönnöysund. June 6th: This morning, the wind having dropped, we left for Brönnöysund, a passage of some 40 miles. We had hoped to stop at Torghatten, a mountain with a most extraordinary hole through the middle of it. According to an old legend, this hole was caused when the Archer, a mountain near Edshaug, aimed an arrow at the Horseman, an island on the Arctic Circle, and poor Torghatten got in the way. What really caused the hole, nobody seems to know, and we had no chance to solve the mystery as Torghatten was completely enveloped in cloud.

The Indreled from this point to Brönnöysund is described as "difficult to navigate for, although the dangers are marked, the channels between them are so narrow, that slight mistakes have on several occasions led to disaster, even with pilots on board," after which a pleasant little P.S. is added to the effect that "the tidal streams run with great strength".

I always think it is so nice to start a passage with cheery advice like this. I worked myself up into such a state of agitation that when we did arrive Brönnöysund seemed sheer child's play to what I had expected and, but for nearly wiping off the Arctic air mail, we had no trouble. I can see we shall have to watch this seaplane. It seems to wait until you are in a really narrow channel, then comes charging down upon you, on its take-off.

On arrival at the harbour, not knowing where to anchor, we tied up to the Shell jetty. As I said to Adams: "What is the use of having a beautiful green leather pocket book, requesting Shell Agents to give us every possible assistance, if we don't use it?" Of course, Adams said it was assistance in getting oil, but that to me was a detail.

The man at the fuel station could not understand us and got wildly excited at my cigarette, but the green booklet was impressive, and I was connected by telephone to the manager. This was rather a set-back, for I could not very well say, "Please, where do we anchor?" I tried to get Adams to speak, but he said I had brought it on myself. Finally, I asked for some oil we did not want and which I suspected they would not have and, fortunately, they had not. The manager was very concerned, and as I magnanimously forgave him, I was able to ask, quite off hand, which was the best anchorage. After he had had further words with his assistant, a man boarded *Perula* and tied us up to a private wharf on the other side. After all a woman is really an advantage.

I quite like Brönnöysund, but Adams does not. We have an ever increasing audience; they even follow us when we go shopping and crowd round the shop door until we come out. I think it is rather funny myself, but he loathes publicity and is getting more and more furious.

Sörvik. June 8th: Arrived here yesterday from Brönnöysund. Rather feeble to do only 30 miles in a day, but we wanted to see the "Seven Sisters", a magnificent mountain range with seven lofty peaks. Like Torghatten we found them enveloped in cloud. "It's no use, Ron," I said. "We'll have to wait for the darned things to clear, we can't go skipping all the local sights. No! it will not do if I have a picture postcard of them, I'm going to stay and see them properly." So we sought anchorage in Sörvik, an inlet about a mile south of the light on Vikholmen. With my usual care I looked up the anchorage under Sörvik in the Sailing Directions, and spent an hour missing rocks that were not there and wondering why the place looked so different. Our Sörvik was finally discovered in another part of the volume altogether. We noticed an ancient looking jetty on the east side, and decided to tie up to it, for, as I said after gazing at the old sheds with their broken windows and buttercups and daisies protruding through the woodwork, "No one has ever used the place for fifteen years, we'll have a night's sleep free from worry and it will save us winding up 20 fathoms of chain after breakfast."

At 1.20 a.m. I was awakened by a voice yelling"'Ello' 'Ello'." A Norwegian woman was rushing about the jetty in a state of great agitation and a Norwegian mail steamer was rapidly bearing down on us. At any moment *Perula* looked like being squashed between the large black hull and the jetty. Out we rushed, clad in pyjamas, the woman cast off our warps and we just managed to escape as the steamer came alongside. Needless to say, there was a lot of rude laughter from the steamer as we, still in our night attire, went off in search of an anchorage.

This morning the weather cleared, so having duly seen and admired the "Seven Sisters," we are about to leave and, before the day is out, should cross the Arctic Circle.

It is a month to-day since we left the Straits, and we have covered 1,400 miles. Our pile of 100 charts is steadily changing order. Almost every day two or three more are taken off the top and put away again underneath. It is most exciting, you get a kind of fever to push on North until you reach the last. If it ever happens, there won't half be a celebration.

CHAPTER V

IN THE ARCTIC

June 8th. Kvaröfjord.

Any moment now we shall be in the Arctic Circle. On our port bow is Hestmandöy, that rocky island shaped like a horseman—the one the archer shot at, to Torghatten's detriment. I cannot say it looks very like a horseman to me, though Adams says he can clearly see the head and cloak of the rider. Anyway, the Arctic Circle passes through it, and we are almost abeam.

I feel quite excited, but I do wish there was a white line or something on the water; they might at least stick up a notice and write "Arctic" on it. I am all ready, pencil in hand, to note the "historic moment" and we have also put a thermometer out in the cockpit to make it look scientific.

We are getting nearer . . . nearer . . . nearer; we are over. 4.56 p.m. B.S.T., which is the same as Norwegian time. *Perula* is in the Arctic, and 23° 28' from the North Pole. Adams has just reported the temperature in the cockpit is 70° F., and in the wheelhouse it is only half a degree off 80. A hot sun is pouring down on to calm blue waters and there is not a cloud in the sky.

To starboard is the Svartisen Ice Field, nearly 400 sq. miles in extent, lying like an immense tablecloth on the rocky mountains. At present the ice is covered with snow and a slight haze hangs over it. This at least looks like the Arctic, but the valleys beneath are rich in grass. Small farms and cottages catch the strong sunlight and this part of the countryside reminds me of England on a clear spring day.

The Red Lion is now starting to show up; this must not be confused with a "local" of the English variety. Norway's Red Lion is a most extraordinary island, 1,444 feet high, composed of reddish coloured rock and taking the shape of a crouching lion. The effect is most realistic and the official name is Rödöy, meaning "Red Island."

We are now bound for Skarsfjord and Holandsfjord where, we have heard, three glaciers from Svartisen extend almost to the water's edge.

Svartisen. Midnight: We are anchored in the most beautiful place I have ever seen, almost at the foot of a gigantic glacier. *Perula* rides alone in milky blue-green water, and all around us tower rugged mountains. The glacier lies just ahead; at the top I can see the snow on the icefields, pink in the setting sun. From it sweeps down the blue ice, like an immense river of breaking foam, casting a reflection on the water that reaches right up to us. As I write, the sun, instead of sinking, changes its mind, to rise again; the glacier is turned to gold.

We are both badly in need of sleep, yet we are sitting in the wheelhouse, fascinated. It is made all the more beautiful by the absence of civilisation; no hotels or shops, hardly a cottage.

As we came in, wondering where to anchor in the absence of targets, a solitary fisherman rowed ahead, beckoning us to follow him. Friendly actions like this are typical of the Norwegian people and they expect no payment. The anchorage he has brought us to is in 10 fathoms, close off a small broken-down landing stage for launches or dinghys.

Now I really must get some sleep. I have an awful job trying to darken my cabin, but with the help of curtains, odd cushions and pieces of cardboard, the result is not too bad.

Crossing Saltfjord. June 6th: This morning we explored the glacier. A marvellous sight; great masses of jagged ice with deep blue crevasses. Small icebergs floated in the water beneath. We had great fun with the camera, using "delayed action" to take pictures of the two of us together on the ice. Having set the camera and focussed it with one of us posing prettily, the other had twelve seconds to get into position, with results that were somewhat disconcerting. I would be in the midst of a wild dash over the slippery ice, when I would lose my balance and go shooting right out of the picture. A nice ride if I had had a toboggan. As it is my hand is cut and several other portions of my anatomy.

Having tired ourselves out on the ice we went back aboard, developed our films and, finding them satisfactory, sailed for Bodö.

We left via the passage on the east side of Aamnöy and through Vaagsbotn into Melöyfjord. In places the channel is less than a cable wide, but it is well marked and not as bad as it looks on the chart. Fortunately, the weather was good for rounding Kunna, for during northerly gales a very heavy sea gets up, making this part of the Indreled practically impossible.

For the last two days we have been in Nordland, considered one of the most picturesque parts of Norway. The scenery has been gradually changing, the mountains have become more wild, peaks jagged and torn, mostly covered with snow during the whole summer.

As the weather was so calm this afternoon we decided to do some jobs at the masthead, a procedure which ended by my emulating, quite unintentionally, the man on the flying trapeze. I had wound Adams up on the bo'sun's chair, with the aid of the mast winch, but thought I would be clever and let him down by hand. I quite forgot that, due to my diet, I now weigh less than he does. The result was startling. I freed the main halyard from the winch, all careless like, and before I realised what was happening, I was away up the mast. As he shot down I, still hanging on to the halyard, shot up. There I clung howling "Help," while he sat helpless with laughter on the bo'sun's chair, which had descended somewhat violently to the deck. In the meantime, *Perula*, left to herself, was charging straight for the rocks. I often wonder what other shipping must think about us.

Bodö. June 11th: Arrived here three days ago. The Arctic sunshine has gone and I am sitting writing in the saloon, wrapped in a rug. The wind. is howling about us and *Perula* tugs and jerks at her anchor chain, which we have shackled to the mooring buoy for greater security. We are safe enough in Bodöhavn, but there is something about the weather up here that is rather frightening. Even on a calm day you feel it is waiting to pounce on you.

Bodö is a busy port, rising up from the shores of a natural haven. It is the capital of Nordland. When the Lofoten Fishery is at its height the harbour becomes exceedingly crowded, but we were fortunate and were able to find a vacant mooring buoy. All along the quayside are ships loading casks of dried fish. Many of the casks have been brought in from the surrounding districts, where you see long trays, racks and also tubs of fish, drying in the sun. Must say it's a bit smelly.

I seem to be spending half my time in Norway saying I am going to a place which, due to my pronunciation, conveys nothing to the Norwegian I am addressing. Bodö is one of them. I have been busily calling it Bodö, only to find it is pronounced more like "Boo der." The trouble is, of course, the two little dots over the o, which make it sound like "er." The Norwegians, however, seem to omit the dots, writing the last letter and "crossing it out". It is a separate and distinct letter of the Norwegian alphabet, like "aa" which is now written å, the former being the old Danish. In either case you seem to pronounce it like the "aw" in awful. They also have "ae" which is a bit like the "a" in care or air.

The best way of learning to pronounce the names of the towns is to tune in to the Norwegian weather forecasts on the wireless, then you kill two birds with one stone. These weather forecasts are excellent and, I am afraid, very much better than our British ones. Just before 10.30 a.m. you tune in to Oslo, and a voice says something that sounds like "vair melling"; needless to say, this is not the correct spelling. Then "Ooslo" holds forth at great length about what the weather is like at the principal places in the Oslo district and also gives detailed "further outlook". A voice will then say something like "Vair vaslingi for Vestland"; that is Bergen, and he goes through the same procedure for Westland. After this comes the bloke at Tromsö for "Nord Norge." Bergen throws in Dogger Bank, Shetlands, etc., and Tromsö, Svalbard.

At 7 p.m. the three stations again give a shorter report and, at 9.40 p.m., another full one. The local stations sometimes give intermediate reports, and shortly after 1 p.m. comes a statement of weather conditions at most European ports and a few in America. Gale warnings are also issued during the ordinary programmes.

I have been trying very hard to understand these reports and have made the following notes for myself of phonetic pronunciation. If the announcer, on reaching your district, says "Paint vair," then you are quids in, the weather is going to be good. If he says "Toe ca," groan, it will be foggy. On hearing "Litten cooling", get a little agitated, if "Steve cooling", get quite agitated, and if "Stack cooling", exceedingly agitated; for Kuling means gale, and each one a bigger one. If he should say "Orcan," lie down and die, because orkan is a hurricane.

I strongly advise any yacht owners visiting Norway to try and learn enough of the language to understand these reports. At present it is not doing me much good, but I am getting better. It is also interesting to hear the different dialects of the three announcers.

Once again, we have had a grand time ashore. On Wednesday the Harbour Master came aboard to visit us and then drove us out to his country house. The Norwegians seem to appreciate nature much more than we do. In addition to a town house, most of them have these country dwellings, where the women and children can spend the entire summer up in the mountains or out in the fjords. The men usually drive out for week-ends or whatever time they can spare from business.

The Harbour Master at Bodö is an old sea captain and his hobby is growing trees. He collects them from various countries, plants and tends them, delighting in the fresh green leaves after the years he has spent looking at little else but water. As we sat on the verandah of his house, gazing out at the fjord, consuming a picnic lunch and liquid refreshments, he astounded us by breaking forth into Welsh. When an apprentice on his first sailing ship he had been wrecked, just south of the Menai Straits.

I do not know if it is usual for yacht owners to have their mail sent out to them, care of the Harbour Master, but we are finding it an excellent plan. You must, however, be sure to have a lot of letters sent at least two weeks before you arrive. Every time the poor Harbour Master sits at his desk he will see the pile. At first he will not take much notice, then he will get rather sick of seeing them and wonder who the damn woman is and when is she coming, anyway. By the time you do arrive (if he has not returned them to England marked "unknown") he will be burning with curiosity to see what the nuisance *Perula* and her owner is like. In this matter my mother is also a great help, for she will probably have written several little notes to the Harbour Master on her own account. They will probably say, "Dear Sir, My daughter is expected at your port. Will you please take care of her and see personally that she receives the enclosed two pounds ten shillings, warm blankets or woollen underwear." When *Perula* is eventually sighted the Harbour Master is so relieved that he hastens to meet you. You can then invite him to dinner and before the evening is over you have made an excellent friend, and one friend always leads to another. Instead of feeling lost in a strange port, you find yourself having the time of your life.

Yesterday, while in search of fuel oil we met Hr. Sannes, and this has proved most fortunate, for he has given me a letter of introduction to Captain Schjelderup, famous Norwegian ice pilot and present owner of *Quest*, one of the ships used on Shackleton's last ill-fated expedition to the Antarctic.

Schjelderup, who originally came from Bodö, is now living in Tromsö, and as he had led many expeditions to Svalbard, I am hoping to obtain some first-hand advice from him.

Hr. Sannes also gave us a delightful day at his country house, followed by a visit to the "Tourist Hut"; one of the mountain restaurants where you can dance and look out on a panorama of islands, fjords and sea, and watch the midnight sun lower and rise again. He has, however, rather disconcerted me by remarking, "See you are well insured for Svalbard. The rates are, of course, extra, but we take out special policies for our fishing vessels going there." I felt rather glad my Insurance Company were not present, for they have optimistically "thrown in" Norway and Svalbard in my usual British waters' policy.

We are learning quite a lot about Norwegian life. For example, a dog licence in some districts costs nearly £4. "Good Heavens," said Adams, "so that's why you all have such big dogs; getting the money's worth, so to speak." Cats are also taxed in places and a wireless licence costs about £1. Both Income and Government taxes have to be paid, as well as a small tax on practically everything bought. As a rough estimate we were told that two months' earnings went to pay the year's taxes.

I think that many English boys and girls would like to live out here, for in the more isolated districts the school year consists of only 12 weeks. In most towns, however, it is usually 37 weeks.

I would not like to drive a car in Norway. In most of the towns it is

"No smoking at the wheel." Out of the towns, of course, you can. The regulations regarding drivers and drink are also stiff; you are allowed one in eight hours. If they suspect you of having more it's a blood test, and next day you pick up the paper and read that Hr. So-and-So has "gone on vacation," without the option. In consequence, the taxis do a good trade.

To-morrow we hope to leave for the Lofoten Islands.

Vestfjord. Midnight. June 12th: We are off North again. This morning it was still blowing hard, the sky was a dull leaden grey and what we could see of the mountains seemed more white than usual; I think snow must have fallen during the night. Adams did not look very enthusiastic when I suggested sailing, but the wind was favourable and too good to miss.

When we got outside I began to doubt my wisdom. The direct passage to the Lofotens meant about 60 miles of open sea, so I used my privilege as a woman and changed my mind.

"Time is getting on," announced the Captain. "I have decided to leave the Lofotens and carry on up the Indreled."

"What about Grötöysund?" asked Adams evilly.

I looked startled, as I had forgotten this channel, which I had previously planned to avoid. "Grötöysund," to quote the Sailing Directions, "through which the tidal stream sets strongly, is only about 100 feet in width and is difficult to navigate, so that this portion of the Indreled should not be attempted without a pilot." Just to make things brighter we went through, without a pilot, at low water springs. I do not know how much water there was; it was "off the clock" on the tide gauge at the entrance. Anyway, I gathered from the chart there would be about 9 feet, with an excellent view of the bottom, we set off.

"Shall I sit for'ard and look for rocks?" helpfully suggested Adams.

"Yes," I agreed, "but look for crabs and pebbles as well; we are just as likely to hit them."

For some 3 miles we twisted and turned between about 33 lighthouses, beacons and poles. Only once, at the northern end, did we hesitate. Confronted with five lighthouses, a beacon and sundry poles, all in close proximity, Adams said, "Where do we go?" "I haven't the slightest idea," replied the navigator; but there are three exits, so we presumably found one of them. The words "Grötöysund O.K." were entered in the log book.

We then had the option of going through an absolute maze of islands and rocks, but on reading "the channel is not well marked," and still being slightly shaken after Grötöysund, we cut through the outskirts.

We are now approaching Tjeldsund and hoping to find anchorage at Lödinghavn.

Klöven. June 13th: Last night's, or rather, this morning's anchorage, was not too bad; close inshore, between an island that does not look like one and the steamer jetty. Had a bit of a "lie in" and left at 10.30 still having breakfast. Fairly tricky navigation in Sandtorgstraumen, further up Tjeldsund, if you read the Sailing Directions and keep religiously to the channel. I did not and it was much simpler. I looked at the chart, there seemed to be bags of water for us, so I cut off the corner and went charging happily along, all on the wrong side of buoys. One of these days I shall come to a sticky end.

I have decided to put the Sailing Directions away. We have got no less than eight books of them for this cruise and they only depress me. Still, they look very impressive in the saloon, especially the Arctic Pilot, which is white and not owned by many people. I am finding the Norwegian Miltabell very useful for the Indreled. It is a table giving you the distance from every place between Stavanger and Kirkenes. There is only one thing to remember, the distances must be multiplied by 4, the Norwegian mile being longer than ours. This Miltabell will be given free by any harbour master or shipping office, and is at the back of a shipping time table.

It has been another rather cold grey day, with tendency to mist. As many of the fjords in this part of the Indreled are wide and exposed to the open sea, it has been a case of compass courses across seemingly open water.

We decided for once to have supper in peace and, at 9.45 p.m., put in at Klöven for the night, having covered 68 miles. It is a small bay off Solbergfjord and was once an important trading station. To-day little remains but a broken-down quay and a cottage or two with the washing hanging out to dry. We are anchored at the far end in 5 fathoms and tied to a post ashore. There is a good deal of traffic in the main fjord; large cargo steamers, a few British and Russian, but mostly Norwegian. After they have passed, the wash sweeps into Klöven, breaking on the rocks and shingle and causing *Perula* to sway about; still it is quite a good anchorage.

Tromsesund. June 14th: We should be in Tromsö in about two hours. We were under way by 10.15 this morning, and if I had used my intelligence could have had the tide with us practically all the way. It was not one of my bright mornings. To start with I omitted about 90° from the compass course and spent some anxious moments wondering why the entrance to Gisund was not there. Meanwhile, a Norwegian fishing boat hovered about, with look-out in the crow's nest and a man at the harpoon gun. I think they were after porpoises. Gisund having been located we took the eastern channel which "should only be used with local knowledge." However, we had no difficulty and eventually reached Gibostad, where the "navigable channel is two cables wide and the tidal stream attains its greatest velocity". The effect of getting the tide with us thus far must have proved too much for me; I remembered my resolve to put the Sailing Directions away and did so. In consequence we arrived in the narrow Rystraum with a 6 knot tide against us. A Norwegian mail steamer was close astern as we met the full strength of the tide and began to go round in circles! Every time the steamer tried to pass us, a whirlpool swept us right in her path and she would have to stop. After much bad language and blowing of sirens on the part of the steamer, and considerable embarrassment on the part of *Perula*'s crew, we managed to keep out of the way long enough for her to pass. Had I read the Directions I would have been warned by the words: "Sailing vessels should always have a boat ready for towing them out of the whirlpools."

We have both been rather on edge all the day. I think it is due to the fact we shall be in Tromsö by to-night and perhaps know the worst, for here our final decision in regard to our cruise is to be made. I have planned, if possible, to see Hr. Hansen at the Meteorological Office and ask him again about the weather conditions and state of the water. We have heard, lower down the coast, that the ice is doing queer things this year and is reported to be in places where it has not been seen for 40 years. I also hope to get Captain Schjelderup aboard and ask him to tell me, quite candidly, whether or not I am completely mad in my desire to sail to Svalbard.

As usual, it looks as though I am going to put everybody to a great deal of trouble on my behalf but I feel it is too great a decision to make unaided. I am quite entitled to set off and drown myself if I want to, but I have Adams to think of and am beginning to feel keenly the responsibility of being "Captain" of even a baby ship.

I think this attitude is perhaps typical of a woman. I have found it in aviation as well. Most of us can key ourselves up to do something spectacular, but when it comes to the steady job of piloting an air liner or commanding a ship, day after day, through all kinds of weather with the lives of passengers at stake; then I think very definitely it is a man's job. I know personally I live on nervous energy, going blindly on without stopping to think until I reach the goal I have set myself. By that time I have probably smoked a few thousand cigarettes, drunk a case of rum and need a rest cure. Of course, I am fortunate in having Adams, for while most of the hairbrained schemes are mine, he, poor man, gets dragged along and provides the necessary stable influence; although, as usually happens in life, I get most of the credit.

It will be heart-breaking if we cannot go to Svalbard after coming so far. To have travelled over 1,700 miles, then have to turn back only about 600 miles from our objective: I think I should weep! To make matters worse, we had a calamity with our lunch. Before leaving Bodö I bought a tin with a beautiful picture of a lobster on it. Granted there were some smaller fish as well, but these, I concluded, were merely decorating the ocean bed. I was sitting at the wheel when Adams appeared, looking somewhat crestfallen, with an open tin in his hand.

"Do you know what it is?" he asked, revealing a mass of small fish, floating in crimson liquid and spice.

"I told you to open the lobster," I said, with some annoyance.

"I have," he explained, "at least I opened what you bought for lobster".

"Oh! Well," I retorted. "I must have changed my mind and bought sardines." I put one of the fish in my mouth—it was full of bones and quite raw.

When I had returned from leaning over the side of the cockpit, Adams said, "Will you have the Norwegian fish balls you bought instead?" I had had quite enough experimenting for one day; I asked for a boiled egg.

CHAPTER VI

THE PARIS OF THE NORTH

Tromsö. June 15th, 11.45 p.m.

We arrived at Tromsö at 6.15 p.m. yesterday and I fell for it at once. The town stands on the shores of a verdant green island, surrounded by snow-capped mountains. Only a few weeks ago the snow was knee deep in the streets, but as we looked at it in the strong sunshine, there was something almost tropical about the picturesque villas up on the hillside, surrounded by luxuriant vegetation.

After inspecting various anchorages, we tied up to a mooring buoy in the north harbour, having narrowly escaped destroying the Arctic air mail which also berths there. Sometimes the tide is quite strong in the harbour, which is usually very crowded. Feeling somewhat nervous, I made Adams grab the first available buoy, before I hit something, for as I always say on these occasions, "For Heaven's sake tie us up quickly, I can't control her." While we were battling with the buoy, the Customs launch drew alongside with a cheery, "Good evening", and "Suppose you will want something out of bond?" Next our mail arrived, followed by the Harbour Master, who wished to see the "Lady Captain," and would have nothing to do with Adams, who had gone up to greet him. While the three of us were having a "quick one" in the saloon, "Tinny Annie's" representative arrived to know if we wanted any provisions rowed out. "Tinny Annie" (which is as near as we can get to this gentleman's name) is the local ship chandler in Tromsö. He is a great godsend, for he will obtain any article you care to mention; get your washing done, your films developed, and everything rowed out to you. When I call upon him he says: "Ah! Good morning, Captain, what can I do for you to-day?" Whereupon he invites me into the back parlour, seats me in an armchair, provides himself with a large book and pencil, and adopts a respectful attitude as if I am about to order the whole of Tromsö. When I ask how much I owe him, he waves the matter aside and says: "Don't give it a thought, Captain, time enough to bother about such trifles when you are leaving." I fear a horrible shock will await me when I do leave, but Tinny Annie's goods and service are of the very best and I can safely leave anything to him.

The Harbour Master apparently did not think much of our efforts at mooring *Perula* and asked if I would not prefer to go alongside the quay. I took a horrified glance at the mass of shipping and hurriedly declined the honour. Finally we tied up alongside a small grey ship called *Zoe* and owned by Captain Johannssen. One ties up to other ships in this matey fashion in Norway, without consulting the owner.

The Customs Officer had very kindly gone in search of Schjelderup for me; we could see *Quest* amongst a crowd of ships moored stern to the breakwater, but her captain was not aboard. About 11 p.m., having given up all hope of seeing him that night, Adams and I went ashore and quite by chance walked straight to his flat. The Customs Officer happened to be passing and took us in. As we climbed the stairs and rang the bell I felt awful. To call on a man at midnight to ask him if I was mad seemed a sure way of getting a response in the affirmative.

At length a tall, well-built man appeared, with tanned face and blue eyes that twinkled with laughter as I haltingly stumbled through my rehearsed party piece.

"So," he said with a smile, "you want to go to Svalbard. First, I must see your boat." I murmured something about not troubling him so late at night, but he waved it aside and said that he rarely went to bed. While he was getting his hat I turned to Adams: "He is a grand bloke, isn't he," I said, for there is something about Schjelderup that appeals to you immediately. He is a man who does real man-sized jobs; cool and calm, with a quiet manner that gives me the utmost confidence. He is a born leader of men, and I can imagine his crew following him to the ends of the earth.

First we went to see the captain of a coal steamer that had just come in from Svalbard. Adams and I fidgeted about the quayside beneath the immense cranes that unload the Spitsbergen coal, while Schjelderup was aboard getting the latest information for us about the ice. He came back smiling.

"The news is good," he said. "The ice lies only 25 miles west of Hornsund on the S.W. coast of Spitsbergen." I fear I saw little that was "good" about it.

Next we made our way back to north harbour. Someone had seized on our absence as a golden opportunity to take our dinghy, but Schjelderup shouted a few curt words. It was back in no time and my respect for him soared even higher.

Perula lay in the sunshine, very small and very white amongst the sealers and whalers. I felt convinced he would laugh outright at her 1½ inch planking, as all the ships here seem to have two or three skins (additional layers of really thick wood) to protect them from the ice. We climbed aboard and he walked silently about, inspecting everything.

"No need to worry, Miss Brown," he said. "You have a boat here that will go anywhere."

"Perhaps the boat will," I said, "but what about her crew?" He laughed. We had sailed from Wales; he thought I was joking when I spoke of our lack of experience.

In the saloon, with charts in front of us, he told me what I was to do. It ran something like this: "You must sail from here to a point a mile or two west of Björnöya (Bear Island); check your course there, then carry on to Spitsbergen. When you approach the ice you will see a white glare in the sky ahead. That is what we call 'ice blink,' a reflection of the ice on the clouds. When you see it, turn west and keep sailing west until you reach the edge of the blink, then course can be shaped for Prince Charles Foreland and into Isfjord." It sent cold shivers down my spine.

I asked many silly questions such as "Suppose I've to keep sailing west for ever?" He patiently explained that owing to the Gulf Stream the ice in summer rarely lies more than 50 or 100 miles west of the southern part of Spitsbergen, and providing you get into the warm current, it is possible to sail right up to the foreland free of ice. "Of course," he added carelessly, "you might have to wait a day or two off the foreland if the entrance to the Isfjord is blocked, but the ice comes and goes; you will get in all right if you pick your time." I murmured something about fog, but this was dismissed with the advice, "Just stop your engine and listen; ice is usually heard." Obviously, a trip to Svalbard was no more to Schjelderup than a trip to the Isle of Man would be to us. He has just returned from the White Sea, having caught about 4,000 seals.

All this was rather more than I had bargained for. Gone was my rest at Bear Island and my quick dash to the southern end of Spitsbergen, for apparently it is inadvisable for us to hit the coast south of the foreland. So we are faced with a really long passage across one of the most lonely and treacherous bits of ocean in the world, bound for a point well up the Spitsbergen coast, which we may not get into for a "day or two." Ice is waiting to pounce on us, with the possibility of a few gales and fog thrown in for luck. Schjelderup says he usually takes about five days for the passage; lord knows how long it will take us, but his influence is such that I would cheerfully go to the North Pole if he told me to.

He has spent most of the time aboard with us, and to-day brought me a very choice halibut from one of his fishing boats that had just come in. I insisted on cooking part of it myself, in the hope of impressing him into taking me on his next sealing trip, but it did not work. He said the way I cooked fish made it sheer poison, and proceeded to get busy himself I hovered about the galley, getting in his way, and handing him various knives with which to cut the fish into steaks, but after unprintable remarks about blunt knives and women in general, he rowed ashore in disgust to borrow a knife that was a knife. He and the Harbour Master have solved the mystery of my "lobster," the small fish in the crimson liquid, which I had saved with the intention of frying. This was greeted with much horror, as apparently these fish are a great delicacy and used as hors d'oeuvres. The two men have spent fruitless hours trying to teach me to bone and skin the wretched little things, after which they are laid in strips on pieces of bread.

The dinghy problem has also been solved. Every time we go ashore now, we leave the oars in an office on the quayside. I do not know who the office belongs to and we never ask permission, but being under Schjelderup's wing, seems to entitle us to do anything we want in Tromsö.

So far we have not been to the Meteorological Office; it is rather a long walk, right on top of the island, and I do not think Schjelderup likes long walks. Also, at times I suspect him of deliberately keeping me away, for having once put the decision into his hands, I feel he is going to send me to Svalbard whether I like it or not. Possibly he thinks the more confidence he can send me away with the better it will be. Every time I mention the Meteorological Office he says he has telephoned them and there is no need for me to speak to them direct. He takes me to see a weather map of North Norway and Svalbard which is posted up in the town, and says, "Look, the sun is shining in Spitsbergen." He probably thinks I do not understand it, although so far there has not been anything alarming about the weather indicated.

I have a great admiration for the work of the Norwegian meteorologists who make such maps possible. For twelve solid months, two or three of them are isolated at desolate W/T stations such as Bear Island. Often they are the only inhabitants and endure the most appalling hardships for the sake of observations, so that sealers and fishermen may be warned of the approach of storms and hurricanes. When their twelve months are up the men are relieved and others take their places.

I keep intending to swing ship, for the compass is sure to have changed in this high latitude, but somehow or other I never seem to have time. So much to do and so much to see. The Lapps intrigue me tremendously as they wander about the streets in their picturesque though slightly moth-eaten costumes. I have been dying to take a photograph of them, but Schjelderup says they do not like it and are apt to get mad at you.

I do not wonder that Tromsö is called the "Paris of the North." There is something very cosmopolitan, gay and friendly about it; and something a little "desperate" too, I sometimes think: a bit like a base camp behind the front line trenches—you know, to hell with life; let the Devil take the hindmost; and let's have a good time while we can. Nobody seems to go to bed, day and night an endless stream of ships leave or enter the harbour. Mostly whalers or sealers, crewed by men "tough as you can make 'em." It is a hard life. Weeks on the ice, working unceasingly, smashing the seals on the head, skinning them on the floes, dragging the skins to the ship and tossing them aboard until the blood and stench would sicken less hardy men. Back in port, their percentage of the catch drawn and "blued in", perhaps in a couple of days, the men seek the next ship leaving, for once a sealer always a sealer; perhaps out of the necessity to get more money or for some strange fascination for the hazardous life.

The way these ships come into the harbour fills me with envy. Full speed ahead they charge straight for the narrowest "parking place," chuck an anchor overboard and, as it catches bottom, the ship swings neatly into place. I am longing to try it but dare not. Anchors are used a great deal here for manoeuvreing. Yesterday a steamer came out of a berth, from which it would have taken me a week to extract *Perula*. With the use of her engines and anchors she twisted her way between an absolute maze of ships.

When the sealers leave, however, a careful watch has to be kept. To-night one charged into the side of *Perula* practically head-on. I rushed on deck prepared to wax exceedingly wrathful, but the men were off for God knows where, they had been celebrating their last night ashore, and as there was no damage other than scratched paint, I found myself merely responding to their cheerful farewells.

For the first time I really feel I am in the Arctic. I haven't much option. The ship next to us has come in with a cargo of ice bears; polar bears as we would call them, and the poor animals are raising hell. On first hearing these blood-curdling sounds, I thought they came from seals and called across to the captain, asking if I might come aboard and look at them. He did not understand me, but later I plucked up courage and went anyway. The crew took my dinghy painter and helped me climb over the high bulwarks. There on deck in a crude wooden cage, half chewed away, were three white bears. One of the crew descended into the bowels of the ship and returned with some seal meat for me to feed them with. The bears growled in the most frightful manner and bit and tore at the wooden bars but, at length, somewhat pacified by the food and gentle words, such as "poor darling bears, what a shame," one of them allowed me to stroke its head, a procedure that brought forth roars of laughter from the crew.

I always have a theory that if you approach animals with love in your heart, they will not touch you. Once in the Canadian Rockies I descended from a car, armed with a large jujube, so that Adams could take a photograph of me stroking a big brown bear. The bear snatched the jujube with a snarl of rage. I fled, Adams dropped the camera, and all we got was a lop-sided picture of my cuff and a blurr that might or might not have been a bear. I must admit my theory does not work out so well in practice, for I have been bitten by several monkeys and once, at the zoo, nearly emulated "Little Albert" with the lion.

I feel very sorry for these ice bears, however. Most people seem to spend their time prodding them with sticks. If I had enough money I would buy them, load them aboard *Perula*, and take them back to Svalbard.

June 16th, 6 a.m.: Our sailing orders have come. At 2 a.m., shortly after I had finished writing the above, there was a hail, "*Perula* ahoy!" Schjelderup and a friend were on the landing stage. Nothing is ready, the compass is not adjusted and I cannot do it now because Adams is tearing the engine to bits in a last minute overhaul. Once again we have sat up all night.

"What is the weather report?" I asked Schjelderup for about the sixth time.

"Good," he replied. "For the first few days the wind will not exceed force 2 or 3, you are to go direct and as quickly as possible."

"First few days and as quickly as possible," I repeated. "I don't like the sound of that, what is coming up?"

"Nothing," he said with a grin.

"I don't believe you," I said suspiciously. "Suppose there is a storm?"

"We don't have storms in summer, and even if there is one, what are you worrying about? You have a sound ship."

"Oh! dear," I groaned, "I wish I wasn't going."

He threw back his head and roared with laughter: "A week from now you will be safe in Spitsbergen."

We said another "Skaal" to it.

Midnight. Abeam Karlsöy: We have started for Svalbard, but I don't think I have quite realised it yet. The day has been one mad rush. Schjelderup took me shopping. I always thought I was pretty wholesale but he is worse. When "Tinny Annie's" boy rowed out the stuff I nearly had a fit. Dozens of cauliflowers and cabbages; joints of meat and hunks of fish; groceries; apples, oranges, and bananas; bottles of milk and cream—the cakes came in a packing case.

"What is it all for?" I asked. "Aren't there shops in Spitsbergen?"

"Oh, you can get things there," he replied vaguely, ordering a few more packets of something to be sent. If I had known we were going to take so much I would have got it out of bond, for this is permitted and there are apparently no Customs Officers in Svalbard. Still, if things are duty free out there I shall be able to buy anything I want really cheap.

Meanwhile, Adams was still working like fury on the engine, having been at it almost solidly for 24 hours. It is the first time he has overhauled it since leaving home. He has cleaned the valves, injectors, etc., and given everything the "once over." Must say she seems to be running very sweetly.

Shortly after 4 o'clock the seaplane came roaring into Tromsö, carrying with it our friend, Jakken Sannes, from Bodö, and also an English newspaper posted by my mother two days ago in Manchester. Makes home seem much nearer, this Arctic air mail, for which, incidentally, there is no extra postage charge. As Sannes was rowed towards *Perula* I called, "Coming to Spitsbergen?" Words that sounded like "No damn fear" floated back across the water. I found he had collected an English explorer, also bound for Spitsbergen, on one of the coal steamers. I thought this gentleman looked rather astonished at my remark, "See you there next week." Possibly he thought he had already left his fellow countrymen far behind.

At last, the engine finished, came the good-bye. Schjelderup held my hand, looking down at me in the queer way he does: very serious, very kind, yet laughing at life in general and Englishwomen in particular.

"Good luck," he said, "and remember I want you back in Norway by the end of the month, before the fog comes." He has been a marvellous friend to us. If we do reach Svalbard it will be mainly due to his help and advice. We sailed at 6.5 p.m., weather fair and calm; barometer 29.7; temperature 56° F. The passage to the open sea is about 50 miles, and for the last few hours we have been winding our way north through the Indreled. As we sailed up Grötsund, I thought I had never seen Norway look more beautiful. I began to wonder when we should sail down these waters again. There was quite a lot of shipping about, mostly large steamers bound for the White Sea.

We had not proceeded far before a small rowing boat pulled frantically across our bows and the occupant, a lone fisherman, held up a rope and looked imploring. It is a common custom in the fjords for power boats to give a tow, and sometimes you will see them with a long string of rowing boats behind. Adams went on deck, caught the rope and made it fast. The fisherman looked rather embarrassed when he found he had hitched up to a couple of foreigners. He could not speak to us, but we made him understand he was to signal when he wished to be cast off. As he sat there astern of us he looked in wonder, first at *Perula* and then at me. He must have decided it was a great honour to be towed by a British yacht, for every time we passed another ship or a tiny village, he straightened his cap, preened like a peacock and looked as proud as punch. After he had been with us for about two hours Adams remarked: "Think he must be coming to Spitsbergen with us." At length, however, the signal came; we cast him off and he departed with delighted bows and waves in the direction of a small village. I must say he would have had a hell of a long row if he had not met us, but these men think nothing of it; they will drift all day down a fjord fishing, and rely on something to give them a "lift" home. Shortly after he had gone a coal steamer passed, so light that her prop. was almost out of the water. "Bet she's bound for Spitsbergen," I said, feeling very like holding up a rope myself.

Now the weather is gradually changing and the wind freshening from the N.E. The fjord is exposed to the open sea and the swell is coming down, causing the water to break on the rocks; it looks rather wild and lonely. I feel worried about the compass, but fortunately our course out of Fugloysveet corresponds with the one we are taking for Bear Island, so I shall get a rough check. Also, I have my pelorus and can always check it from the sun.

Adams has not turned in yet; he is getting the sails up, for it looks as though we shall get a bit of a tossing outside.

June 17th, 3.30 a.m.: I am sitting alone at the wheel wrapped up in a rug. At 2.15 the north end of Spenna abeam; Adams streamed the log, then departed below for his four hours off so once again I shall be up all night. It is a queer thing, but sleep does not seem half so necessary out here; it must be the constant daylight.

We are just passing Fuglöykalven Fyr and heading out into the open sea. The weather is quite good, wind N.E. about force 4 and the sea slight. The barometer has risen (thank Heaven) to 29.74. and the temperature in the wheelhouse is still 56° F. It is probably colder outside but the engine has warmed things up in here.

I have been trying to analyse my feelings now we are leaving the land behind us and setting out on this 600 mile passage. I feel that I ought to be scared stiff. We have never attempted such a long sea passage in *Perula*, and I know that ice is waiting for me, yet strangely enough I feel quite cheerful and content. I do not take any credit myself for this apparent feeling of "bravery"; it is probably the "Spirit of the North" (taken both ways). One learns a lot from the men of North Norway. The sea is their life, they take it as it comes. Mostly they love it, and loving it have no fear; my greatest ambition at the moment is to be like them. The conditions are helping me; the sun shines down on *Perula*, the wind fills her sails, and so we set out for Svalbard.

CHAPTER VII

SVALBARD SEAS

June 17th, 8.30 p.m. Our second day at sea.

I finished my night watch with the aid of a novel. We have both taken to reading at the wheel; I know it is "not done," but it does help to pass the time. The only trouble is that Adams likes "thrillers" and I a rather lurid love story. In consequence we have each to buy separate books.

At 6.15 a.m. Adams relieved me and I turned in, still in doubt as to the fate of sweet Cynthia, who had been captured by a masterful sheik in the desert. I was grudgingly awakened at 10.15, ate my porridge, took a sight, looked at Nories and my novel, and the novel won. "I'll work the sight later," I said. I am not the only one who is lazy; Adams has announced his intention of growing a beard.

During the afternoon, however, I did make myself attend to navigation. It was a bitter blow. I discovered my azimuth tables ended at latitude 60° N., and with much grumbling had to resort to trigonometry. I always hate the ½ log haversine formula. I try to divide the wretched haversine by two mentally and forget the "one over." I shall stop being posh, hold my arm above the compass, squint at the sun along it and guess the azimuth. Of course, I might have used my hand bearing compass—if I had not said: "It's only a sticking pivot; leave it to me."

By 4.57 I declared we were 8 miles east of our course, but did not do anything about it, for the following reasons : Firstly, I think our deck watch must be of the female sex: it is always changing its mind. We have now "lost" the British time signals on the wireless, and do not seem to be having much success with the Norwegian ones. A most frightful buzzing and pipping goes on for about ten minutes, and as I seem to remember something about an error of four seconds in time causing a corresponding error of one mile in longtitude, it does make things a trifle uncertain.

Secondly, I cannot read my sextant accurately, owing to scratches and the cracked magnifying glass. I have a dreadful habit of shooting the sun without a glass in the end of the telescope, because "I can see it much better that way, Ron, and I don't think it will matter very much."

Thirdly, if by some miracle my sights are approximately accurate, I expect the tide south of Bear Island to put us back. In any case, really accurate sextant work is almost impossible aboard a small yacht. Still, it looks superior, and the resultant position is a guide to be "born in mind," in case your dead reckoning does not take you where you hope it will.

We have now "broken" our first 100 miles by log and the needle is starting to go round all over again. The sun shines out of a pale blue sky and I have had to put my yachting cap on to keep the glare out of my eyes. It does seem rather wonderful out at sea, watching the sun sweep round the horizon without ever sinking, only knowing it is "night" when it is on the wrong side of you, so to speak. All day the wind has gradually dropped until there is not a breath of air and not a ripple on the water.

I certainly never expected peaceful conditions like these and it started me philosophizing.

"If this is the Arctic it's nowt but a blinkin' duck pond. You know, Ron, these foreign places are all the same. Take Honolulu; we went there expecting to find Hawaiian belles in grass skirts, and what were the first things we saw?"

"Two factory chimneys and some Japanese," he replied.

"Then look at the Amazon; people said if we as much as dangled a finger in the river an alligator would snap it off, but what actually happened when we got there?"

"We bathed in the river every day," he responded.

"Mark my words," I said learnedly, "the Arctic is the same. Nothing to it. When we get to this Longyearby place Schjelderup says we are to go to, we shall find a large town with super cinemas; even the Sailing Directions say 550 people lived in Spitsbergen in 1930." I then went to the barometer to take the reading for the log book: "29.7—hell! It's falling," I gasped.

"Serves you right," said Adams, "you ought to know by now never to speak disrespectfully of the weather."

Although it is so calm the weather is getting much colder. Adams has just brought my supper up and the hot food completely fogged the wheelhouse windows. I do not want to wrap up too much yet, though; worse may come and my best eiderdown is still being reserved.

June 18th, 4 p.m.: I feel despondent. I have had some shrimps that were three days old; perhaps they have not agreed with me. Anyway, I have a morbid idea we are not going to find Bear Island. The beastly place is only about 10 miles long, 8 miles wide and usually obscured in mist. A bonny landmark after 240 miles of open sea, with a cock-eyed navigator. I got another position at 6 a.m., 8 miles west of our course, this time. At least I am consistent about the distance. Adams did not look impressed. "It is not me," I said, "it is the tide."

The barometer has now fallen to 29.69, the sky is covering with cirrus and the sun is pale and faint through the mist of cloud. I rather fear a depression is coming but am trying to console myself by thinking it is merely the low pressure area that lies between Norway and Spitsbergen; an extension of the Icelandic low. Here the sky is nearly always overcast, the monthly mean of cloud amounting to eight-or nine-tenths, with an average of only about seven clear days. Anyway, I believe depressions usually pass south of Bear Island, so even if there is one, we should be sailing out of it and the overcast sky will enable us to see the ice-blink, for we are now approaching the possible ice-line. It does not look as though I shall get any more sights, but what is the use of the darned things anyway? What we do want is a deep sea lead to sound for the Spitsbergen Bank. I could kick myself for not bringing one.

Adams say he has seen some whales. "Quick, Win, damn big ones, spouting," but I do not know whether I believe him. They have always gone by the time I arrive on the scene.

9 p.m.: I knew it. We are lost. Somewhere between the Barents and Greenland seas. I don't know what the hell to do. The log shows 250 miles, having been put out shortly before leaving the Norwegian coast. The visibility is good, and even allowing for the log to over register, we ought to have sighted the island two hours ago. According to my first position we were 8 miles east, and according to the second, 8 miles west. Of course, they may both be right, about 13 hours elapsed between them and we might easily have been set 16 miles in that time. It is now about 15 hours since I got the last position, so we might be 30 or 40 miles west by this time and may have passed the island without seeing it. If I keep on and we have passed it we will be in the ice. If I alter course east, and we are not where my navigation says (which is more than probable) we shall also be in the ice. I dare not change course for Spitsbergen without a bearing of the island, and now there is no sun to get another sight. Moral: "Gather the rosebuds while ye may, to-morrow may be a rainy day," or "Do not ignore Nories for novels."

One hope seems to remain—the deep sea lead we haven't got. Bear Island lies on the edge of the Spitsbergen Bank, and if I could obtain a sounding it would be a great help. I have therefore just instructed Adams to make the necessary. "Go below," I said, "find all the odd pieces of rope and string we have, join them on to our ordinary lead line to make it about 50 fathoms. And oh," I added, "bring up the flat iron in case our lead is not heavy enough."

He is now busy tying himself and everything else into knots and I am anxiously awaiting the result. It will be a miracle if it works, but we can at least try.

June 19th, 3 a.m.: We have sighted Bear Island. I was never so pleased to see anything before. We were quite lucky to spot it. About 10 o'clock last night we put the engine in neutral ("Don't stop it, Ron, it might not start again") and both went on deck to battle with the newly made "deep sea lead." It was not very successful. Having both got exceedingly cross and completely tangled up in it I chanced to look up to the N.E. A narrow golden streak lay on the horizon, caused I supposed by the sun lowering behind the grey clouds. At the north end of the streak was a sharp black edge.

"Don't want to raise false hopes," I said, "but look over there; it may be land."

"I believe you're right," replied Adams. "It is too sharp and low for cloud. It's worth investigating?"

After two hours the island came into view. "Never insult my navigation again," I said with dignity. "I knew perfectly well we were to the west; I don't know what you were worrying about."

We went nearer to get a really good bearing. Patches of snow and ice lay on the low lying northern part of the island, southward of which was a dark high plateau, terminating in a sheer cliff, off which a detached pillar of rock rose from the water, almost hooked at the top. It must have been the cliff which we first sighted.

Bear Island was officially discovered by a Dutchman, Willem Barents, in 1596; though Norsemen had probably found it long before. After a battle with a polar bear, which his men succeeded in killing, Barents named the island Beeren Eylandt. Later it was christened Cherrie Island by an Englishman, but it is now known as Björnöya; the Norwegian for Bear Island. During the 17th century, walrus hunters and whalers visited the island, and for most of the 18th century Russians hunted and wintered there. Later Norwegians wintered there frequently, but the walrus were, by this time, being either exterminated or driven away. In 1882 an attempt was made to colonize the island, which ended by everybody dying from scurvy. After this the Germans had a "do" at running a fishing and hunting station. Björnöya became part of Svalbard and Norwegian Territory after the Treaty of Paris in 1920, and to-day is only inhabited by the staff of the Meteorological and Wireless Station. It is, however, frequently visited by our British trawlers, and we were looking forward to seeing some of them, but it must be the wrong time of the year for there was not a ship in sight.

With any encouragement from Adams I would have put into Sörhamn, or South Haven, where there is fairly good anchorage, except in winds from a southerly direction. Still, there would not have been much point for, according to the Sailing Directions, the cliffs may only be scaled with some difficulty. Even if I had got up without breaking my neck it would have been a horrible walk to the wireless station at Tunheim, on the eastern side, for the island is composed mostly of rock, ice, lakes and bogs. There is anchorage near Tunheim in Austervaag, where there are the remains of an old coal mine, but the wind was freshening from the N.E. and putting in there would not have been advisable. In fact, Bear Island appears a rather doubtful sort of haven; shelter in the lee of the rocky cliffs being about all you can hope for. It is rather a pity, for we heard that one of the wireless operators speaks English and I would have liked a chat with him and some more information about the weather.

At 12.45 a.m., having got my bearings, I set course for a point 30 miles west of South Cape, Spitsbergen, for I want, if possible, to clear the ice. We cannot afford to be trapped in ice, it would crush *Perula* like matchwood. Adams is now fast asleep below and, I must admit, I do not feel very cheerful watching the land disappearing after such a brief sight of it. We are on the bank, the tide seems to be running strongly and we are tossing about a bit. I feel rather tired. I must not forget the magnetic variation; from practically nothing it is now increasing rapidly.

6 pm. Bear Island has disappeared and we are alone with the sea once again. The barometer has dropped to 29.59 and I have just entered the wind as being north, force 5. The sea is getting fairly rough; a few "white horses" knocking about. We are making rather poor time under mainsail, staysail and power, just about holding the wind; "close hauled" I think you call it, I don't pretend to know these seafaring terms. We have not got the mizzen up, we seem to be going better without it and, to quote a skipper in the bar parlour of the Gazelle, "Indeed to goodness *Perula*'s mizzen is nothing but a bloody pocket handkerchief". Sometimes I wonder why Bill Campbell of Dickie's thinks so highly of it. He says it does not "balance," but it will prove one of the most valuable sails we have.

It will be pretty grim if we cannot get into Isfjord when we reach Spitsbergen. Imagine having to turn back and face another week at sea. We are being very careful with our fresh water. I have just had a bath in the Arctic Ocean, heated up in a kettle, of course! The temperature dropped 8° yesterday; I would hate to be in an open cockpit. It is not so bad in the wheelhouse, we have a good fug up, but even so we both keep watch wrapped in rugs. In fact, I have fastened my rug round my waist and walk around looking like an eastern gent in robes.

THE JOYS (?) OF YACHTING !

I keep looking anxiously ahead for ice-blink. Fortunately, the sky is completely overcast, so we should see it before encountering any ice. The sea is about the coldest and most depressingly grey colour I have ever seen; still, with a bit of luck we may sight the South Cape soon after midnight. Hell's Bells! We have just had a near "do." I had to put the wheel hard a'starboard. A damn great log, at least 12 feet long and 3 feet diameter, was about to crash into us. It was a good half tree, sawn neatly at either end, rolling round and round, half hidden by the waves. It might have done considerable damage had it hit us in this sea. I wonder where it has come from. I will have to put this writing away and keep a better look out. It is the second log I have seen and in any case this blasted weather is getting worse. The "glass" has fallen again. I definitely do not like it.

Midnight. It is frightful. I am scared to death. I have just recorded the wind as north, force 7 and a sea "gone mad". It is chucking itself at us from every direction, no rhyme or reason to the waves. The barometer is down to 29.5 and still falling. The log reads 366 miles; we have covered 26 miles in the last ten hours and are now practically hove to. The weather has been gradually getting worse and worse. By 6 o'clock the wind had increased to about force 6. We talked of running back for Bear Island but we were about 80 miles away. "Oh! Hell," I groaned, "why didn't we put in at Sörhamn while we had the chance?"

By 8 o'clock it became evident that something would have to be done about the mainsail. It had seen us through our November gale in Wales and we were loath to part with it, for we did not know how *Perula* would ride without it. We discussed reefing, but we had never reefed a sail before. Our mainsail is only 360 sq. feet and of heavy canvas, so it stands up to most blows. "It will be easier to take it down," I said, "and try her under mizzen and staysail." A bonny place, the Arctic, to start learning seamanship. I began to realise what a complete B.F. I was to have set out on this passage with so little experience.

The wind was howling and shrieking. God knows how Adams got the sail in; the deck was a mass of spray and his limbs were frozen almost stiff. I was at the wheel with engine throttled back, dodging the waves as best I could. At length the mainsail was down and the mizzen up. *Perula* seemed to be riding better and we felt a little more encouraged. It did not last long. The weather got worse and we realised something else would have to be done. Adams thought we might be better without the staysail, as it seemed too big for the mizzen. I was horrified at the idea of him going for'ard in that wind and water, but he said he thought he could do it. Having lowered and lashed it on deck, he staggered back, soaked to the skin, his fingers cracked open with the cold.

Now we are heading about 4 points off the gale, under mizzen and just enough engine to give us steerage way. It is bloody awful trying to steer, and we are taking alternate hours on and off. We tried to manage two hourly watches but could not stick it. Adams has just relieved me and sent me below to rest. I wanted to stay in the wheelhouse, but he feels it will take our minds off conditions if we go below for our hour's rest—the wheelhouse is just a sheet of water. I can hardly write and moving about is almost impossible. You have to make a series of lurches; one down the companion; one to the saloon door; then a wild dash that ends with both arms round the mast. We have a root bunk out and I am in it now; it is the only place. I am trying to think of Schjelderup; to capture some of his confidence and laugh as he would. This would be nothing to him. But he would know what to do: we don't. It seems so far away from everything out here, no help for miles, just the sea and somewhere ahead a coast of ice. I wish I had not come.

June 20th, 9 a.m.: We have covered 9 miles in the last nine hours. The wind is now N.N.W., force 8, barometer 29.39, still falling. We are both exhausted; I have not the heart to write more.

1 p.m. We have sighted a coal steamer, the first ship we have seen. Gosh! It was a good sight. She was proceeding slowly and passed us on the starboard hand. It has cheered me tremendously. For one thing we must be right for Spitsbergen, also she will report seeing us should there be any anxiety on our account.

I had to laugh a little while ago; a rather large-sized wave crashed on deck, uprooted the meat-safe and sent it hurling aft, where it jammed for the moment, waiting for the next wave to finish it off. Adams, in response to my agonised shriek, came bounding up from below and, clad in pyjamas, rushed on deck and managed to grab it in the nick of time. As he dragged it and himself safely into the cockpit, I gave him one look. "Well, you are a B.F.," I said, "risking your life for six lamb chops and a pound of butter." Funny how things affect you at sea. At the time the saving of that meat-safe seemed to be the most important thing in the world.

But fresh danger threatened. We noticed that the same wave had dislodged the dinghy and she too was sliding perilously down the deck, minus part of her lashings. Adams had to dash to the rescue once more and, after a fearful battle, managed to get her back into place.

I hardly like to say it, in case I am tempting providence, but I do believe the wind is easing slightly. The barometer is still falling, however; it is 29.3 now; I shall stick a piece of paper over the damn thing in a minute. I do not mind admitting that I would not like to go through another night like this last one. I think I spent most of my time alternately calling upon the Heavens and my mascots. As I have no less than four mascots I was kept fairly busy and looked a bit like a Christmas tree.

First I would rub my St. Christopher medal and murmur: "Please look after us." This medal was given to me by a lady when I was en route for

South America and I always fasten it to my belt when on travels, for St. Christopher is, of course, the Patron Saint of travellers.

Next I consoled myself with my bracelet of monkeys' teeth, the gift of an Indian chief in the jungles of the Amazon. He had said, through an interpreter: "Tell the white woman that while she wears it no harm can befall her."

Then there is my "lucky button," cut from the jacket of a naval officer by his wife, an old school friend whom I had not seen for years. She had sent it to me just before we sailed with the words: "Wear it, Win—it carried him safely through the war." So I polished the button and said to it: "Please make the wind drop."

Lastly, there is my newest mascot, a little pair of wooden shoes given me by Mrs. Sannes in Bodö. She could not speak English but she had smiled through misty blue eyes, unpinned them from her dress and fastened them on my jersey. I had stammered: "Takk" (thank you), and since then I have always worn them. As the barometer falls lower, I keep rubbing the shoes and saying: "Please make it rise." You will notice that I am very polite when addressing my mascots.

I really do think they are working, for the weather is definitely getting better and better. Cynical people will say the depression is passing, but I still say it is my mascots. I am going to open up the engine a bit more; think she will take it now. Riding rough weather seems to be very much a question of speed, and I think Bill is right about the mizzen; it is useful.

June 21st, 1 a.m.: Our fifth day at sea. It is still rough and blowing quite hard. The barometer is down to 29.29—I don't think it will ever rise again. The log reads 418 miles, but as I mournfully said to Adams: "Don't expect we have moved much, it's just the water sweeping past us." Some times the sky ahead has been literally black; I felt that if it would only rain or snow it might be better. Occasionally there has been a brighter patch and I have cried joyfully: "Look, Ron, it is brightening to the west, the depression is passing." Then the clouds would bank up again. Once, to port, they were so dark and heavy I thought it was land. It was an awful shock. "Hell!" I said, "is it Greenland or the east coast of Spitsbergen?"

The gale has lasted now for over 27 hours, but I do think it is easing. My attempt to increase speed was quite impossible; we shipped wave after wave, quite green. I had to be content just to crawl ahead. We have got a little water below but nothing to worry about. We are both somewhat black and blue with being thrown about and my arm is cut, but I do not remember doing it.

10 a.m. I think we can see Spitsbergen. I feel I could turn somersaults. The weather has cleared, the skies are blue, and rising behind a purple haze to starboard are ghostly white peaks, faint and unreal. But I do not think it is cloud. No, I am sure it is land. Spitsbergen. Strange we should sight it to-day, Tuesday, for it was on a Tuesday, six weeks ago, that we left the Menai Straits.

Now we are here I don't know whether to laugh or cry. My one thought is that it has been worth it—the gales, the heart-breaking fatigue. I am so excited I don't know what to do; even the barometer is going up. I wish you could see Spitsbergen as I see it now. It is like a fairy-tale land; white and misty in the blue water. Something about it gets hold of you; hard to put it into words. I am not sure where we are, but we must have passed the South Cape, so I am changing course to the north.

2 p.m. I changed course too soon, we are in drift ice. About half an hour ago fantastic white shapes appeared in the water ahead; some like antlers or branches of trees, almost transparent and washed by the sea into the most delicate forms. "

What are they?" I asked in wonder.

"Ice," said Adams grimly. "Better turn west."

"They are beautiful," I said. "Let's go a bit closer and get some pictures."

Larger pieces appeared; tiny icebergs. "Bergy bits," I said, with superiority, for if you want to be posh never call ice, "ice." Each shape and size has its own name—floe, brash, growler, pancake, etc. If you hear of a glacier "calving," do not expect veal for lunch, it is merely shedding baby icebergs.

Adams is sitting for'ard, keeping a look-out for the larger floes and signalling me where to steer. The ice is glistening blueish-green in the sunshine and gives the impression we are in a sea studded with diamonds. Inshore, however, it seems to form a close pack, and a coal steamer has just appeared slowly boring her way out. Looks as though she is going to pass close to us. I am going on deck to wave.

Back again. It really was funny, the captain nearly fell off the bridge at the sight of us. I cannot make out where the steamer has come from, but we had better follow her west and get out of this. We can't have far to go now and should reach Isfjord to-night. I shall not be sorry.

June 22nd, 2 a.m.: We are still at sea. We reached the coast about midnight; all we could see was a flat mass of white, streaked with black patches of rock. The weather had clouded up again and a mist hung over the ice. The mountains we had expected to get our position from were obscured in a layer of cloud, which merged into the snow. We could not tell high land from low, the entire coastline looked exactly alike and there was not a single landmark. First I mistook Prince Charles Foreland and started in for what I thought was Isfjord. Black shapes started to dance up and down in the water ahead. We watched fascinated, thinking they were large fish leaping. I had to put the wheel hard over. Our "fish" were rocks.

Mirage and refraction are very misleading, both in Northern Norway and out here. We would try to sail between "two islands," to find ourselves trying to penetrate a mountain range. An open passage looked blocked and a blocked one clear. It is difficult to give an idea of the utter desolation, of the helplessness we felt. Not knowing where we were, our charts were useless, except to try and recognise things by, and we had some very lucky escapes.

We tried another opening; wide and with high land on either side. It looked quite clear and we felt certain it was the fjord, for we were heading east. All at once a sheet of white appeared in front of us. At first we thought it was ice but it proved to be the low land covered with snow and stretching across the entrance. "Bellsund," I said in triumph, "we have hit the coast too far south". I looked at the chart. It is Bellsund all right, high ground either side, a low flat strip of island running N .W., practically blocking the fjord; beyond it water and high ground in the distance. It is a great relief, we were both feeling very dispirited, but it is all right now and we will be in by morning.

I am following the coast northwards and Adams has turned in; he looks fagged out. We have not had any rest as, thinking we should soon be in port, we have been cleaning ship. It has been an awful job, the water below was worse than I thought. The fireplace was a miniature duck pond and the saloon carpet wet through. It will take days to dry things up and the brasses are beyond words. Never mind, to-morrow night we will be at anchor and able to have a damn good sleep.

9 a.m. Lord alone knows where we are. I thought we reached Kapp Martin rather quickly, but as we turned north, the coast looked all right; a ledge of flat ground with mountains rising up beyond it. I was keeping well offshore to miss the shoals and had to keep taking a bit more off my course, but put it down to magnetic disturbance of the compass.

Adams relieved me about 5 a.m. and I wakened an hour ago fully expecting to see Isfjord. Instead of the fjord entrance the coast seemed to stretch endlessly ahead. It is rather terrifying, the wind is strengthening again and the water lashing the shore. A wilderness of ice, cold and cruel, but above all so desperately lonely. There is not a sign of any living thing; we might be in a dead land. Queer I should say that. Adams says that years ago these northern regions were thought of as the "other world," the land of the dead. If only there was a tree, a blade of grass, something living; there is not even a bird. Adams has helplessly suggested turning back for Norway. I feel I could sit down and weep.

Forlandsund, 9 p.m. About noon we saw a beacon; this was indeed a find. Beacons are few and far between in Spitsbergen, where there is only one lighthouse on the coast and two small ones in Isfjord. "It looks like Fuglehuk," I said. "If it is, we are miles too far north."

We were going into the log, reading and trying to work things out, when Adams cried: "What's that?"

To the northward was a small dark object on the water. I seized the glasses. "Allah be praised, it's a boat," I said. With the engine flat out we made towards it.

"What are you going to do?" asked Adams.

"Shed my dignity as a navigator and ask where we are," I replied.

"It is no use, they won't speak English," he said. I had not thought of that but, with a desperation born of sheer necessity, I declared that I would speak Norwegian.

Fortunately, the boat was fishing; we managed to catch up with it and, with my party piece prepared, with the aid of a dictionary, I went on deck. Our arrival caused great excitement, and the entire crew of the fishing boat assembled on deck. Amongst them I noticed a small man wearing a pot hat and armed with a camera.

"Kan De mig veien til Isfjord?" I shouted; hoping it meant what I thought it did. The crew regarded me open mouthed; the gent with the camera took my picture, raised his "pot" and bowed. I repeated it with no better success.

"Jeg ser efter Isfjord?" I tried.

Again the gent in the "pot" took my picture and the crew bowed.

After about ten minutes of this, almost hoarse and clinging to the rigging as *Perula* rolled in the swell I cried: "Oh, dear! How can I make you understand I want Icefjord?" In the agony of the moment I used my own language. The result was startling. The Captain beamed, "Icefjord, Madam?" he said in perfect English, "I will direct you there with pleasure." It was my turn to gape open-mouthed; then I started to laugh with sheer relief Apparently my efforts at Norwegian had been mistaken for Russian or Chinese.

That old skipper was marvellous to us, offered his own charts and did all in his power to help us. It was Fuglehuk we had passed and we were cheerfully heading for latitude 80° north.

"Well, I suppose the Great Ice Barrier would have stopped us eventually," remarked Adams sarcastically, "but it seems rather a pity to be only about 600 miles from the North Pole and not visit it!"

We started the weary trail back. As it was blowing up the skipper had advised us to take the Forlandsund, the inside passage between Prince Charles Island and the mainland. According to the Sailing Directions this charming bit of nature was named Foul Sound by a gentleman named Poole in 1610. I don't think it has changed much since. It has a bar with depths of about 12 feet, if you happen to get the right spot. The bar is considerably more shallow elsewhere. just as we approached it the sky turned a murderous black and ahead everything blotted out. "If that is snow, we are sunk," I groaned; for navigating in an Arctic snow storm is, I believe, worse than fog. Fortunately it proved to be rain, and we could more or less see through it as we groped along, keeping as near to the island as we dared. We could see the bottom quite clearly, and Adams kept calling hard to port or starboard as the water turned a lighter green. The wind was howling against us and throwing up a nasty sea on the banks. We expected to bump at any moment, and once we missed a rock by a couple of yards, either I or the chart being at fault regarding its position. Immense glaciers, sheer cliffs of ice, lined the shore and at times we had to swerve violently to avoid icebergs which had broken free.

As we proceed along the sound, I am beginning to realise what happened. Probably the ice extended further west-ward than we expected and this, coupled with the tide, which sets northward and which, of course, I had forgotten, caused us to make land about the middle of Prince Charles Island. Adams vows we were at the foreland and perhaps even in the southern entrance to Forlandsund, but I know now that my "Bellsund" was definitely Prince Charles Island. Although I am now looking at it from the other side I can recognise it; high land at either end of a flat stretch of snow. The chart bears this out, for the courses round Kaldneset and up the island coast are roughly similar to the northern exit of Bellsund. Anyway, it's done now and it is no use arguing about it.

So we spend our seventh night at sea, but we shall be in . . . . No! I better not say it.

Look out for ice; Brown in Main Street, Longyearbyen and Lapp settlement at Lyngen

CHAPTER VIII

THE "OUTSIDE" WORLD

Longyearbyen. June 27th.

Shortly after 6 a.m. on June 23rd we turned into Adventfjord, a small inlet of Isfjord. It was only a matter of minutes before our outward passage would be completed and as we hauled in the log it read 698 miles, making 741 from Tromsö. I departed below to put on my yachting cap, and my return to the wheelhouse was greeted, as usual, by Adams' sarcastic "Ah! the Captain is on the bridge." He had shaved his beard off but left a moustache that had started all Spanish but finished up Ronald Coleman, after much debate and looking in the mirror.

We both felt very excited as we surveyed our surroundings and wondered where to anchor. On the southern shore were some small tents, above which fluttered the swastika: a German Expedition, and "Look, Ron, they have an aeroplane; how the devil do they land it there?"

We made towards a coal loading jetty, but the anchorage did not look promising and we decided to proceed further down the fjord to a second jetty, off which a few boats appeared to be moored. Along the hill that rose up from the shore were steel pylons, connected by cables along which ran an endless procession of buckets. The surrounding mountains had the usual patched effect; dark streaks of earth and rock showing through the snow, but beyond the valley at the fjord head, the scenery changed to the unblemished white of the Arctic.

As we approached the second jetty, I gave a shout of joy. Anchored just off it was a large Norwegian whaler and, at the masthead, flew a red ensign. "A British Expedition," I cried. "Gee, it's good to see your National flag." Adams spotted a mooring buoy, we tied up to it and stopped the engine for the first time since leaving Tromsö. My ears started to sing at the sudden silence; we had listened to the engine for over a week, and it had never given us a second's anxiety.

"Well, we are here at last," I said. "In Advent Bay." Adventure Bay they used to call it. We both agreed we had had our share of adventure reaching it. In just over six weeks we have covered 2,462 miles—quite a few of which we had no need to cover!

"What shall we do now?" I asked, full of enthusiasm.

"I'm going to bed," said Adams; he never has any soul.

We had just got to sleep when a frightful knocking awakened us. Adams departed to the wheelhouse, cursing heartily.

"What is it?" I called. "Dunno," he replied. "There's a bloke here getting very excited, I can't understand him very well, but I think a coal steamer is coming and we are on its buoy."

"Hell," I growled, "are we never going to rest?" However, our visitor, who had come in a motor launch, tossed us a rope and towed *Perula* to an anchorage, west of the jetty in about 10 fathoms.

It was not worth going back to bed and I was dying to go ashore and explore Longyearbyen.

"Don't see your super cinema," remarked Adams.

"Oh, the town is up beyond the hill," I replied, attiring myself in my Sunday best; which included a new pair of navy trousers and white suede shoes. I really did expect to find a large town. "I wonder if one wears a white cover on a yachting cap in the Arctic," I debated, as I viewed my clean one, which I had ironed with great difficulty the previous night. I always loath ironing aboard a small yacht; a primus is no place to heat an iron and the iron shield invariably gets rusty.

"I don't think it will matter much what you wear," said Adams.

I gave him a disgusted look. "No need to appear like a damn savage," I said, powdering my nose. "Besides, it is a big place, they will be very excited to see us and we have the dignity of the British nation to uphold." I did not know Longyearbyen! It was previously known as Longyear City, named after an American, John M. Longyear, who started the mine there. Doubtless the name was approved by the settlers, who considered that no where on earth could a year be longer.

We rowed ashore, shelved the dinghy on the beach, climbed over sundry rubbish and stepped, ankle deep, into slimy mud. My new shoes were ruined. We looked at a few wooden sheds dotted around us; the workmen that passed us by with hardly a glance and the tractors that ploughed through the quagmire.

"Where do we go now?" asked Adams, with an amused look at my horrified expression.

"The town is up the hill," I persisted, with as much dignity as possible, having tried to jump a puddle and landed in the middle.

Going up the hill was easier said than done, and before long we were breathless and filthy. There was coal everywhere, on the ground and in the air, as it swung down from the mines on the overhead cables. In one place the buckets crossed the "road," and a notice of warning requested you to "se op." I dodged beneath, feeling sure a load of coal would descend on my head. The "town" in view, I nearly had a fit. It was situated on a slope, and lining the two "streets" were rows of wooden buildings, mostly painted with oil and resembling old army huts. Outside them hung dead birds, odd blankets, clothing and muddy boots. One hut I noticed bore a painted cross, and was apparently the hospital. Near it were two or three glass frames in which a few lettuces, etc., were carefully tended, reserved, I suppose, for the sick. A building rather resembling a bicycle shed proved to be the fire station and, on the right, in the shadow of a mountain, was a small wooden church, painted white. The mountain was a reddish colour and along its side was a mine structure and the usual steel pylons. We found later that this mine, closed down after a disaster some years previously, was still on fire—hence, I suppose, the reddish colour.

The other side of the town sloped down to a valley, composed of water and pebbles. Across here also, coal buckets ran to a mine on the opposite hillside. Some dark specks wandered about in the distance, and later we discovered they were reindeer, grazing on the patches of moss. The real piece de resistance, however, was an immense mountain of tin cans. I never thought there were so many cans in the world. They rose up in a magnificent mass, alternately glinting and patched with rust. "There is no doubt what Longyearbyen lives on," I remarked.

As we wandered dismally along the street, still ankle deep in mud, men brushed past us carrying kit bags, possibly just arriving or leaving on a coal steamer. Nobody took the slightest notice of us. Fortunately, we met our visitor of the morning, and he pointed out the post office and the one shop. Both were closed. In fact, we paid about eight visits to the shop before we found it open; then all we could buy, other than miners' requisites, were some Turkish cigarettes and "penny bars" of chocolate. Actually, the shop only opens for about three hours on five days in the week. This was, of course, posted up outside, but we had been unable to read it.

We were more successful with the wireless station and news of our safe arrival having been despatched home, we made our way back to *Perula.*

As we rowed by the vessel flying the red ensign I wanted to call but Adams said it was too near lunch time. Back in the saloon, having left my best shoes in a bucket of water on deck, I threw myself mournfully on to the settee.

"For heaven's sake mix me a drink," I said.

"What's the matter, didn't you enjoy your nice little walk ashore?" asked Adams evilly.

"Enjoy it," I wailed, "I've been to a few godforsaken places in the world but never have I seen anything to equal this; it is awful, awful beyond description. To think we have come all these miles, fagging ourselves out in disgusting weather and all to reach this place; it's cruel . . . . Mix me another drink."

"What will you have for lunch?" asked Adams consolingly.

"A lamb chop would be nice," I said, brightening.

"We've no fresh meat or vegetables left," he replied. "Don't you remember, you finished them yesterday and said you'd buy more this morning."

"Open a tin," I started, very quietly, "empty the contents"; gradually my voice rose, "then take the empty can ashore and throw it on to that blasted pile," I ended in a storm of rage.

Those were my impressions of Longyearbyen up to June 24th. Then the sun came out, a gloriously hot sun, that let us walk about without overcoats and dried up some of the mud. This time we went ashore in sea boots. I looked at Longyearbyen with new eyes and found myself liking it. "You know, Ron," I said, "people can make a home anywhere, it's not half as bad as I thought, and what's a bit of mud, anyway".

While we were in the town a man spoke to us, asking if he might come aboard and see *Perula*. He said he had passed us in a launch the previous night but had not liked to trouble us. I remembered him quite well. I had been preparing to turn in, when Adams had called me on deck to see a baby seal which was swimming around us. While we were watching the seal, the launch had circled round and a tall grey-haired man had hesitatingly smiled across at me, looking as if he wished to speak to us but was too shy. I had been on the point of inviting him aboard when I remembered I was not properly dressed. On this second meeting he told us he was the "Sysselmann". We did not know what that meant, but he spoke excellent English and was obviously a man of distinction. He accepted my invitation aboard to supper, and I was delighted at having found a friend, for I liked the Sysselmann very much.

"Now you've done it," said Adams, as we walked away. "What are you going to give him to eat?" I had not thought of that, and the problem became even more alarming when, on consulting the dictionary, we discovered I had invited the Governor of Svalbard to share our bully beef.

We had not as yet spoken to our fellow countrymen of the Red Ensign. On seeing a gentleman who resembled a retired colonel, cleaning his teeth over the side, I had hastened to the cockpit prepared to smile across in friendly fashion. Perhaps it was an unhappy moment to choose; anyway I met with no success.

That evening we met Einar Sverdrup. I have the greatest admiration for Hr. Sverdrup, to me he has one of the finest characters of any man I have met. Our first meeting, however, was not exactly successful. We were just going back aboard to prepare for the supper party when a man stopped us, asking if we had everything we wanted and if there was anything he could do for us. “Dear me,” I thought, “who is this awful looking man?” I think Sverdrup had just come out of the mine. He was wearing muddy knee boots, an old jacket and breeches, no collar or tie, and low over his forehead he had pulled an ancient cloth cap, back to front. On his face was a few days’ growth of beard and moustache. Yet he talked with authority, had a spontaneous humour and blue eyes that I decided were rather nice. “I’ll ask him aboard for a drink,” I thought. Then I looked again. “No,” I decided, “not with the Governor coming—it would not do at all”. So after a few more words and an awkward pause, he departed and we rowed back aboard.

The supper party was quite successful. Our guest was very interested in *Perula*, as he was designing a ship of his own in which to carry out his work as Governor of Svalbard, for this entails a fair amount of travelling. In addition to Vest-Spitsbergen his territory includes Nordaustland, Barentsöya, Edgeöya, Kvitöya, Kong Karls Land, Hopen, and Björnöya. Visits have to be made to different parts of the coast and to various islands in the course of administration and the enforcement of game laws. During the spring he had crossed from the west to the east coast of Spitsbergen by dog-sleigh. The ship he is planning, however, is to be considerably larger than *Perula*; some 70 tons and built specially for penetrating the ice.

It was interesting to hear something of the early history of Spitsbergen and the controversy that existed between England, Holland and Norway, for the sovereignty of this northern land. Often fierce fighting has occurred between ships of the different nations, but with the decline of the whaling industry interest was lost, and in 1715 Russian trappers were practically the only inhabitants. Later, Norwegians came back, but these

Arctic regions had, for too long, been No Man's Land, a hunting ground for all nations.

With the animals in danger of extermination, they are to-day, under Norwegian rule, protected, and a licence is required for hunting. The animals include the polar bear, the blue and white fox and reindeer. Hare and muskox have been imported. The bird-life includes about thirty species, mostly sea birds, and there is also the snow owl and ptarmigan.

The Governor told us much about life out here in the North. Longyearbyen is the principal settlement, with a population of about 600 men, 60 women and 50 children. Most of the men are employees of the "Store Norske Spitsbergen Kulkompani," about 400 being miners and the remainder engineers, office staff, cooks and outside men for the construction of new mines, etc. Some of the women are employed as waitresses in the canteen, nurses in the hospital, etc., but only the engineers, foremen and office staff are permitted to have their wives and families in Spitsbergen.

We asked about the one shop and told of our predicament regarding food. The Governor explained that everything was controlled and rationed by the Mining Company and that it was not possible to buy food in the ordinary way, but he asked us to call on him next morning and said he would take us along to see the Food Controller.

Before leaving he very kindly consented to sign our log book, for, as I said to Adams, "You know what people are like; there are no Customs to stamp papers here, and when we get back they may not believe we have been." I had just finished my old log book with our arrival at Spitsbergen, so I handed it to the Governor, with an inward prayer he would not ready the last entry, namely: "June 23rd, 1938, 6.45 a.m. Anchored Longyearbyen—what a hell of a place!" Beneath it he wrote the following words:-

> "24/6/ 38. jeg har varet på besök ombord i *Perula*, hvor jeg fikk en udmerket aftens. Jeg har den störste beundring for hvad *Perula* har utrettet, seilet fra England over til Norge og defra til Spitsbergen.
>
> Longyearbyen
> (Signed) WOLMER MARLOW,
> Sysselmann."

We did not quite know what it meant, but gathered it said he had been aboard, the bully beef was O.K. and that he admired *Perula* and her voyage from England to Spitsbergen. Anyway, we were delighted with it and took it to the post office next day to be stamped with a nice seal that said, "Longyearbyen, Svalbard," and in the centre the longitude and latitude, 15° 35' 00" E.; 78° 13' 04" N. I also bought 30 postcards, similarly stamped, which I despatched to my kind, but possibly doubting, friends, and upon which I wrote: "Look where I am."

After the Governor had left us, our baby seal paid us another visit. He comes most nights and we have christened him "Sammy the Seal." As he swims through the water a cloud of seagulls hover above. Suddenly he will dive, small fish leap out of the water, and the birds swoop down with greedy shrieks, catching them in mid-air. Sammy has taken a great fancy to the dinghy. He rubs up against it and appears very partial to the varnish. He is not in the least afraid of us and lets us stroke his head, rolling over in the water like a kitten.

"Catch him, Ron," I said, "he'll make a fine picture if we can get him on deck."

Adams got in the dinghy and battled nobly. "He's so damn slippery," he said. "Oh! blast it—" as Sammy, his funny little face screwed into a paroxysm of rage, gave a snort, a spit, and bit Adams. I fear I was rather unpopular for laughing. After that Adams tried to manoeuvre him into a bucket, but it was no good, Sammy would not fit in.

Next morning, after several enquiries for "Sysselmann," we eventually arrived at "Government House", a brown wooden bungalow on the hilltop overlooking the bay.

A maid opened the door and showed us into a room. We both stood still and gazed in amazement; we might have walked straight into an English drawing-room. English pictures and books, an English programme on the wireless. An open fireplace replaced the large stove that is usually found in Norwegian homes. I looked at the beautifully furnished room, the tasteful decorations, the cushions and flowers, then at the pale Indian carpet and my muddy sea boots. I whispered in horror to Adams: "Had I better take them off?" but the Governor came in, the maid brought a tray of tea, cakes and, how wonderful!—fresh milk.

On the radiogram was a photograph of an attractive woman. The Governor, seeing me looking at it, remarked: "My wife, she too is English."

Unfortunately, we have not met Mrs. Marlow, for after spending the winter with her husband, she has returned to London for a holiday. I feel very proud that one of my countrywomen has the courage to live away out here; through the constant darkness of winter, the storms and the shrieking wind, sharing the life of this Arctic settlement. It takes some doing when you have been brought up in a comfortable London home; to leave our English capital for a bleak and lonely little bungalow, which for month after month is practically buried in snow. Hester Marlow not only came to the North herself, but by her great character and personality, she has brought here the very spirit of our country, a tiny corner of England in Spitsbergen. As I sat in this room, so far from home yet so "at home," I felt very grateful to her.

Our visit in search of food was, to us, rather an affair of mystery. I gathered the gentleman we were looking for had gone to have a bath, but the Sysselmann took us into various offices, where everything was very businesslike, and I understood a parcel would be sent to us. We then went to the mine bakery, where a man in white overalls was busily extracting the most beautifully crisp brown loaves from enormous ovens. We waited some minutes in the cheery warm atmosphere, sniffing in the delightful scent of baking bread, until he was free to attend to us. He told us he spoke English, French, German and several other languages, and gave us a sample of each, as he tossed loaves, rolls and cakes into large paper bags with cheerful and wholesome abandon. Rather to our embarrassment, our offers of payment were waved aside; like everything else the bakery belonged to the mining company.

It was marvellous to have fresh bread again; cakes, rolls and butter for tea. I began to like Longyearbyen.

In the afternoon we took *Perula* out across Isfjord. The scenery was magnificent. The two sides of the fjord vary tremendously; along the northern shore are bays where great walls of ice rise sheer from the water, towering up almost as high as *Perula*'s masthead. The water beneath is a mass of floating white shapes—icebergs that have broken free. On the other side we did not see a single glacier. Barren flat-topped mountains, having a most extraordinary striped effect; "Tiger mountains," I call them.

We crossed to the snow-covered glaciers. There is something profoundly fascinating about clean, crisp snow, unmarred by a single footprint. They tell us that the call of the north is almost irresistible; once men have lived out here, they must come back. "You too will come back," one man said to me, "the snow-covered mountains will call you." I believe they will; I am rapidly falling for Spitsbergen.

Poor Adams was again sent off in the dinghy to indulge in some photography, while I threaded *Perula* in and out of the ice and posed on deck. As usual we both got very cross, and Adams's temper was not improved when, in hot pursuit of me, he rowed straight into an iceberg, and went backwards over the thwart. With memories of advice in the "Arctic Pilot", I called brightly across to him: "That was very clever—every endeavour should be made to receive the blow on the stem, the part of a ship best suited to the purpose." Most of the night was spent developing the films.

On Sunday we once again visited the small hut that formed the wireless station. One of the operators is new to Spitsbergen and we have become friendly with him. Tall and rather shy, he is thoroughly delighted with his surroundings. "Is not it beautiful?" he will say, "I am so happy to be here." In his off-duty he goes for long walks and when we meet him he will cry: "Look, I have found another flower; I have found five different kinds now. It is wonderful, wild flowers growing here in the ice and snow."

At one time there was considerable vegetation in Spitsbergen, but to-day it is very scanty and consists principally of saxifrages and mosses, although I believe the polar willow and some berry bushes are to be found in places.

I was rather horrified to discover I could not obtain a weather-forecast at the wireless station, at least not the kind I wanted. A brief notice, giving particulars of wind and ice, was pinned to the door and that was all. The Met. station is situated on Kapp Linné, at the entrance to Isfjord, but is more of a reporting than forecasting station. With thoughts of the gale we experienced coming over and with the return passage hanging rather like a millstone round my neck, I sent a prepaid wire to Schjelderup, "Please reply on day weather suitable for us to return." Having done this I felt much happier. We were again in Schjelderup's capable hands, and as I said to Adams: "When the reply comes we will have to leave whether we want to or not, and there will be no time to think about it." I delayed my wire, however, until late on Sunday, for the Governor had invited us to supper and I did not want the reply to come during the party.

We duly arrived at the Governor's doorstep, and I was standing on one leg endeavouring to shed a sea boot, prior to putting on the remains of my best shoes, when an amused voice remarked, “Good evening, we do that inside.” Having nearly fallen over in embarrassment, I looked up to find a dark boy ringing the bell. He would probably be very cross at being referred to as a “boy,” when he was in reality a fully-grown man, but I shall always think of him as “my nice dark boy”. He is very earnest, rather an idealist, and I should imagine much younger than the rest of us. He proved to be a fellow-guest, Hr. Ross, a mining engineer, and we were told the director of the mines was expected. I was rather excited about this for I had heard a good deal about the director in Tromsö.

“I thought you had met him,” said the Governor.

“No,” I replied, “I have only met you, the wireless staff and an awful-looking man on the jetty.”

“What was the man on the jetty like?” asked the “dark boy,” his eyes twinkling.

“Oh, it could not have been the Director,” I said, with conviction. “He was, er . . . rather untidy-looking, medium height and had a moustache.”

“It could not have been the Director if he had a moustache,” said the Governor. Just then the door opened and a good-looking clean-shaven man walked in, attired in a smart lounge suit. “I don’t think you have met Miss Brown,” said the Governor. I rose to greet this stranger and, as we shook hands, I chanced to notice his eyes. I turned a deep and horrible crimson.

“We have met,” said Sverdrup gaily, “but Miss Brown does not recognise me. I had not shaved before—she thought I looked terrible. Is not that right, Miss Brown?” Such is the understanding of Einar Sverdrup. They say in Svalbard he anticipates everything before it happens and no situation has ever found him at a loss. Yet he said the words with such charm that my embarrassment fled and we all roared with laughter.

I shall never forget that evening: myself and the four men seated round a polished table, lace mats, beautifully served food and wine. “Is it really Spitsbergen?” I thought. “It seems like home.” Although Ron and I were complete strangers in a strange land, we felt we were amongst friends whom we had known all our lives.

I think this feeling is perhaps best explained in Sverdrup’s words: “It is only ‘outside’ the world that we are natural and act the way we are or ought to be.” I sat next to him and as he talked I began to understand something of this man, who is admired by all who know him. On the surface he has the characteristic toughness of the north, a little relentless and "hard boiled"; he has to be, to keep 600 miners working in a place like Longyearbyen. Yet underneath he knows and understands his men and concentrates on making life as pleasant as possible for them. He told me that the midnight sun lasts from April 25th to August 24th and that temperatures as high as 15° C. have occasionally been experienced. The average temperature in July and August is, however, about 5° C. During the winter the sun is below the horizon from October 25th to February 16th and it is, of course, completely dark. A temperature of - 50° C. has been recorded, but - 25 or - 30 is usual.

"Gracious," I said. "Is it terrible?"

"Cold weather rarely feels bad because there is no wind," he explained. "The worst we have to face is when it is between - 15 and - 25 and it is stormy. Then you sometimes feel there is little, very little, between you and the other world. On such days it is not possible to keep the temperature above zero inside the houses. It has happened that my wife, to prevent our bulbs, tulips and hyacinths, from freezing, has been obliged to have them in her bed overnight." The idea of sleeping with tulips tickled my fancy immensely, but later I was sorry that I had laughed. It is a queer world, we always want something we haven't got. On the Amazon the endless green drives you almost mad: you call it "green hell". I guess out here in winter it must be very like a "white hell." Not a sign of anything green, no trees, no grass, Just snow and darkness. It would be rather wonderful to see a bulb growing. I admire Mrs. Sverdrup.

Every winter Spitsbergen is completely cut off from the rest of the world, hemmed in by ice. I asked how long this lasted.

"In years with good conditions," he replied, "from the last days of October to the first days of May."

"Gosh!" I exclaimed. "What does it feel like when the last boat leaves in October?"

"When you are very young and more or less filled with romance, there sails away quite a lot with the last boat," he replied, with a smile. "I believe I felt myself as Robinson Crusoe, the very first time I saw the smoke of the steamer disappearing in the south and knew it would not be back again within eight months. Now I have been here for 12 winters and 17 summers, I am glad when I see the last boat off. Every one then will quieten down and life will be again regulated in an ordinary way. Also it is often cold, dark and stormy at that time of the year, and sometimes the ships are caught by the ice. I am always glad when the last ship is safely out of the harbour."

"And the first ship," I asked: "How did you feel when the first ship came?"

"Dear Win," he answered sarcastically. "Many, many years ago, in 1710 or thereabouts, I was filled with excitement, all kinds of hope and a fever made me quite unfit for work . . . ."

"Idiot," I laughed, "you know perfectly well what I mean."

"Well, I don't know what to say," he replied. "I am marching along, trying to make the men work and smiling at my own efforts. I know very well that when the first boat is here, none will work for 24 hours. They are like children that day and, you might laugh, but I feel like as if they were all my kids."

"Does the darkness get on your nerves?"

"No, I don't believe the darkness gets on my nerves," he answered, "but to work in the darkness does. When it is dark and stormy, when you can see nothing and you've got to have everything running. When your foreman says it is too dangerous to run the aerial trainway and you say not to stop it, because that would stop the whole mine—well, I believe that things like that, in the long run, work on your nerves."

I thought of the coal buckets that even in daylight caused me some apprehension. What would they be like in howling wind and darkness, running in an ever menacing procession to and from the mines; over ground piled deep with snow.

"Hell's bells," I said. "If that only gets on your nerves in the long run, what is your greatest problem?"

Sverdrup grinned and started to sing that German-American ballad: "How gan I all dos dings exblain to dat small jacob Straus?"

After dinner we returned to the lounge and as whiskies were poured out Adams remarked: "Can't understand the way you drink whisky in Norway." Norwegians invariably pour out a small whisky and add a large bottle of soda.

"How do you drink it in England?" they asked. Adams held up three fingers. "So much whisky," he said and, holding up one finger, "so much soda."

"To-night we will drink the English way," cried Sverdrup, highly delighted at this procedure. After several "Skaals," it was discovered that the Governor's supply, at this unusual call upon it, had run out. The "dark boy" departed to fetch his own supply and possibly Sverdrup's as well. When he returned we started to play bridge—strict Culbertson! But I fear I fell asleep at the card table during the second hand. The evening finished with Adams and Sverdrup arguing heatedly about the Irish question—neither of them knowing the first thing about it!

I woke up at 11 a.m. next morning, still fully-dressed. "S'truth!" I thought, "the galley looks different?" I blinked and looked again. I was in a comfortable bedroom, and soon a maid arrived with tea and informed me the others had finished breakfast some time ago.

"I have broken a great record coming here," I said to Adams later. "Yes," he agreed, drily, "probably the first Englishwoman to be 'three sheets in the wind' in Spitsbergen."

On Monday the wire had not come and we spent the morning talking to Ross. He explained many more things about their lives and the various problems they have to deal with. We were in the drawing office and all round hung plans of the coal mines, showing the various seams, workings, etc. A man was at work on a drawing-board and appeared to be taking no notice of us.

"Food is of course one of our main problems," said our friend. "We store fresh meat and fish in the mines, for they keep a constant temperature of - 3°C. all through the year and act as, how do you call it—refrigerators? In this way we are able to dispense largely with tinned meats. Vegetables like carrots, onions and potatoes are stored, and many fruits. It was thought that lemons could not be kept, but we find we can keep them for months and they are, of course, invaluable." He then went on to explain about some other fruit, but neither Adams nor I could discover what he meant.

"A lot of them," he said, "purple or green, with stones in them."

"Plums?" I said.

"No," he replied. "It is in my mind, but I cannot think of the English name."

"Damsons?" said Adams.

No, they were not damsons, so we tried blackcurrants, without success. The "dark boy's" forehead was furrowed in deep thought, as is often the way with small details, the solving of the name of the fruit became almost a matter of life and death. We puzzled and puzzled. Meanwhile, the man at the drawing-board was steadily working, to all intents and purposes ignoring us completely and, I concluded, not understanding a word. Quite suddenly, without so much as looking up, he said "Grapes," very much in the tone of voice anybody would have said "Raspberries!" We gazed at him in astonishment, but he calmly went on working. "Thank you," said Ross, "it is grapes." The gentleman paused to bow briefly, then got busy again.

"What is it like working in the mines?" I asked. "Are they like ours?"

"No mines are alike," he answered. "They cannot really be compared, but our mines are in a hillside, where yours are under more flat ground. Then our ground is frozen to a depth of 300 metres, and we believe a frozen roof to be a great advantage. We are not much troubled with gas and there is no water."

"Do you ever have trouble with the men?"

He shrugged his shoulders. "Not really," he replied. "We did have food strikes. The food is always good, but it is not easy to give great variety. As the men sat eating a few would start to stamp on the floor, in their heavy mine boots, until all joined in and the noise was terrible. The strike generally lasted for twenty-four hours; one shift off for every man, but Hr. Sverdrup, he is wonderful, he issued rubber boots, so now they cannot make the noise and all is well."

Later I asked Sverdrup about it. "Yes," he said, "we did have food-strikes, but now all of us have more sense. You know, Win, and please understand it and do not blame the workers, for it is always easy to blame other people, but it is not always just; it was not in reality food-strikes. Of course, the food here can, as in other places, be more or less good; as a rule, everyone is satisfied. When we had these strikes it was other things at the bottom. In most cases the nerves were too hard pressed and something had to happen, that the whole bunch might get some fresh air, literally, or what you call it. Excuse me if I have expressed myself poorly —it is your impossible language and my impossible way of handling it."

"But Einar," I said, "did you really stop the strikes by giving the men rubber boots?"

He smiled. "Well, have you seen a cat fail a mouse?" he said. "So it was."

Besides the mines at Longyearbyen there is one in Bellsund and the Russian workings in Grönfjord, which is also off Isfjord. The Russian mines are named Grumant City and Barentsburg. In the first there are about 500 people and in the second 1,400. The Russians export some 400,000 tons of coal a year and the Norwegians 300,000. Sverdrup is inclined to think, however, that the coal seams have been overestimated, and there are not the milliards of workable tons of coal in Spitsbergen that most people imagine. In addition to the miners in these settlements, there are about thirty hunters, sometimes accompanied by their families. During the summer fishermen come and even a few cruise ships, but we are too early for them.

I would like to be here in spring. I believe the country is lovely. The Governor's sledge fills me with envy—a beautiful "saloon-de-luxe" model, complete with windscrew wipers. It must be grand to be pulled over the snow by the huskies. At present these poor dogs are housed in cages of wire netting, and sometimes they throw back their heads and howl like their brother wolf, longing for the snow and freedom again.

When our parcels of provisions arrived, I was completely overcome. Fresh fruit and vegetables, tomatoes, chocolates, cakes and a bottle of milk, which last caused me to say, "Oh, Ron, do you think I ought to take it? It's usually reserved for the sick." Not only have we the very best of the mine supply, but our friends have shared with us their own personal supplies, luxuries sent out specially to them from Norway. They will not allow us to pay for anything. I must say it is damn decent. There is a grand spirit out here—a kind of courage, unselfishness and comradeship that makes the settlement a pretty good place to live in. I think we in Europe could learn a lot from Longyearbyen.

Isfjord. June 28th, 9 p.m.: This morning we went round the mine quarters. A shift had come off and the men were busy washing themselves in preparation for bed. Elsewhere a woman might not have been welcomed at such a time; here no one thought anything about it. With a brief knock Sverdrup took us into a comfortable little room, where a curly haired lad sleepily smiled at me from his bed. "They are nice rooms, aren't they?" asked Sverdrup. "It is my ambition that no more than two men share a room and gradually the old barrack-like huts are being replaced for these new ones, with separate rooms."

The miners receive between 17 and 18 kroner per day, from which they pay 2 kr. 50 per day for board and room. There is a resident doctor, his services, medicine, etc., being free, but if they want to have toothache they must arrange it for the summer, at the annual visit of the dentist. The men also have free fares from Norway to Spitsbergen and back again, being paid 4 kroner a day when travelling. Holidays are given as in England and extra pay for working on holidays, Sundays, etc. The usual eight hours a day is kept to.

We saw the kitchens, beautifully clean and well kept, the canteen, etc., Sverdrup has even provided his workers with a little cinema.

"Why don't you let the men have their wives and families out?" I enquired.

"For many reasons, economic and social," he replied. "Do not forget that everything we need must be transported to Spitsbergen, whatever you can think of from the cradle to the grave. Suppose something should happen to our supply, or if the houses should burn? Then again, all we have here are the mines. Think it over. What would you do with the children when they are grown up? Let them all be coal diggers? But the mines could not take all of them. They could go down to Norway, but that wouldn't help; they wouldn't get a day's work; they would be 'foreigners' in their own country. In fact, people who have been working here only some few years, very seldom get work at home, because we have the same trouble in Norway as you have in England—unemployment. Then there are lots and lots of other problems arising in this connection. It is not good for women and children to stay in such an isolated place. I have always admired women and especially women going with their men to difficult places, but generally, it is too hard for them. The men, you know, have their work, more or less, generally less, chosen by themselves, and it does not matter very much where in the world they are."

"You like being here, don't you, Einar?" I asked.

"Yes," he replied. "I would not like to go back to Norway for good."

"Don't you miss anything out here?" I asked.

"Nothing at all, Win; what you miss in the one place you gain in the other, and besides, is there really so much to miss around in the world? Do you miss anything from England when you are sailing, for instance, in the Norwegian fjords; or do you gain?"

"No," I said thoughtfully, "I don't miss anything and I do gain. I gain a lot; better weather, magnificent scenery and the kindest and most hospitable people. You know, Einar, I have spent two summers now in Norway. I am beginning to feel I 'belong' to your country."

He took us to see a new road he was building. "See," he said, "the very first road to be built in Spitsbergen." It was just a piled-up track of mud, leading along the valley to a new mine they are opening at the far end. "We shall open the road any day now," he continued. It may seem funny but I felt terribly thrilled about the road. I felt there ought to be a tape stretched across it and cut with due ceremony.

It is an achievement to build a road out here; it must be rather nice to have a little country of your own to build and work for. It would be disheartening, though, to work all summer, planning and building, only to have most of your efforts undone in the storms and darkness of winter. “You should see it,” said Sverdrup, “when daylight comes again. We have thrown everything out; for you can’t do much in darkness, and you never saw such a mess as we have to clear up. But one day I will have grass growing and proper streets.” I believe he will.

We saw the store houses where the food is kept; not all together but divided up in case of fire or accident. Ten cows are kept to provide milk for the children and sick, and there are 150 pigs, for many reasons.

During the winter communication with Norway is, of course, impossible except by wireless. The men can receive no letters, little news of their families at home. The Governor is working for the installation of a wireless telephone, but Sverdrup is against it. “A telephone in our little isolated world would only bring unrest,” he explained. “You will be called on the ’phone whenever something is wrong and you will ’phone yourself to make sure, and you can do nothing at all to help. You have got to stay where you are whether you like it or not. Think about that, Win. I have seen people go crazy for less than that.” I did think about it. I imagined a boy out here, shut in by ice and darkness, his mother, perhaps dying in Norway, asking for him. The tragedy is still there whether he knows about it or not, but ignorance might easily save his reason.

These are only a few of the problems of life in this settlement; there are many others and most of the responsibility falls on one man. All summer he has to work out and order what will be required for the mines and the men during the winter isolation. Nothing must be forgotten. It is a pretty big responsibility, not many men could do it. I take my hat off to Einar Sverdrup.

About 1 p.m. our telegram came. We were sitting in the staff club, in a cosy smokeroom with big leather chairs; a bookcase lined the wall, and I had turned on an ancient gramophone that wheezed: “On the beach at Waikiki”: rather incongruous in a setting of arctic snow. The men were beginning to come in for the dinner interval; some were already playing billiards, and the Wireless Operator had found another flower. I felt so happy, so at home with them all. Then the white form was handed to me and my heart missed a beat. I tore open the seal.

"First five days favourable, Schjelderup."

I handed it to Sverdrup.

"You must have dinner with us first," he said. "It is not good to start out without food and it will save you cooking aboard."

I sat at table next to him, the dentist's wife and myself being the only women among some thirty men. The man who had said "Grapes" smiled across at me, the "dark boy" came in later and also smiled. I ate my soup, and thought: "600 miles of that awful sea." I ate my meat, and thought: "First five days favourable. Which five days? Have I read it right. It's blowing a 'liten kuling' now."

Sverdrup made no reference to the coming passage; he poured me out a glass of beer and cheerfully enquired for the hundredth time, "Are you going to join my Club?" We have joked a good deal about his Club. Members pay a subscription of 100 kroner, the money is invested and the yearly dividend divided between the non-smokers. I think Einar has formed the club to stop himself smoking, and I strongly suspect he is the only member to draw the dividend, in spite of his assurance that three members got it last year. Every time he asks me to join I reply: "Am I hell as like! Providing you with a dividend!" Whereupon he laughs, and says: "But of course one day you will join and I might have the pleasure of saving you and your soul."

At last the meal was over. We had coffee in the smoke-room and somehow Sverdrup got us out without any "good-byes," for which I was truly thankful. I think he must have guessed how I feel about such matters, for he said: "We shall have to call at the Sysslemann's, Win. You must say good-bye to him."

On the way we encountered the two Englishmen who had returned in the whaler flying the red ensign. We just "looked through" each other and passed without a word. "You English!" said Sverdrup. "You have not been introduced, you will not speak. You make me laugh. Some day I am starting an hotel for crazy Englishmen. They will all keep to themselves and be no trouble."

The Governor appeared rather concerned at our departure. "Send a telegram," he said, "we should like to know you are safe in Norway." In Longyearbyen they are not seafaring men like those you find in Tromsö. Here *Perula* is considered very small, and I think many of our friends have serious doubts for our safety. One day the "dark boy" said to me: "I admire people who take their life in their hands. You must have done that coming here in so little a boat." Of course, I laughed, and said there was no danger in summer, but my "job's comforter" sadly shook his head, and answered: "Even in summer we can have bad storms."

As I trotted down the hill between Adams and Sverdrup, I felt horribly sad. Would I ever see Longyearbyen again, these friends with whom I seemed to have lived a lifetime in five brief days? It was unlikely I should ever return; Spitsbergen is a long way from England, yet I knew I should never forget them, and when I was back home many of my thoughts would still be out here.

A launch was waiting at the jetty; our dinghy in tow. There were cans of oil and water for *Perula*, more food for us, including a beautiful cake baked by the Governor's housekeeper.

"You are coming aboard for a last drink, Einar?" I asked.

Again he understood and shook his head. Probably he had watched me fidget through dinner; my nerves were keyed up and I was itching to be off. Once I started I would be all right.

"The coal steamers will look out for you," he said. "Don't forget to wire, will you?" Then, with a brief good-bye, he turned and walked back to his outside world.

As we hauled the dinghy aboard, fierce squalls rushed down the mountains, and at 4.45 p.m. *Perula* sailed out of Advent Bay. I looked back at the place I had once thought "awful beyond description" and which now I hated to leave. We turned out into Isfjord.

The "tiger" mountains and the glaciers are fading into the distance. The weather has calmed down and I have never seen Spitsbergen looking more beautiful. Her snow-covered peaks rise into a blue sky streaked with silver and gold. A faint mist hangs over everything, and again I feel this land is mythical, almost ethereal.

After nearly two months of heading north we are bound south again. Here to-day, gone to-morrow. It is typical of life on the sea; typical of life itself

Perula at foot of glacier; *Perula* at Isfjord, Spitsbergen

CHAPTER IX

BY THE GRACE OF GOD

June 29th, 4.30 pm.

At 9.40 last night Kapp Linné was abeam and we headed out to the open sea. With the land 5 miles astern I changed course to 199° compass. "That should clear the ice," I remarked with satisfaction. By 11.15 white shapes surrounded us so I changed course to 215°. We were still in the ice and by midnight we were sailing 235°. Adams and I looked at each other.

"It seems to be much worse," he said anxiously.

"I don't mind it on the east of us," I replied, "but look at those blasted big pieces to the west. We'll get trapped if we don't watch out."

The ice was certainly much further up the coast than it had been when we came. We picked our way as best we could and, after a bit, it got better and at 1.15 this morning I returned to the original course. About an hour later Bellsund was abeam. The wind was now freshening from the east and we were under full sail and power.

Adams turned in and while I was sitting alone on watch I saw an immense fish leap vertically from the water and fall backwards. It gave me an awful shock: I am sure it was nearly as big as *Perula.* I changed course to 166°, running approximately parallel with the ice-bound coast and some 15 to 20 miles off it. I felt it was worth dodging through the ice, as it was rather essential to get a bearing of the South Cape before changing course for Bear Island. Eventually Adams relieved me and I had my four hours off.

I woke to find Hornsund abeam and risked taking another 10° off our course. The coast looked beautiful; needle-like peaks or "spits", that lead to the name Spitsbergen. Glaciers lined the shore, but to the south the country changed, the mountains being flat topped or more rounded.

The barometer began to fall and, as the day has progressed, I have become more and more worried about the ice. Our track is now a series of zig-zags and it is almost impossible to keep account of our position.

We have lost sight of the coast and keep sailing further and further westwards, but still the blink can be seen. There is a kind of low dancing whiteness on the water beneath it. I have looked at it through the glasses and nearly had a fit. It is ice; not the detached pieces we have been seeing, but great solid masses, stretching for mile after mile. Mostly it is low and flat, but here and there it piles up into hummocks. On the outskirts are some dark streaks in the blink, showing lanes of open water I suppose, but to the south and east it seems to form an icefield. I fear the hot sun of the last few days has broken up the polar ice and these strong easterly winds are bringing it round the South Cape.

There is something fascinating about it, and something frightening, too. I am beginning to wonder if we shall ever get round it. It is getting quite rough and the waves are breaking on the detached ice that surrounds us. The pieces are a good 6 feet above the water and sometimes they break apart as the spray flies over them. It is getting more and more difficult to avoid them as they crash about in the rapidly mounting sea. I think I shall have to slow down; it is a pity, for we have covered over 150 miles in 24 hours and were congratulating ourselves that we should be across in four days.

June 30th, 9 p.m.: At 9.40 last night the wind backed N.E. and started to blow really hard. The glass fell another two points and things began to look nasty. Fortunately we had got round the worst of the ice, but a few odd pieces were still crashing about. We throttled the engine right back, but we were still going too fast. We debated about getting the mainsail in and as usual left it too late.

Having, more or less, gone back on our course, we were now taking the seas on the port quarter, and water poured over the wheelhouse. I looked at the mast; it was bending right over and the track slides were tearing out of the sail. I looked at Adams.

"I'm sorry, Ron," I said, "but the sail will have to come down."

"I know," he replied. "I'll go and do it."

"Can I help?"

"No, I don't think so." We both knew the half-frozen canvas, the strong winds and flying spray were beyond the strength of a woman.

I sat miserably at the wheel trying to heave-to and keep *Perula* as steady and dry as possible as Adams struggled with the sail alone. He was soaked to the skin and blue with cold. One minute I'd see him working for'ard, then a wave would come and blot everything out. Sometimes I shut my eyes not daring to look at a deck I felt certain would be empty. But there he was, his arms tightly wound round the mast. The suspense was awful; I felt helpless and useless. "Oh, hell!" I groaned. "Why am I a blasted woman?" I think I drank about a quarter of a bottle of neat rum while he was out there.

At last the mainsail was down and Adams safely back in the wheelhouse. He staggered below to change, for he had not dared to go out encumbered by oilskins and seaboots.

We proceeded under mizzen and staysail. It was not a bit of good; the wind and sea were beyond description. I really think we were doing about 8 knots under such reduced canvas. We tried to back the staysail and heave-to. We had never tried this before and found that the sail was too big. *Perula* swung broadside and I had to use engine to bring her back. I was doing this when there was a horrible jolt. The engine faltered. We looked at each other. "My God!" said Adams. I pushed open the throttle; the engine roared back to life.

We went on; the weather got worse and worse. Even if *Perula* could go on, her crew could not; we were both completely exhausted and sat in miserable silence. At first I tried to make bright conversation; it sounded inane. As wave after wave crashed on the wheelhouse I began to wonder what we should do if it carried away, how we should block up the hole. Then I realised that if the wheelhouse went we should probably go with it. "It is finish," I thought. "It can't hold much longer."

It was the first time I had wondered what the end of things would be like. Once or twice in the air the ground had come up to meet me, but there had been no time to think—I had been too busy trying to save my 'plane. Strangely enough, I don't think I was very frightened now. Of course, I'd had a lot of rum, but I have always been horribly afraid I would be afraid.

When I was a tiny kid I was taken to the theatre and something happened on the stage that made me realise, for the first time in my young life, that some day I would have to die. I never saw the rest of the show and for weeks I was scared.

It is rather a blow to one's dignity to realise the world will go on quite well without you. On this occasion I thought to myself, "Perhaps it won't be so bad, at least we shall not have to fight any more."

I think that Adams too was thinking on the same lines. He sat at the wheel, very silent and looking utterly wretched. He was not afraid for himself, I know that, his actions on deck proved it. He was thinking of his people at home; of me, perhaps. I staggered to my feet, put my arms round him and said a few daft things, but he took no notice, except perhaps to look even more grim. I sat down again and had another rum.

Then we remembered the sea anchor: how we had read of people putting them out and going to sleep. We had never used one before, but read up in a book what to do. Our sea anchor is a hefty affair and was specially made for us by the Fleetwood Trawler Supply Company, with 4 fathoms of half-inch chain, 15 fathoms 4½-inch warp, and a canvas drogue 6 feet in diameter. In the Straits they had laughed at it, asking if we thought we were the *Queen Mary*.

I do not know how Adams got it out. Bit by bit he dragged it up the deck. His fingers split with the cold and he had to keep coming back to the wheelhouse to thaw out. I tried to rub life back into his numbed hands, but he cried out in pain. We were rather puzzled to know what to do for a float, until I thought of a life-belt.

By 5 a.m. the sea anchor was out, the staysail down, and the engine stopped. It was now a full N .E. gale, but *Perula* lay remarkably well under sea anchor and mizzen. For a few moments we watched, then having done all we could, we staggered below and fell into our root bunks.

"I don't want to dishearten you, Win," said Adams, "but while I was on deck I found the mainsheet over the side." I remembered the faltering engine.

"How much has gone?" I asked.

"I should think about 3 fathoms," he replied.

"Three fathoms of 2-inch yacht manila round the propellor," I groaned.

"It may not be round the prop," he said. "The engine has run for an hour or two since."

"Was the end chewed up?" I asked.

"Yes," he admitted.

"Oh, well," I said, wearily, "what the hell does it matter— time enough to worry if we see this lot out." With that we both went to sleep for nine hours.

We have been riding to the sea anchor now for almost 17 hours. One gets quite used to it. We are both in our root bunks; it is the only safe place. We sleep, read, eat and sleep; actually it is the best rest we have had all the cruise! Sometimes I stagger up to the wheelhouse to look at the barometer, but it is depressing. Waves seem to tower up, almost to the height of the masthead; the saloon is infinitely more reassuring. We have drawn the porthole curtains and turned the wireless full on to drown the shrieking wind, but if it doesn't give gale warnings it plays hymns.

The words "sterk kuling" (fresh gale) have come over the air from the shore stations, but I really feel that, exposed as we are to the open sea somewhere W.N.W. of Bear Island, we are having the "benefit" of a good full gale. Fortunately, it is a long sea, but sometimes a wave breaks on deck with a sickening crash that makes *Perula* shudder. One has just forced the skylight open and a cascade of water has descended into the saloon. I had to laugh. Adams sat up quite peeved, and exclaimed: "It shouldn't do that with a sea anchor out!"

As we lie here, I have thought quite a lot about Longyearbyen, and all the things they have to fight. It helps me somehow. Einar once said: "You know, Win, it is a funny world." A box of chocolates has reminded me of his words— violet chocolate creams. The Governor gave them to me just before we left. They had been sent out to Mrs. Marlow, but arrived just after she had sailed. The box is now full of sea water and Adams says I'll be sick; but think of it, here I am, in an Arctic gale, eating chocolates from London. It is a funny world.

Sometimes to cheer ourselves up we sing our "theme song". It is strange how a song helps you along, as "Tipperary" did in the war. On the Amazon we had " 'Ol Man River" and "Ain't it grand to be blooming well dead"—with modifications of course!

For this cruise we decided on "I've got my love to keep me warm", but we have changed "love" to "rum," and with due apologies to the composer, our version runs:—

Duet:	The wind is blowing, The snow is snowing, But we will weather the storm.
Adams:	No matter how much it may storm,
Brown:	We've got some rum to keep us warm!" (pause for action)
Adams:	I can't remember It worse in December, Just watch those icicles form.
Brown:	What do we care if icicles form? We've got some rum to keep us warm. (pause for action)
Duet:	Off with our oilskins, our boots of gum, We don't need wrapping up, we're burning

with rum.
(more action)

Brown: My throat's on fire,
The waves rise higher.

Duet: But we will weather the storm.
What do we care how much it may storm?
We've got some rum to keep us warm.
(no action—bottle empty)

Funny what does amuse you at times like this: it kind of lets off steam.

I think I'll go to sleep again, my novel is no good anyway, I've never read anything so depressing, everybody is dead or dying. I don't know how the author will finish it.

July 1st, 8 p.m.: When we woke this morning it was blowing as hard as ever. We managed to get some breakfast and went back to our bunks. By afternoon conditions improved enough for us to go on deck and examine the propellor. The rope is round it, three blasted fathoms of it.

"What are we going to do?" said Adams.

"Sail," I said somewhat grimly. "But first we must get the sea anchor in, and how we are going to do so without any engine to manoeuvre, I don't know."

We went for'ard, seized the tripping line, gave a mighty heave and nearly went over backwards.

"Hell!" said Adams. "There's nothing there."

We sat down on deck and laughed until we cried.

The sea anchor had gone at the bridle and with it the lifebelt bearing *Perula*'s name and yacht club. She had ridden out the gale with nothing but a mizzen and a trailing warp. "Oh! Ron," I gasped between laughs, "do you remember saying 'It shouldn't do that with a sea anchor'? Little did you know what words of wisdom you were speaking!" Actually it was perhaps fortunate we did not know it had gone; we should have been hairless, tearing down doors, etc., to make something to replace it.

I pulled myself together.

"Ron," I said, "it's serious about the lifebelt, though. If a coal steamer picks it up we'll be reported missing."

"And we daren't start the engine," he groaned. "It may be weeks before we reach Norway. What will they think at home?"

"The sooner we take advantage of the wind the better," I said. "Fogs and calms will be here any day. Come on, let's get these damn sails up."

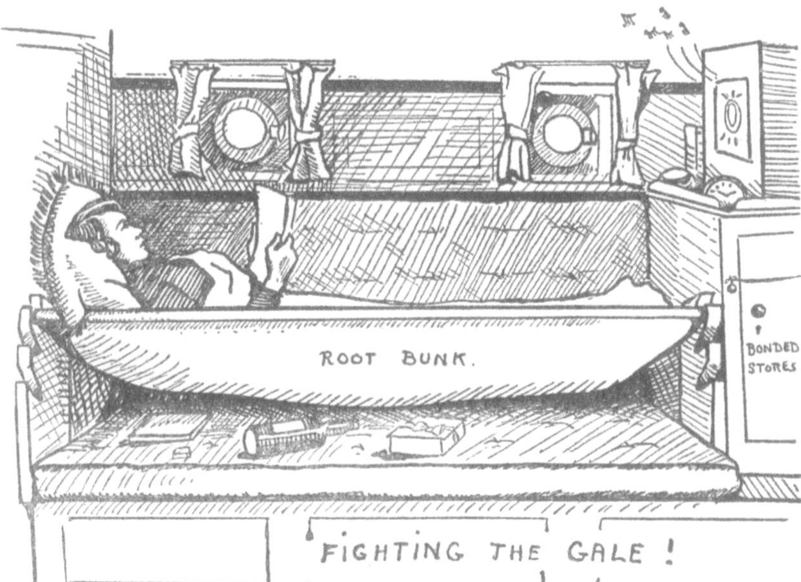

We had hove to heading north, for the dinghy, being on the port side of the deck, it had seemed easiest to get the sea anchor over on the starboard bow. Having hoisted the sails I went to the wheel. Would *Perula* turn round? Would she hell! The wind had fallen light and we could do nothing with her. Adams dashed about, prodding the sails with a boathook. "Oh! dear, what shall we do?" I wailed. "We are going back to Spitsbergen!" I think it took us a good hour to turn her round.

So at last we are on our way; I must say it seems horribly slow after power. The knot tying the log line to the register is hardly turning. It gets to the top, stops to think a bit, and then goes round. I try to console myself by thinking that in the old days people had to rely on sail. I suppose we might reach Norway—by Christmas.

July 2nd, 4.30 a.m.: We have covered 15 miles in about 12 hours, and now we are becalmed. The sky is completely overcast and the sea a flat oily grey. I have not the slightest idea where we are. The log read 206 miles when we hove to, but we had changed course so often for ice that by the time I had worked up our D.R. position, the chart resembled a jig-saw puzzle. At a rough guess I have put our drift down as 60 miles S.W. during the 36 hours we were hove to, but with not knowing when the sea anchor carried away, it is really impossible to estimate it.

Adams is leaning over the side, trying to clear the propeller with a knife tied to the end of a boathook. The water is quite clear and we can see the mass of manila wound round and round the shaft. It is no joke lying out there in the cold leaning over the side, the rail sticking in your tummy and your head hanging down, trying to manipulate a long boathook. I have not even the strength to hold the boat-hook in place against the pressure of water, let alone saw through a mass of rope that has become as hard as steel. Adams has gone through three knives and a saw blade already. He hasn't a dry pair of gloves left and now his hands are bleeding. It is pretty grim sitting here at the wheel doing nothing. I want to dive in with a knife, as I did that time in the Straits, but Adams will not hear of it. He took the temperature of the water, it is nearly freezing. If I covered myself with grease I might do it, but he will not listen. He is probably right.

I spend the time working out how much food and water we have. It is water I am afraid of The supply pipe was broken on the jetty at Longyearbyen, so we just took two 4-gallon cans and told Einar we were O.K. I don't know how much we have, the tanks are certainly less than half full. All fresh water has been reserved for drinking and we cook and wash in salt water.

Every now and then Adams comes into the wheelhouse. "Any luck?" I ask. Sometimes he has a tiny bit of frayed rope, but more often than not nothing. We are carefully trying to keep any bits he cuts free, so that we can measure up how much has been cleared and how much is still on. We know the length the complete mainsheet should be. He is tired, sick and bruised all over, having been working at it for over 12 hours. I do not think I have ever felt so disheartened in all my life. If only I could do something it would be better.

Adams is just coming in again. I wonder if he has got any more off. No —I can see by his face—he looks utterly weary and dispirited. "Oh! hell, what shall we do?"

2 p.m. We have risked starting the engine, it seemed the only thing to do. Adams got more and more exhausted, yet he would not give up. In the end he was so weak I had to sit on his feet as he worked to stop him falling overboard. I made him go below and lie down for an hour, but when he tried to get up again he just collapsed. He looked ghastly; I thought he was going to be seriously ill.

I kept going to look at the propeller and wondering what to do. I reckoned he had cleared 2½ fathoms. I wondered if we dare start the engine. If it had run with 3 fathoms round the shaft, it ought to be all right with only half a fathom round. But there was no telling what damage had been done; possibly the whole shaft was strained. Suppose the tail-shaft forced out. This had happened to a boat at the Straits. She sank. It would be crazy to take such a risk; we had at least a sound ship and were in no immediate danger. We would get to Norway some time and we might even sight a coal steamer. Then I looked at the log. We had covered 3 miles in seven hours. I thought of the water and the possibility of the lifebelt being picked up. I took a coin out of my pocket. "Heads engine; tails sail," I said. It was tails. I thought again. "Best out of three," I said and got two heads.

Adams staggered up from below.

"How do you feel about risking the engine?" I asked.

"I'm all for it," he said. He turned it over by hand while I watched the propeller. It seemed to go round all right. We cleared a passage aft and carried down various things to block the hole in case the tailshaft should be forced out.

"Ready," I said.

"Yes," he replied. "I'll go out and watch while you start up. Put her in gear for a few seconds, then back to neutral again, and we'll see if the prop stops with a jerk." He went out and leaned over. Now for it, I thought, and pressed the starter button. The engine sounded all right, but of course it is the shaft and not the engine. Very gently I put her in gear, then pulled the wheel back to neutral again.

"The prop is still spinning with the momentum," cried Adams, "I think it is all right."

We have decided to make for Bear Island at half speed. I should imagine we have 70 or 80 miles to go, but it is all very uncertain. A misty-looking sun came out for a few seconds and I rushed on deck with the sextant, but the errors are too great and it is only a single position line. There seems to be a horrible humming noise going on underneath the floor boards. Feels a bit like sitting on a bomb, waiting for it to go off.

July 3rd, 9.30 p.m.: We have not found Bear Island. After about 90 miles we saw some black and white birds, and I felt really hopeful.

"We're back at Puffin Island," I said, cheerfully, as they flew by, their wings going nineteen to the dozen.

"We can't be far off land," said Adams. "I wish the damn things would fly straight—I'm trying to watch where they go." Then we ran into fog patches.

"It must be here; Bear Island is always in fog," I said. It was no use; we kept on for another two hours and then I swung *Perula* round.

"Norway?" said Adams.

I nodded. "Fruholmen, it is the nearest, then we'll go into Hammerfest." Another 220 miles of open water, that is supposing we were at Bear Island. We might have been north, south, east or west of it.

We have to cross the line where the magnetic variation changes from W. to E. I have drawn dozens of pictures trying to find out what will happen if I add when I should subtract and vice-versa. After about an hour of —"Now if we have passed Bear Island, as I think we have, and I lay off a course from a point E. of the island and subtract variation as we go along, and we are in reality W. of the island and I should be adding it, will it tend to decrease the error?"—the answer as far as I am concerned is still a lemon! I have drawn a line from the middle of Bear Island to Fruholmen and left variation severely alone, for the present, at any rate.

At 3 p.m. we turned on the reserve fuel tanks. We have not filled up since Bodö. We still have plenty, but it always gives me a sinking feeling to turn on a reserve tank. We have turned on the reserve water, too. Still, we are getting along now, if only at half speed. The log reads 416 miles. The wind has been steadily freshening from the N.E. and the barometer is beginning to fall. I have turned on the wireless for the Norwegian weather-forecast . . . Kulingvarsel . . . Gale warning . . . Björnöya . . . Bear Island . . . ostlig liten kuling . . . easterly "little" gale! Well, I suppose I ought to feel thankful it is only a "little" one, but we have no sea anchor and we cannot heave-to properly under our present staysail and mizzen.

July 4th, 3 p.m.: It was another weary night. We got the mainsail in at once and managed to reef the staysail. It was not really satisfactory; it would have been better double-reefed and there is only provision for a single one, but I felt we might be able to heave-to if we had to.

Fortunately, the gale was mild compared to the last and we were able to keep under way. The wind veered E.N.E. and then E. It threw up a nasty beam sea, and as usual the wheelhouse was in a sheet of water. We both stayed up all night and took alternate hours on watch. During our hour off we lay on the wheelhouse settee, but I did not sleep at all. In the last three nights I have had about two hours; I think I have got past it.

At noon to-day the wind suddenly decreased to light variable. There was something rather ominous in the way it did so. A nasty swell still persisted from the east and the glass was falling rapidly. Now the wind is freshening from the west, blowing against the swell; the violent motion is getting on our nerves.

I still do not know where we are. I took 2° off the course last night and another two this morning. I feel that between variation and leeway something ought to be done. We have covered over 480 miles now and the shaft is holding up nobly.

10.30 p.m. At 7 o'clock this evening we picked up still another gale warning. Will there ever be an end to our troubles? Adams looked just about fed-up.

"We can't be more than 30 miles off land," I said. "Perhaps we'll get in before it."

"I am beginning to think we shall never get in," he replied, dejectedly. "We ought to have seen the coast by now."

I, too, had hoped we would sight something by this time. I began to wonder if we could possibly have missed Norway altogether. It was an awful thought; I asked him to take the wheel and rushed below to consult the chart. I came back smiling. "I've worked it out, we can afford an error of at least 60 miles either side and still sight Norway soon."

He did not seem impressed. I did not blame him; he must be "all in", going out there on deck, bringing the sails in, sawing at the fouled propeller. He has been splendid. I shall never forget what he has done; my part seems very miserable in comparison. "What the hell are you standing there for, looking like a wet Whit-Sunday?" I said. "Go below and read; your face is enough to put anyone off." He went like a lamb.

We have run into bad visibility now, the most frightful rain squalls, and the sky is literally purple. I have never seen anything like it. I feel horribly worried. I have gone into the log reading again; we have covered 220 miles since we changed course for Norway. If we were at Bear Island, we should be at Fruholmen now. I keep getting up and peering ahead, but . . . . It is land! A damn big mountain, almost on top of us. "Ron! RON!! Come up, it's land." He came dashing up and is standing here beside me. We are both looking at it, and saying "land" over and over again, like a couple of blithering idiots. I am half-laughing, half- crying; I never thought I would see it again.

Noon. July 5th: It is one thing to sight land and quite another to know what land it is. I looked at the headland that towered up through the mist.

"It's North Cape," I said.

"Shouldn't it have a horn?"

"It's got one."

"Well, it doesn't look like a horn to me."

"Go below and bring up that picture postcard of it," I said crossly. We gazed at the highly-coloured card and the mournful grey landscape. "It is North Cape," I snapped. "Don't argue." We consulted the chart; decided to put in at Gjesvaer and turned west. The tide was running strongly against us and the wind beat against us in squalls. "We're going backwards," I groaned. We lowered the sails and opened up the engine, but it seemed we should never get round the headland. We were both fagged out and exceedingly bad tempered. After a further dust-up, Adams departed below, on his dignity.

As we proceeded I began to realise it was not North Cape after all. "We must be to the east," I thought, "or we wouldn't have reached land in 220 miles." I read up the descriptions for the whole north coast of Norway and was no wiser. "Surely it can't be Russia," I groaned. Suddenly small islands and white breaking water appeared ahead. Adams had by now returned to the wheelhouse and I turned to him in triumph: "I know where we are—Nord Kvalöy." He looked at the chart and then at me. "You're a grand navigator," he said. "First it was North Cape; now it's Nord Kvalöy. We've made pretty good time— 140 miles in about two hours."

We had not got a large scale chart but I felt convinced it was Nord Kvalöy, because here start the islands and skerries that line the west coast. The gale must have carried us much further to the S.W. than I allowed for, well over 100 miles, and we must have changed course for Norway considerably to the S.W. of Bear Island. We headed *Perula* back east, but Adams did not look at all convinced. We saw two fishing boats in the entrance to a fjord and I turned towards them. "I'll ask, to make sure," I said. Rocks were now popping up in the water around us, but at length we reached the boats. With memories of my last efforts at Norwegian, I went on deck with a chart, waved it about and pointed. One of the boats stopped, the men hauled up their nets, launched a small boat and two of them rowed across to us.

"Speak English?" I enquired. They shook their heads.

"Hammerfest?" I said. They broke forth excitedly in their own language.

"Tromsö?" I tried. They nodded and pointed down the fjord. They came aboard and drew a pencil mark on my general chart, showing the passage we were to take. I said "takk" then pointed to the saloon and made the usual drinking motion. They pointed to their fishing clothes but I beckoned and they followed me down and, of course, bumped their heads. I poured out two whiskies and, in my gratitude, they were very large ones. I put the glasses on the table and went to the galley for a jug of water. When I came back the two Norwegians were spluttering and running at the eyes; the whisky had gone, downed in one.

After they had recovered their breath there was great excitement and much gesticulation. I offered them another drink, but they shook their heads and kept pointing to their boat and then to the bottle of whisky. "They want the bottle, Ron," I said. "We might as well give it to them." They would not take it. At last it dawned on me; they just wanted to take enough for their two mates to taste and that was all they would accept. Finally, they departed in great delight with much bowing and hand-shaking. I turned to Adams and started to laugh.

"Think of it, Ron, *Perula* has brought us back to within 5 miles of where we left the coast outwards; if we had kept straight on instead of turning west we would have been back in Fuglöysveet."

We started for Tromsö, down the west side of Vannöy. It was rather nerve-racking with only a general chart, but it did not seem worth going right round the island to Fuglöysveet. At length we reached Grötsund and "home ground" so to speak. Once again I have sat up all night, not out of necessity, but just to sit here and look at Norway. It is grand to be back. The weather has cleared; snow-capped mountains, green grass, a blue sky. The sun is blazing down and we have carried the cushions, etc., on deck to dry. There seems to be a terrible vibration now we are in smooth water; I fear the shaft is badly strained.

We left Longyearbyen last Tuesday and it is Tuesday again to-day. Rather a coincidence: outward we left on a Thursday and arrived on a Thursday.

Tromsö is coming into sight, soon we shall turn into the harbour. I must go and put my yachting cap on.

The diver at Tromsö and Tromsö — *Perula* looked small and white among the whalers

Perula at Jokelfjord

CHAPTER X

THE ROOF OF EUROPE

Tromsö. July 11th.

We came into the harbour here at 12.40 p.m. on July 5th and made towards *Quest*; Schjelderup had invited us to moor alongside when we came back. The harbour was crowded, the tide running strongly, nobody appeared to be aboard her, and as I looked at the narrow space into which I had to manoeuvre my nerve failed. I saw the little grey motor boat we had tied up to last time; she was in comparatively clear water. "Let's go back to *Zoe*," I said. While Adams was making us fast I went below, turned off the water, looked at the time and noted it down on my cigarette packet, beneath the log reading of 600 miles. As I had finished my log book at Svalbard and had not got another with me, particulars of *Perula*'s voyage south were dotted about, on the Governor's chocolate box, various novels and odd scraps of paper. Having decided the water had had time to drain, I stopped the engine.

We were back, my work was finished, something seemed to snap and I went into a complete daze. I remember vaguely the Harbour Master rowing out to greet us, seizing my hand and saying, "Welcome back, Captain, congratulations on a fine voyage." I remember staggering ashore to telegraph my mother and our friends at Longyearbyen of our safe arrival. I was so tired I kept tripping up on the pavement and Adams said I must pull myself together or people would think I was drunk. I spent two kroner on cream cakes, took them back aboard and ate them. Then I went to sleep.

About 17 hours later I woke with a start to find a man in my cabin. It was Captain Johannssen, and he was standing with a tray of breakfast in his hands. Knowing how tired we should be, he had prepared it aboard *Zoe* and brought it for us to have in bed. It is grand to meet people like that. Later a telegram was brought to us: "Well done, congratulations, greetings," from the Governor.

We searched Tromsö for Schjelderup without success. He was not aboard *Quest* nor was he in his flat. Eventually we found that he had left for Svalbard shortly before we arrived here. As we sailed in on the west side of Vannöy, he probably sailed out east of the island. We both felt very disappointed. Somehow it does not seem like Tromsö without his cheery laugh, his "*Perula* ahoy," at all hours of the day and night.

I went completely gay at "Tinny Annie's." Cauliflowers (imported, wrapped in cellophane) at about 1s. 6d. each; small cabbages at 1s.; new carrots 6d. a bunch (we'll want four bunches for lunch); fresh lettuce and tomatoes; fruit, etc. We have not brought nearly enough tinned goods and out here they are very expensive; except, of course, for the Norwegian canned fish and milk. I dread getting my week's bill; I feel convinced it will be over £4.

On Thursday we took a really good look at *Perula*. She might have been out in two English winters. The wheelhouse, hatches, etc., were almost bare of varnish and so were the masts. The topsides would have to be repainted. The floor boards of the dinghy were smashed and there was other minor damage. Fortunately the weather was good and we set to work, scraping, rubbing down and varnishing. We could still see the rope wound round the propeller shaft and we consulted the Harbour Master regarding this. I was in favour of taking *Perula* up the slip, but apparently this would be very expensive as a special cradle would have to be made. After consultation with the shipyard it was decided a diver should go down. He would come to the harbour where we were moored and it would cost about 50s.

I spent the day in a fever of anxiety, wondering what we should do if the shaft was badly damaged and we could not sail home. At length a kind of Heath Robinson affair appeared; an old wooden hull on which was erected a hut. This contraption was being towed by some men in a rowing boat. It was made fast a few yards away from us, a heavily weighted ladder let down into the water, and a rope passed underneath our keel. Meanwhile the diver sat inside the hut, looking as miserable as sin, while one of his mates put the finishing touches to his attire: lead-weighted boots, gloves, a large knife strapped round his waist and, lastly, the helmet was put on; the glass window having been immersed in a bucket of water. With slow deliberate strides he came out of the hut, climbed slowly down the ladder and flung himself backwards into the icy water, reaching for the rope under our keel as he went.

"Oh dear!" I said to the foreman, who spoke English. "Won't he be cold?"

"Not with all the clothes he has got on," he replied, turning the handle that pumped the air.

Adams and I stood on deck awaiting the verdict. It could not have been more than five minutes, but it felt like five hours. At last the signal was given; the diver was coming up. On reaching the ladder he paused for a few seconds, then climbed slowly up; his helmet was removed and for the first time he smiled.

"He says there is no damage," said the foreman. "There were only two turns of rope left round; he has cut them away and examined the shaft." I heaved a large sigh of relief Apparently the vibration was either my imagination or perhaps the effect of a loose end of rope whizzing round. We all went below to celebrate and I gave the diver a "double." In spite of the foreman's assurance I felt sure the poor man was cold!

With the anxiety gone the days passed pleasantly. On the Friday the Harbour Master came to supper and we spent a very cheery evening together. He was greatly interested in *Perula*, but there was one thing he did not like; the open cockpit. He felt we should have a cover for it, even if it was self-draining.

"Is your lavatory working properly?" he asked later.

I looked somewhat startled. "It is the most useful part of a ship," he continued. "Many times a lavatory has saved my life."

"Oh dear!" I thought, "What's coming next?"

"Often when I was at sea," he went on, "we would have a great storm; the waves would crash down on us until it seemed my ship would be wrecked and my passengers be drowned. The lavatory saved us. From it we pumped out oil on to the water and the oil made the waves flat." I had never thought of a lavatory in this connection before, but it sounded a good idea and ours was duly inspected and approved.

We spent a good deal of time drinking coffee with Captain Johannssen. He always makes it himself, grinding the beans each time. We have a good eight cups a day and with each he shakes his head sadly and murmurs: "No good for belly!" Captain Johannssen was one of a party of three, the first men ever to winter on Jan Mayen, that desolate island between Norway and Greenland. For the sake of meteorological observations they endured the most appalling hardships, the hut they had built almost completely covered in snow. Hurricane followed hurricane, their anemometer was blown down and many instruments destroyed. Even the inside of the hut was a mass of ice where the snow had blown in. Yet this quiet, unassuming man, rather lightly-built, takes his adventures as a matter of course and shows me his photographs as we in England might show our holiday snaps.

Yesterday he took us for a walk to the top of the island. It was very beautiful; the midnight sun reflected on a placid lake, surrounded by green trees and wild flowers, On the far side stood the Observatory for the Aurora Borealis, and on the left of the road the Meteorological Station. Coming down we went into what appeared to be a lovely park. Johannssen halted before a large cross.

"Your people," he said. "I thought you would wish to see them."

I read the inscription: "In memory of the crew of S.T. *Golden Deep"*, followed by the names of eleven British fishermen who, on November 6th, 1932, perished when their steam trawler struck the rocks in a storm. Silently we stood out here in the Arctic, so far from home, thinking of those men. Having sailed these waters, I realise a little of what our fishermen have to face. We are here in summer, in constant daylight; they come in winter. Perhaps for an hour at noon the sky may turn a dull grey, after which it is dark again. Our summer gale would be nothing to a winter hurricane. From our British ports away out to Bear Island, not a light on the island to guide them, just darkness, snow, ice and wind. They must be grand men. It is typical of Norwegian people that flowers should bloom on this little spot. In some countries the graves of foreigners might be neglected, but not in Norway. It was cared for and tended as if it was their own. We have now been here a week. I have had a letter from my mother in response to my telegram. It says: "Dear Winifred, you have not stopped at Bear Island, you have not even been to North Cape, I do not know what you are thinking of." This, I might say, is a long letter. She may write at length to harbour masters, but "letters" to me are usually a scrawl on top of a newspaper. I read her remarks out to Adams and we roared with laughter. "Well, I'm not going back to Bear Island," I said, "but we'll go to North Cape, to please her!" So to-morrow we start on a cruise of Finmark.

It is now midnight and high time I got some sleep in readiness for to-morrow. Oh, hell! Adams has just reported the approach of visitors. "Americans, I think," he said. The saloon is in a frightful mess and he is throwing everything into the galley in a wild endeavour to "tidy up." They are alongside now. I must thrust this behind a cushion. We shall be up all night. It is Tromsö all over.

July 12th. Lyngenfjorden, midnight: We were up all last night. Our visitors were not American, but a Dane and an English girl. The Dane was a correspondent for some American newspaper. After a party aboard *Perula*, we finished up at their hotel. At 11.50 this morning we left for the fuel station, expecting to fill up and carry straight on, but either I or our Sailing Directions were at fault. Perhaps I have read them wrong, but they appear to give the tide in Tromsesund in exactly the opposite direction. In consequence, we spent the afternoon tied up to the Shell jetty, waiting for the tide to turn.

We were under way again at 4.35, and we have now turned into Lyngenfjorden. The rocks at the entrance were almost white with sea birds. Lyngenfjord is reputed to be one of the beauty-spots of North Norway. The sun shines mistily through a layer of cirro-stratus, to starboard blueish glaciers fill the mountain-tops and waterfalls crash down from the melting snow. I should feel poetical but I am too tired. These parties will be the death of me!

July 13th. Valan: At 4.40 a.m. we anchored off Lyngseide, S.E. of the jetty in 8 fathoms. After a brief sleep we rowed ashore and set out for the Lapp encampment, some twenty minutes' walk from the village. The Lapps form about 1 per cent. of the population of North Norway. They are nomads, often driving their herds of reindeer over the mountains and across the fjords. During the summer months they camp near the towns, making souvenirs, etc., for the tourist trade. They are mostly short in stature and they slouch along in their pointed and upturned shoes of skin. Most of them wear their national costume. The men wore tunics of blue cloth or fur that reached down to long woollen hose or thigh boots of skin. On their heads were blue caps, often having an enormous red pom-pom. From studded belts about their waists hung knives, etc. The women also favoured red and blue with scarfs and embroidered bonnets. Some rocked or carried babies in small leather cradles. Wisps of blue smoke rose from the camp fire, and round about stretched huskies, tethered by large pieces of wood fastened round their necks. Inside skin tents, children played with the most adorable huskie pups that looked like little balls of white, fawn or black fur. One old woman, who I am sure was about 90, was peacefully enjoying a pipe. We tried to take a photograph but she was completely camera-shy, burying her head like an ostrich. An old man, however, on finding us trying to take his picture, became exceedingly wrathful and shrieked "Money, money." After we had bought a knife he was carving from reindeer horn (for 1s. 6d.), he became appeased and proceeded to pose in the most impossible positions. On the walk back it rained and we had to stuff the various souvenirs we had bought beneath our clothing. At 3.35 we sailed again, and as usual the 13th day of the month proved unlucky. The wind freshened, accompanied by blinding rain squalls which blotted out the land. Although we were in comparatively sheltered water, it was quite rough and *Perula* rolled her scuppers under.

"Have you seen the saloon?" asked Adams.

"Not lately," I replied. "Why?"

"It's only about a foot deep in water," he said. Thinking we were in the fjords we had left the ports open. Photographs, books and papers were swimming about. After a violent argument as to whose fault it was we sought anchorage. "There is a good one just there," I said, pointing to the chart, but when we got "just there," no anchorage was apparent. The flowers chose this moment to upset on my best shoes and we found the milk had turned sour. We had only had four hours' sleep in the last two nights and it was 11.30 p.m. before we found anchorage here at Valan, Kvaenangerfjord, S.W. of an island in 10 fathoms. *Perula* is now playing "ring a roses" round her anchor.

July14th. Sörröysund, 11.30 p.m.: I woke at 10 o'clock this morning to find a simply marvellous day and decided to go down Jökelfjord. This decision was made with some apprehension, as at the head of this fjord is the only glacier in Norway which "calves." The Sailing Directions informed me that the procedure "often causes so heavy a sea to get up as to endanger small vessels." Also, apparently, large boulders had a habit of descending from the hillside.

The only excitement we did have was of a rather different nature. We had practically reached the fjord head and I had decided there was "nothing to" the place, when the water suddenly started to flurry and a terrific squall rushed down the ice-covered mountain and hit us good and proper. All the cushions, etc., we had carried on deck to dry took wing and floated gracefully through the air, then, with a "plong," fell into the fjord. (Language unprintable.) Hearing my "Oh, dear me" Adams, who was having a bath (why will these things happen when one of us is having a bath?), rushed up to the wheelhouse, clad in a towel. I took a flying leap into the dinghy, which we were fortunately towing. I was wearing shorts and had bare feet, the dinghy was half full of water and the icy blasts seemed to penetrate my bones. You know what it is like when a man chases his hat. It was the same with me. I was chasing cushions all over the fjord. Just as I thought I had got one, a fresh gust of wind swept it from my grasp. After a frightful battle, the dinghy, cushions and all, ended up on the rocks and Adams had to use quite a bit of engine to prevent *Perula* sharing the same fate. In the end I managed to retrieve everything and, very cold, wet and cross, returned aboard. "You did look funny," remarked Adams. I gave him a withering glance and replied: "Go and look at yourself in that towel before you talk."

The squall died as suddenly as it had come and after remarking, "Well, I suppose the glacier is beautiful, but after Spitsbergen I call it a miserable affair," we decided to take advantage of the good weather and push on to Hammerfest. Kvaenangenfjord is very open and exposed to the sea. Winds blowing from N.E. through E. to S. usually all blow out of Kvaenangen, often with considerable violence, and are known as Kvaenangenvind or Kvaenangsvind.

Having rounded Brynilen we were completely exposed to the open sea save for a mile or two when passing south of the islands Loppekalven and Loppa. We looked out on the stretch of blue water to the north. "Let's go back to Svalbard," I said. I had vowed at Tromsö that I would never make the passage again, but now the sea looked inviting. I thought of those misty white peaks. For two pins I would have headed north.

"Don't be so damn funny," said Adams, and brought me back to earth.

We rounded Silda Point, sailing on across Loppenhav and we have just come into Sörröysund . The weather is squally again and the tide is running strongly. Adams is asleep and, as usual, I am seizing my watch as an opportunity to write. I wonder why we do sail all through the night when we need not. It's daft.

Rolvsöysund, 4 p.m. July 15th: As we proceeded up Sörröysund this morning I remarked, "This damn compass is cockeyed." I had suspected it for some time, then I chanced to look at a notice on the chart. My Norwegian is not good, but I gathered there was abnormal variation of 7° in an easterly direction, south of Gaashopen, which then became 5° westerly between Vatnholmen and Gyfjordveggen, and back to 7° easterly at Hjelmen and Haaja, all in the space of a few miles. "Blasted place," I said, throwing down my dictionary. "Thank goodness it isn't foggy."

We arrived at Hammerfest at 6.15, having covered 102 miles since leaving Valan. It was still very squally, the place looked bleak and weather-beaten, mostly jagged rock with little trace of green. Dismal looking buildings formed the town and there was a small harbour, but it was too crowded for me, so we tied up to a buoy, close off the quayside, at the

N.E. side of the bay. There was no shelter, the wind rushed about us and I felt tired. "If this is the northern-most town in the world," I said, "I'm sorry I came."

When I woke at 9.30 a.m. the wind had dropped and the heat was almost tropical. I killed a couple of mosquitoes and felt better. When we went ashore the Harbour Master's son was waiting to greet us. He took us round the shops and saved me having to say "Ba-ba" in the butcher's—my sheep act which usually produces the desired lamb chops. Having spent about 5 kroner in the cake shop, our new friend and his father accompanied us back aboard. We were disappointed to hear that all our mail had been returned to England, the Harbour Master having concluded, from the Tromsö newspapers that we were returning south.

We left Hammerfest at 1.15 and we are now heading for North Cape. The tidal streams need a bit of working out and it is best to get local advice. If proceeding north it appears best to leave Hammerfest just before half flood. We could not have had better weather; cloudless blue sky, calm blue sea, and a heat mist hangs over everything. The mountains have become lower and more barren, flat tablelands rising almost perpendicularly from the sea, with barely enough foreshore for an occasional Lapp hut or tiny fishing village. I am writing this sitting on deck in the sunshine wearing shorts and half-sleeved jersey, yet our latitude is over 70° N.

Midnight.—We are at North Cape, sometimes called "The Roof of Europe". We have arrived at the appropriate hour; one should always see North Cape at midnight; it is "done." The midnight sun is not much novelty to us now, and to-night it is shining mistily through a layer of cloud. Something else has appeared that is causing us far more excitement: "Good Lord, look, Ron, it's the moon. Well, I'm blowed, haven't seen the thing for weeks." It speaks of England and dark nights; of a short brilliant Arctic summer which, like our holiday, is drawing to a close. We have agreed that North Cape shall be our turning-point. For a few minutes we are lingering, looking at this rocky headland that rises some 1,000 feet above us. On the eastern slope of the Cape is a pointed crag or spur, named Hornet, and "They are quite right, Ron, it is like a rhinoceros." I felt rather tempted to go ashore, there is temporary anchorage at Hornvika on the east side, but we have learned too much of this Arctic weather not to take advantage of its peaceful mood.

I should imagine the passage from Hammerfest to North Cape can be the very devil. It is mostly exposed to the open sea and the tidal streams run strongly. We are told that when strong winds or heavy seas oppose them, it is impossible for small craft to weather this part of the Indreled.

Now we are turning back; I've just taken a final look at North Cape and said to Adams: "I don't know why they call it North Cape—there's another bit of land to west of it, sticking out much further north."

I am worried about the compass, the thing seems to be about 20° out now. If it had been foggy, we should have "gone through" an island. I must adjust it.

July 16th. Hammerfest: We got back to Hammerfest at 11.38 this morning, just in time. The most disgusting rain-squalls blotted everything out. Rather strange the weather should be so bad, for the barometer is high. The Harbour Master's son says it is because "the sun has gone freckled this year." Think he must mean sunspots.

The weather did clear this evening and we climbed up to the usual mountain restaurant. A French cruiser had come in and the sailors are everywhere; seems odd to hear the French language here amongst the Norwegian. To-morrow we leave for Altenfjord.

July 19th. Stjernsund. Noon: We left Hammerfest at 10.10 a.m., July 17th; managed to get the tide with us through Straumen and had a pleasant passage down Vargsund and into Altenfjord. Anchored off Bossekop was a ship painted black with cream funnels.

"Good gracious!" I said, "what is she? Looks like a destroyer."

"She's flying the White Ensign," said Adams, after inspection with the glasses.

"Oh dear," I said, "ought we to dip to her? Get the book on flag etiquette."

"It depends," he replied, after consulting same. "If she is a man-of-war or a Royal yacht . . . . "

"We'll dip in any case," I said, "and be on the safe side; besides, we are in a foreign country and it is nice."

As we approached Adams went aft and dipped our ensign. "They've answered it," he remarked, in a somewhat astonished voice.

Ashore that evening a man came up to us, shook hands and said his name was Westminster. He asked if we had come from the North Pole "Oh no!" I said, "from Spitsbergen." He seemed amused, was extremely kind, offered us every assistance and invited us to visit him aboard. As he had gone I turned to Adams: "The first Englishman to speak to us since we left home—makes you feel kind of homesick, doesn't it?"

"Do you know who he was?" replied Adams. "The Duke of Westminster—that ship is his yacht, *Cutty Sark*.

"Back aboard *Perula*, a visitor arrived, Commander Mack, complete with latest newspapers and wireless news. As we sat in the saloon, he asked: "Anything we can do for you? Would you like a bath?" This may sound odd, but to anyone on a small yacht it is the most understanding and hospitable offer that can be made. We departed to *Cutty Sark* for supper.

Next morning the launch again carried us to *Cutty Sark*. Mack was waiting with an amused smile as the launch came up alongside a most precarious rope ladder. "Hell's bells! Have I got to get up that?" I was duly assisted aboard and we spent an enjoyable morning, yarning in his cabin.

I was having a quiet sleep on *Perula's* deck that afternoon when the launch again returned carrying a note from Mack: Would we have "high tea" with the Duke?

"Oh dear!" I cried, womanlike, looking at my soiled navy trousers. "What shall I wear?"

"Come as you are," said the officer with a grin. I put on my best white sweater. It was terribly hot and Einar had called it my "icebear party suit."

We had a grand evening, after which we went with Mack in a car to watch the fishing. The party were fishing every night from about 9.30 to about 4 a.m. Forty-pound salmon seemed quite common.

I was surprised how fertile the interior of Finmark is: green trees, wild flowers, but the mosquitoes are a nuisance. Veils have to be worn when fishing and mosquito nets are advisable if sleeping ashore: seems odd in the Arctic.

Mack, of course, seized the golden opportunity to lower colours aboard *Cutty Sark* and catch me napping.

"The sun doesn't set, you didn't lower them last night, and besides you've got a large crew," I exclaimed with indignation, as he laughingly told me off.

"Always follow the senior ship," he said. *Perula* has been wearing her colours night and day for almost two months, but then I fear she often does, even when the sun does set. I can never decide which is the worst of two evils—to leave them up all night or put them up when I get up, usually about 10 or 11a.m.!

Having dipped after another debate, we are now sailing away. Before we left, the Duke sent us three salmon and we have a marvellous parcel of provisions. It means a lot to the crew of a small boat to experience kindness like this. I shall never forget *Cutty Sark* and the great hospitality and charm of her owner.

Seglviken (we think), 11 p.m.: About 9 o'clock this evening we were sailing along in a slight swell, N.E. of Brynilen, when I suddenly saw a blanket of grey rolling in from the sea. "Hell, Ron, I'm afraid its fog."

"Oh, just mist out to sea," he said. But I did not like it, our compass was all over the shop and there was a lot of shipping about. I searched the chart anxiously for a possible anchorage. The coast was barren and bleak, rock that was torn and polished by these pounding northern seas. There were a few creeks but they gave no shelter and rocks were about. I was debating what to do when the fog closed in. A great steamer was close astern of us and set up a mournful howl on her siren. Adams went aft to listen. "Oh, dear," I groaned, "if I change course she will do so too and if I don't she won't." So we spent some entertaining minutes being dogged by a shrieking siren and a large black hull, that every second I expected would loom up in the fog and crash into us. At last Adams reported she had turned seawards. At that moment a misty shape charged straight across our bows at a good 8 knots.

"My God! Did you see that?" I said.

"It's a fishing boat," he replied.

"Can you still see it?"

"Yes."

"I'll follow it then." It was easier said than done. We set off through the fog, engine flat out, only to lose sight of it in the finish.

"A pretty kettle of fish," I said. "Heaven only knows where we are now!" I decided to make towards the shore; I knew it was all wrong, but it does help to know you can get out and walk if need be. We groped our way along slowly. Then the fog kind of changed colour and we heard the noise of breaking water. "It's here," said Adams. "Try to follow it round into Kvaenangenfjord," I said. "There's anchorage just inside."

We sailed south. "Look!" I said. "Rowing boats— we'll ask."

My "rowing boats" turned out to be buoys marking nets. "We're losing the coast," cried Adams. I turned east.

"We're losing it again," he reported. I turned N.E., then almost N.

"Do you know where you are?" he asked suspiciously

"Go and sound," I said with dignity, not having the least idea.

"Five fathoms," he called, and cast again. "Hard astern —1 fathom," he yelled. I had already put the engine hard astern, for a nice pretty farmhouse had loomed up a few yards ahead.

"We'll drop here," I said.

"But where are we?" asked Adams.

"Don't be a B.F." I said crossly. "There's a house, what more do you want?"

Having consulted the chart and our changes of course we think we are in Seglviken, but I admit it is the first time I have anchored in a place and not known where I was. Anyway we are in shallow water, out of the traffic, and when the weather clears the mystery may be solved. We have had supper and Adams has just asked me what I am going to do now. I'm going to bed; what's the use of worrying?

July 20th. Nordlenangen. Midnight. It was Selgviken. We were anchored at the head of the creek; good holding ground, sand. By 11 this morning, the visibility had improved considerably. Patches of fog hung about but you could see. We sailed an hour later and as we were crossing Kvaenangenfjord the fog came down on us again.

"It's your blasted fault," I said, politely, to Adams. "It was your idea. We should never have sailed—the weather report was condensed 'toeca' (taake=fog)."

"We have only got 3s. 6d. between us," he replied. "You know it is essential to get back to Tromsö; besides if you hadn't spent 15 kroner on an oilskin for yourself . . ."

We had expected to reach land in an hour and a half; the time was up and still we had not seen it.

"What's that?" I suddenly asked.

"Just a sheep bleating," said Adams mildly. "Hell's bells," I groaned. "I'm down to navigating by farm animals?"

Fortunately the weather cleared again; we proceeded along Kaagsund and started across Lyngenfjorden. The blanket of white appeared ahead again. It was most annoying; the sun was shining overhead and we could see the tops of mountains above it, yet once in it we were completely blinded. "I'm fed up," I said. "I'm turning back to where it is clear." Then followed a hectic race against the rolling fog, that ended with anchorage in Langfjorden, off the west shore, 3 fathoms, sand. We stayed there three hours, during which time we had tea and Adams made several journeys up the mast, to see what the weather looked like.

Eventually we sailed again and were just rounding Nordklubsen when the fog came down worse than ever. I followed the coast round to the south'ard for the anchorage in Nordlenangen.

"You've looked at the chart, haven't you?" asked Adams.

"Yes," I snapped. The navigable channel was barely two cables wide, we had to pass between two poles and there was a good cable of shoal ground either side. I don't quite know how we got in, but we did, and we are anchored by three fishing boats, south of the poles. A beastly swell is sweeping down and it is decidedly uncomfortable. We have no bread left, no cakes, no cigarettes; only tinned stuff, a little butter and a few potatoes. We cannot see the shore and the 3s. 6d. is burning in our pockets.

Tromsö July 21st.: It was still foggy when we woke this morning. About 11 o'clock I gave a cry of joy: the sun was breaking through.

We passed the Dane and his girl friend heading north in a motor boat and paused to yell greetings. About 2.45, in Grötsund we were excited to see a brigantine heading north under power and flying the red ensign. It was *Mary Fortune*, but her owner did not appear to be playing the bagpipes. She had been in Norway the previous year, but this was the first time we had encountered each other. I went out prepared to be all matey —I always forget I'm British—but my cheery wave apparently met with little success.

We anchored here at 6.15 p.m. It is nice to be back. We have covered 521 miles during the last nine days. I am having great difficulty with my new log book. Having bought it out here, all the headings are in Norwegian: haven't the slightest idea what I'm entering up.

Hammerfest - midnight (the northernmost town in the world) and North Cape at midnight

CHAPTER XI

TROMSÖ TO AALESUND

July 24th. Vestfjord. 4 p.m.

We left Tromsö on the evening of Friday, July 22nd. "I wouldn't sail on a Friday," said the Harbour Master, when we went to say good-bye to him. Strange, this superstition so many seafaring men have, regarding the bad luck that will dog your voyage if you sail on a Friday. I've known captains be in port, their ship ready loaded, yet they would not leave until the fateful day was over, at one minute past midnight. The Harbour Master told us such harrowing stories of what had befallen vessels that defied this superstition, that I really got the jitters.

At 6 p.m. the tide was with us, at midnight it wasn't. We could have waited until next morning, but Heavens above! if we listen to superstition we'll get nowhere; besides, we have sailed on dozens of Fridays.

It was a glorious evening as we sailed out of Tromsö harbour and headed south down the Indreled under power. "We'll go to the Lofoten Islands," I said. "We missed them coming up and if we sail on through the night we can afford the time." So the following afternoon, with Rotvær abeam, we changed course to the S.W. The compass was driving me hairless again, but we managed to pick up Skarvhausen and proceeded to the westwards between a maze of small islands and skerries.

Lofotöyene are a rocky chain of island mountains, rising up some two or three thousand feet from the sea. The passages between the islands are narrow and tortuous. The tidal streams rush through them with great violence, forming whirls and eddies, and fierce squalls rush down the mountains. In short, Lofoten is not a particularly cheering district.

I looked at the mountains that rose up to starboard, the sharp-pointed summits that even our rather conservative Sailing Directions declare have been "aptly compared to a row of shark's teeth." They were like shark's teeth. I remembered seeing them before when we left Bodö, rising from the water, white and pointed; rather cruel-looking beneath their covering of snow. Most of the snow had now gone and there was nothing alarming about the sharks' teeth in the evening sunshine. To the S.E. the coast of Norway appeared a misty purple, while the islands in the foreground were silhouetted, almost black in a sea-like glass.

We turned up Raftsundet and then down Ulvaagen, a creek on the eastern side of Store Molla. The passage became more and more narrow —a ribbon of water, barely 100 yards wide, between the mountains. At the end it opened out into a magnificent lake. I thought I had never seen anything more peaceful and beautiful. "We'll anchor here, it's lovely," I cried, little guessing we were in the very jaws of the shark. We sounded, but the water was too deep and we were compelled to go back and anchor by one of the small islands near the entrance.

We had just finished supper when we heard a faint whistling sound.

"Hell! What's that?" I said.

Next moment it was blowing like fury from the south. We rushed on deck and made things fast. We had a stern warp out, the wind was on our starboard beam, and *Perula* was tugging against warp and anchor. "We'll have to get out," I shouted to Adams. No sooner had I said it than the wind dropped completely and all was peace again. "Well, I'll be—" I remarked. Clouds had gathered and rain-storms passed up the main fjord.

"Just a squall," I said. "It's brightening now. I'm going to bed."

Adams told me later he had a presentiment, and sat in the wheelhouse reading a book. I was awakened by the whirr of the self-starter, made a choice ejaculation, leapt from my bunk and rushed to the wheelhouse. The wind was howling and shrieking, this time from the north. I arrived just in time to see our anchor uprooted like a feather and the stern warp, acting like a pivot, swung *Perula* round straight for the rocks. "Quick," I yelled, "cast off that warp." The rope was wet and tight; for when Adams makes us fast, he does make us fast. "For Heaven's sake cut it," I shrieked, for we were almost on the rocks. Fortunately, he always keeps a knife and marline spike strapped to both the main and mizzen masts. Even so he hesitated; he is very fond of warps, always playing with them and coiling them up. This particular one must have been his favourite; to him it was sacrilege to cut it, and besides, he told me afterwards, he was thinking how much it had cost!

Meanwhile, I was frantic. "Cut it, you fool!" I screamed. With an inward groan and a tender last look, he slashed through it.

We were almost touching the rocks, for a moment *Perula* hesitated; then with engine flat out she slowly turned to safety, dragging the anchor after her. It was not particularly warm in silk pyjamas, but I mopped my brow: it was about the closest shave we'd had.

We wound the anchor up and headed out into Raftsund. The sound acted like a funnel and the wind shrieked down it, throwing up a nasty sea.

I looked at the dinghy, which we were towing; it was leaping about like something possessed and shipping water.

"What shall we do?"

"Don't you think you'd better put some clothes on?" said Adams. "You might catch a chill."

He was quite right, but sometimes I feel I could murder him (he says the feeling is mutual).

With trousers and jersey hastily pulled over my pyjamas, I studied the chart for an anchorage. We decided to try Valöyhavn, on the eastern side of the southern entrance to Raftsund, a small haven in the shelter of some low-lying islands. The Sailing Directions said the entrance was easy. Perhaps it was—when you knew which entrance it was. I didn't. I looked at a maze of small islands, lost count, and groaned. "Oh dear! Which two do we go between?" So we had to go past the lot and start again from the other end. After several remarks such as: "Well, I think it is," and "No, you are quite wrong," we headed gingerly through a narrow passage between two of the islands. The swell broke on the rocks and the seaweed swirled about. Targets were painted on the rocks in the entrance. "We'll drop here," said Adams, "and tie up to that post." After much for'ard and astern work, I eventually succeeded in putting *Perula* broadside across the narrow channel.

"You aren't in the right place yet," he said, "you want to be about six yards to the right."

"Put the blasted boat there yourself," I replied, crossly. "I'm sick of going up and down."

By the time we had finished arguing the wind had carried us down the channel, and we were practically jammed between an island and a big rock.

"Blasted place," I groaned. " It's all your fault for sailing on a Friday." After much difficulty *Perula* was extracted. "I've finished with targets," I said. "We'll anchor in that pool, head to wind in a decent and respectable way."

"You can't," said Adams, "it wouldn't be safe with it blowing so hard, the anchor would drag."

"It's never dragged before, when it's been left to itself," I said. So down went our full 30 fathoms of chain, after which I retired to my bunk.

An hour later I was wakened by a frightful ringing. "What's that?" I called.

"The alarm," said Adams. "Thought I'd better set it to see if the anchor was all right."

An hour later it rang again. "It's your turn," he called, sweetly, "I went last time."

"Listen," I said, very ominously, "if this boat is going on the rocks, an hour won't stop it—if that damned alarm rings again, I'll throw it at you." With that I got peace.

I woke at 10 o'clock this morning. I found various rocks had popped up around us, but the anchor was still in the same spot. I made a mental note that anchorage should, if possible, always be made amongst low-lying islands and not in places surrounded by high ground.

At 11.55 we left for Trollfjorden. The entrance of this fjord is about half a cable wide and almost a mile long. Sheer precipices of bare rock tower up on either side; had there been anything to tie up to it would have been possible to take *Perula* alongside. As I gazed up at these great walls of rock, I felt like a tiny ant. Names were scratched and painted on the sides, where people had paused in their desire to leave something of themselves written upon nature.

"Shall we put ours on?" said Adams. "I've got some red paint I don't want."

"We are not tourists," I replied, crushingly. The tide was running strongly against us, forming small whirlpools and eddies; it took almost full engine to keep steerage way.

Trollfjord is actually a larger and grander edition of Ulvaagen. At the head, the passage opened out to form the same kind of lake, almost completely shut in by mountains. The reflections on the water were exquisite and the usual waterfalls thundered down from what seemed like the very heavens themselves.

"You row back in the dinghy,"I said to Adams, "and take a photograph of me bringing *Perula* out."

"What!" he said. "Row a bally mile?"

"It will do you good," I said; so off he went. When we eventually got back to Raftsund he asked: "Where shall we go now?"

"Back to Bodö," I replied, "to a safe harbour and comfortable mooring, before the sharks' teeth really bite." So we are heading back now. I really intended to take the open sea passage all the way, but I've changed course for Grötöysund; might as well go through the Indreled, it is more reassuring.

Bodö. July 28th: We tied up in Bodöhavn at 3 a.m. on July 25th, after more anxious moments with Grötöysund, which seemed to look different coming back. In consequence, I arrived at Bodö in a bad temper, to find only one vacant buoy and a fishing boat making towards it. I opened up *Perula's* engine, and after an exciting race we won by a short head. Adams leapt on to the buoy and shackled our chain to it in triumph. The fishing boat circled round and then, to my great disgust, she also tied up to the buoy. I went on deck, seized a fender and glared fiercely, for although Norwegian fishermen mean no harm, they usually have no respect for paintwork, their own planking being mostly bare wood treated with oil.

The skipper looked at me and must have thought I looked savage, for he produced a whole row of old motor tyres and fastened them between us. This procedure caused me much remorse; I smiled sweetly and invited him aboard for a drink.

Having put on his best clothes, he duly arrived. We could not speak a word to each other, yet for about two hours we held a most enjoyable "conversation," though how we did it I shall never quite understand.

It was grand to be back in Bodö and to meet our old friends again; we celebrated by having strawberries and cream for tea. "Gosh, Ron," I said, "imagine having strawberries in the Arctic!"

Yesterday we drove out in Hr. Sannes' car to see the Saltstraum, said to be the strongest tidal stream in the world. The countryside smelled sweetly of new-mown hay; long racks of it stretched across the fields, drying in the hot sun or being loaded on to quaint little pony carts by the country girls.

On arrival at the Saultstraum I felt rather disappointed—it looked so calm and peaceful, not at all like the raging torrent I had expected. As we sat in the hotel having lunch I looked down on the stretch of water that has taken so many lives. Situated between Straumöy and Knaplundöy, the channel is about a mile long and a quarter of a mile wide. It leads from Saltfjorden to Skjerstadfjorden, a large and practically land-locked basin, which is partly filled and emptied by the tide twice a day. In consequence, the amount of water that rushes through Saltstraum is enormous. Houses on the banks are said to tremble, and whales have been driven back when trying to force a passage through against the stream.

As I looked at it an old fishing boat had just passed through and another was about to make the passage. Idly I watched. The second boat had just got about half-way through when I saw the tide turn. There was no mistaking the turn, from slack water a great wave started to sweep northwards towards the boat, which would make a few yards headway, only to be swept back. As the tide strengthened the Saltstraum became a mass of overfalls; curious black circles appeared, the cavities of immense whirlpools. They were carried along with the stream in the form of inverted bells, diminishing gradually until they disappeared, only to be replaced by more. Following each other, like so many pits in the sea, these vortices have drawn down numerous boats and men. Fishermen say that if they see the approach of a whirlpool in time and are able to throw something like an oar into it to break the continuity, the water will rush in to fill the cavity and the boat will pass safely over.

We were now watching the fishing boat with decided apprehension.

"Why don't they turn round and go back with the stream?"

"They can't, they have left it too late," explained our friend, Hr. Johnsen. "To turn would mean losing all control and being swept on the rocks or dragged down."

The way that skipper did get out was one of the neatest bits of seamanship I have seen. With engine full ahead he steered his ship clear of trouble while he was being swept backwards, making about 3 knots astern. His greatest difficulty was not to turn. First they would be swept broadside one way and then the other; one second we would groan and think he was finished, the next second he had regained control again. At length on reaching quieter water he did risk turning and was carried safely out in Saltfjorden, where he dropped anchor. He had got out just in time. The Saltstraum had become a raging torrent. Officially the strength of the tide is put down at 16 knots. Seeing it at Springs, we considered 20 knots a conservative estimate. Only for a short time, at slack water, is it possible for a ship to pass through, a signal being given from the shore.

After lunch we walked down to have a closer look at it. The noise of the rushing tide reminded me of Niagara Falls and spray rose above the fjord like a mist. On the gates of the small farms were nailed tin collecting-boxes: relief for the widows of the fishermen that lose their lives. Just as the tide begins to turn these men sweep fearlessly down to the edge of the channel in small rowing boats. Apparently many fish are to be caught so, almost daily, the men risk their lives for a good catch, heedless of the danger.

As we walked back to the car I indulged in a little unintentional "bull fighting" and was eventually escorted to *Perula*, patched with sticking plaster. It was undignified, for much as I would like to enlarge the proportions of my "bull" (for the purpose of the story, I mean), I must confess it was in reality a small calf, a pretty, piebald calf, grazing in a meadow, tethered by a long rope to a rock. "Oh, how lovely!" I cried, daft like and, holding out my hand, walked up to him. He seemed pleased to see me at first, rubbing his head against me affectionately. "The sweet little pet," I said, but next minute it was, "The bloody little so and so."

UNINTENTIONAL "BULL" FIGHTING!

My "pet" had jerked away, snorted, and commenced to charge round and round me. The day was so hot I was wearing a summer frock and no stockings. "Look out, you idiot," Adams shouted; but before I could do anything the tether rope was wrapped firmly round my legs, cutting into my bare ankles, and my "bull" had me at his mercy. It really was ridiculous. There I was howling for help and all tied up while a wretched little calf, no bigger than a large dog, did his best to toss me. My only consolation was that his horns had not yet begun to grow. "Serves you right," said Adams, after I had been rescued. "I'm always telling you not to touch strange animals."

The early hours of this morning were also unfortunate. The first fishing boat had left our buoy, but another had come, a large grey vessel of some 70 tons. We turned in early in the hope of getting a good rest before pushing south on the morrow. I was awakened by a frightful bumping, shouting and tramping of feet. After each bump *Perula* shook and trembled, her timbers groaned. "Suffering catfish!" I yelled and tore on deck in my night attire. The wind had reached gale force and it was pouring with rain. Fishermen were rushing about *Perula*'s deck trying to save her, and soon the air was blue with English and Norwegian Curses. Another and larger vessel had tied up to the buoy on the other side of us. As these two ships were tossed about in the rising sea, straining at their mooring warps, we were being crushed between them. A large rowing boat with the usual pointed prow was jammed under our counter, trying to knock holes in it. To make matters worse all the mooring warps had got tangled up with each other. Finally, they managed to free the ship which had arrived last and, much to our relief, started the engine and took her away; a very decent thing for them to do with a gale blowing. We staggered down to the saloon, cold and soaked to the skin. "For God's sake, give me a whisky," I said, "a large one—neat."

It is now 10 a.m. and we are going ashore to say good-bye to our friends. I do hate these good-byes. It's horribly depressing.

Stigfjorden. 11.35 pm.: We have passed out of the Arctic. Half-an-hour ago we once again crossed that imaginary circle, this time heading south. I felt rather miserable about it, then suddenly I looked up; a big star had appeared, as though to welcome us back. Adams was just turning in. I called to him: "There's a star, Ron, do you want to see it?" He came rushing up. Just as the moon had caused us excitement at North Cape, so did the sight of this star, the first we had seen for weeks. It is surprising how you miss them. A heated argument started as to which star it was. Adams would have it that it was a planet; I got cross and said: "Use your sense, the damn thing's twinkling."

He has now turned in again and I am alone with my thoughts. One or two other stars have appeared, and when I look back I can see that red glow in the sky: the midnight sun which for us, is now only a memory. It is still shining in Spitsbergen, still shining at North Cape. I feel rather like turning back. Ahead the grey mist of twilight steals over the fjords and islands; it reminds me of a November afternoon in England. I have just plugged in the compass light for the first time since we left Aalesund, and—there ain't no light.

We shall have to overhaul our navigation and riding lights; clean the glasses and trim the wicks, a nice job for someone. I expect I'll be able to palm it off on Adams, though! The lighthouses are not yet lighted, at least not in this part of the Indreled, they will be further south and possibly on the coast. It is rather disconcerting in the half-light; a white fishing boat crossed our bows and she was not easy to see. The Norwegians tell me it is usually bad these last few days before the lighthouses come into action again, especially on a wet or cloudy night. Of course, large craft, steamers, etc., already have their navigation lights up, and I think we will put ours up to-morrow. Perhaps this coming of darkness again may prove a blessing: we may get some sleep at night. I am beginning to feel rather tired—as if a good holiday would do me good.

Möihavn. July 29th: We arrived at Brönnöysund at 12.25 p.m. and went alongside the steamer quay for water, whereupon a large steamer appeared and the assembled crowd had the pleasure of watching Adams and me tearing along the quay with our warps, dragging *Perula* after us. The Harbour Master rushed to the rescue, and next minute the entire town seemed to be dragging our ship, and I, having been left well behind, began to wonder where she would end. She was finally made fast to a small jetty north of the quay.

In the afternoon we were invited to coffee at the Harbour Master's home. As we approached he came out to meet us, accompanied by his two pretty little girls. To my horror the youngest took one look at me and burst into tears. Apparently her father had told her that an English lady and gentleman were coming to see her, and at the sight of my trousers and yachting cap, she had cried in disappointment, "Oh, Daddy, they are both gentlemen!"

We were tempted to remain overnight at Brönnöysund, but the weather was perfect, so we decided to carry on to Torghatten and see the "hole" in the mountain while the going was good.

We anchored here in Möihavn at 5.30 p.m. up beyond the second island in 6 fathoms. We had debated about taking *Perula* to the small inlet where landing for the mountain is effected, but the anchorage is very temporary and we did not deem it wise to leave her there unattended. We set off in the dinghy, doing our usual brother-and-sister act. My "bull fight" wound had turned septic and Adams had put his knee out, otherwise all was well. Having rowed about a mile-and-a-half (aren't we ever going to get to the place?) we arrived at some steps, the lowest of which was about 5 feet above the dinghy.

Eventually I was hauled ashore and we limped off, like a couple of sleuths, tracking footprints in the hope they led to the trail up the mountain. Having climbed some 450 feet, we arrived at the hole, a natural tunnel about 500 feet long, with a height of about 240 feet at its south-western end. Our voices echoed strangely, water dripped on our heads from the domed roof, and about the floor were many boulders that looked suspiciously as if they had crashed down. To the S.W. we looked out on miles of sea, the islands and skerries which form a "Skjaergaard" and protect Norway from the full force of the North Atlantic and Arctic seas. To the N.E. lay Brönnöysund and a panorama of fjords and mountains, framed in rock. A magnificent view, well worth climbing up to see.

As we walked back a farmer beckoned to us. On a small table were dishes of fruit and cream—a kind of yellow raspberries gathered by the children.

We are now back aboard; the sky is covered with cirro-cumulus, giving the typical mackerel effect, and the reflection on the water is marvellous. As we were rowing back to *Perula* there seemed to be two complete ships, one on top of the other. We are staying here for the night and pushing on to-morrow.

July 30th: We are still at Möihavn. This morning we picked up a gale warning, so decided to stay "put." It is now blowing hard, but the holding ground seems good and the low islands that surround us are free from squalls. It is quite pleasant to have a day's rest.

Stokksund. August 1st: We left Möihavn at 11.25 a.m. yesterday and spent last night once again tied up alongside old *Fanny* at Edshaug. We took the north-eastern entrance into Nordsalten, between Korsholmen and the mainland. Narrow, but quite O.K. Marius rowed out to meet us and there was great excitement and much handshaking although, of course, we could not understand a word the other said. He took us to his house and we sat devouring eggedosis, with biscuits and coffee. Hr. Jacobsen was away but we gathered that another "Englishman" had been sent for.

Having had to row for miles, our interpreter eventually arrived. He was a Norwegian who had spent about 30 years in America; consequently, he was more at home with our language than his own. The result was rather amusing. When asked by the Norwegians to interpret our remarks, he replied to them in English, or rather broad American, and they were no wiser. Poor Marius got more and more excited and enraged as the evening progressed.

After a farewell party aboard Perula we sailed at 5 o'clock this morning. I turned in again, leaving Adams on watch, and when I woke he was looking decidedly shaken. He had taken the inside passage, westward of

Strömö and described it to me by saying: "S'truth, Win, I could have spat on either shore!" Vulgar, but apt, I gathered.

All day the wind freshened.

"It's going to be a foul night," said Adams.

"It can't," I replied, "look at the glass, it's over 30 inches."

Then we picked up a gale warning and we could not have been in a worse part of the Indreled. We had crossed Folla and were winding between the islands and rocks to the sou'ard. "Stokksund is our only hope of a decent anchorage," I said, after consulting the chart. "Sixteen miles to go and only three hours of daylight left to make it in."

The first hour we covered 4 miles; the second only 3. I was now in a thorough state of agitation and my eyes hardly left the clock.

"One hour's light and 9 miles to go."

It may not be really dark for another two hours," said Adams hopefully. We opened the engine up to full speed. It was blowing harder and harder from the S.W. every minute. At the end of the next hour we had only done another 2 miles and the seas were sweeping over us.

"That's torn it," I groaned. "It's a most intricate passage and now we've got to go in at dark."

I had never navigated after dark in Norway, although I had often marvelled at the number of lighthouses, the last number in the Norwegian list of lights being 2,160; there having been several a, b, c and d's. Most of the lighthouses in the Indreled are small white towers or huts situated on the fjord bank. Red is also a popular colour, to show up against the snow, I suppose. The arcs of light are usually red, white and green, and as there are so many lighthouses, I feared it might be confusing. Actually nothing could have been more simple. Navigation became a matter of keeping in paths of light; changes of course, shoals, etc., being denoted by a change of colour. No sooner did we pass one lighthouse than another appeared to guide us, as we twisted and turned down narrow channels and between rocks.

I thanked Heaven I had Norwegian charts for, with the light-sectors being shown in colour, the briefest glance was sufficient to get the hang of things. I really think it is easier to navigate the Indreled by night than by day. When you think that in winter, darkness envelopes the northern part of this country both night and day, well, I suppose it is essential to have a really competent system of lights.

Safely in Stokksund we have dropped anchor off the north eastern side of Kirkholmen in 10 fathoms. It is blowing really hard, but the island is low, shaped like a horse-shoe and gives good shelter. As usual we did not take a long enough warp ashore and had to row back for more, after which Adams slipped on a piece of seaweed in the darkness. "Go on, laugh—don't mind me," he remarked with dignity. His clothes are now hung up in the engine room to dry.

Stokksund. August 2nd, 10 p.m.: We are still here; it is still blowing and there are still gale warnings. We spent the afternoon painting the topsides from the dinghy—literally, as the last of our paint had upset in it. I don't think we shall ever get the floorboards clean again.

Trondheim. August 6th: We arrived here on August 3rd and, after much debate, moored in Skansen, on the west side of the town. Trondheim is a most confusing place to arrive at, if you only have a large scale chart, as we have. Having passed west of Munkholmen, we surveyed about a 2-mile stretch of breakwater, docks and lighthouses.

The Sailing Directions were not much help to us; they spoke of various basins, inner and outer, but we had not the slightest idea which they were. Also, as I had not looked in the glossary on page X, I did not know the "elv" meant river, and, in consequence, Nidelv and Elvehavn caused me more confusion. I gathered that Trondheim was practically surrounded and very much cut up by water, also that various bridges were waiting to pounce.

"We'll start at one end," I said, "sail along the outside and have a good look at it." We headed south to commence at the western end.

"Yachts," said Adams, suddenly.

"Yes," I replied. "Yachts, mooring buoys, a restaurant and a swimming bath—it will do us fine."

Skansen is a clean little harbour and most of the local yachts are kept here. I should imagine a nasty swell might come in with some winds, but there is a railway drawbridge should you wish to seek better shelter in the inner basin beyond.

We have to take a tram ride to get to the town, but the conductor is very nice; he helps me on and off the tram and salutes respectfully. As usual we soon made friends and have had some enjoyable times with members of the Trondheim Sailing Club. Hr. Wold took us out for a sail in his racing yacht *Sonja*, and I was fast becoming converted to motorless craft—until the wind dropped and we had to row home. He also took us to a supper dance at the Britannia Hotel. I made a special note of the

Britannia, because it is not only a fine hotel, but the first I have visited in Norway where whisky and soda, etc., can be bought.

Yesterday we went to the railway station, and having arrived at the booking-office, paused in some embarrassment.

"You ask," said Adams.

"It's not my place to ask," I replied with hauteur. Eventually he walked up to the office, tapped politely, and rather red in face asked for: "Two to Hell, please."

The booking clerk looked at us. "Week-end, I suppose?" he remarked. "It's the same price, 1s. 9d. Return."

There is, of course, no fire and brimstone about Trondheim's Hell—not even a devil—just a sleepy little village a a few miles from the city. Quite unintentionally it got its extraordinary name, leapt to fame, and now the Norwegian State Railways do a roaring trade selling tickets to tourists as souvenirs. As we walked away chuckling, I thought of the booking-office clerk. Funny job, dishing out tickets to Hell.

For the last three days I have been saying, "We must go to see the Cathedral," and Adams has replied: " Yes, I suppose we ought to." So this morning we went. Trondheim Cathedral is a magnificent building where the coronation of the Norwegian sovereigns is solemnised. It was erected as a memorial to the martyr king, Olav Haraldsson, and in 1030 consisted of a little chapel built beside a medicinal spring that had its rise beside St. Olav's burial place. This spring still exists inside the wall of the high altar of the Cathedral. The Cathedral has had a mixed history—built up only to fall in ruins again. The restoration began when Norway regained national independence, and is still being carried out.

I loved Trondheim market. It is situated in a big square through which our tram route passes. It is the first time we have really been able to buy fresh summer fruit and vegetables, all ridiculously cheap. Having taken a bus-ride (good for your liver) to see Lerfossen waterfall, which is well worth the visit, we are pushing on south to-night.

Haröfjorden. August 8 th, 4 p.m.: We spent last night anchored at Oro, a small island E.S.E. of Hestskjær light; 5 fathoms, solitary but satisfactory.

This afternoon we paused to swing ship. It was not very satisfactory: someone had painted the pelorus with bicycle enamel. After remarks such as, "The damn thing's stuck," "Bring some paraffin, a hammer and a screwdriver," the "adjuster" got busy and finally gave a large groan.

"What's up?" asked Adams.

"Only deviations of 15° or so," I replied.

The Arctic seems to have made a proper muck of the compass. With not having soft iron correctors, I naturally expected to find deviations on changing latitude, but 15° just north of Aalesund was a bit thick. The compass had appeared to be all right at this point of the outward journey. "It's beyond me," I said, and having got the readings, left it at that.

By this time we were both somewhat tired and hot, so we changed to bathing costumes, put the engine in neutral, and dived overboard. Some minutes later local shipping was horrified to see a yacht drifting unattended down the fjord and the crew swimming after it in hot pursuit. One of these days we shall get left behind.

Aalesund. August 21 st: We arrived at Aalesund on August 8th at 7.35 p.m., and—we are still here. As we came into the harbour we were surprised to see a local steamer that had just left the quay turn round and put back. "What has she done that for?" I asked. We soon found out. Two figures disembarked and hurried across the quay in our direction, waving and shouting. It was Captain Christiansen and his wife. Having seen us coming in they had decided to abandon their own trip.

Hr. Solbjörg's car dashed up to the landing-stage steps and he and his wife got out. "Welcome home," were the words these very good friends greeted us with; and believe me, this little town has become a second home to us. We could not have had a better time—invitations every day, picnics, sunbathing and swimming parties at the sailing hut, with dancing in the cool of the evening.

Not only have we been royally entertained, but *Perula* herself has come in for a good deal of attention. Captain Christiansen insisted on setting-up the rigging himself and Hr. Loe, instructor at the navigation school, on hearing our compass was giving trouble, rowed out to see if he could help us. We had not met him before, yet he offered his services in an honorary capacity and, having found a maximum deviation of 17°, adjusted for us.

In a little loft near the quayside the sailmaker was equally busy. A sturdy new sea anchor and a new lifebelt were being made to replace those lost in the gale. "Storm can come now," he said when they were finished and, having paid him about 40 kroner, we carried them off in great delight.

We contemplated grounding *Perula* to scrub the bottom, which was like the Amazon jungle, but we could not find a suitable place; still, I've got quite a lot off during my morning swims. Adams somehow found time to overhaul the engine and, with *Perula* more or less ready for her North

Sea crossing, I wrote to the Meteorological Office at Bergen asking them to let me know when there was a chance of two days settled weather.

I cannot speak too highly of Hr. Petterssen's kindness. Almost every day I receive letters, telegrams, or telephone messages from him. I said we could sail any day, on or after Monday the 15th; it is now the following Sunday and still he advises us not to leave. First it was fog; news came in of ships aground and even the local mail steamers were hours late. Then came severe gales, "kulingvarsels," and even the occasional mention of the word "storm" on the radio.

Once again I feel that one should leave Norway early. Had we been a few days earlier we could have had a marvellous crossing. Now, I sometimes, wonder if we shall ever get back. Summer is over in Aalesund, soon the sailing hut will be closed for the winter and the ducks will be devoured.

I have been very interested in the Sailing Club ducks. The birds are treated in a lordly manner all summer, having their own pond on Gaasholm. They are very tame and everybody feeds them and call them by name, then—on the last day of the season—the men sit down and eat them for supper.

"I don't know how you can do it. I couldn't," I exclaimed to Solbjörg. He grinned and replied: "You wouldn't get the chance; the supper is for men only."

Last Sunday was the final Regatta, a terrible day, but the date had been arranged during our previous visit and the members would not disappoint us. In driving rain and squalls we followed the races in the Shell launch and saw some really grand sailing. I expected the boats to be dismasted any minute. "Blimey," I said, as I drank a glass of beer in the comfortable cabin, "I'd rather be in here than out there."

August 19th was Adams's birthday, and I happened to mention this, not realising what the result would be. He promptly became known as "Birthday Child"; a title which apparently entitles you to say "Skaal" as much as you like at everybody's expense but your own.

The party started with champagne at the Town Club; women are not normally allowed in here, but the hostess allowed us to use her private room. In the evening, after dinner at the Solbjörg home, an immense and beautiful cake (suitably inscribed) was brought in and the "Birthday Child" reigned supreme until the last stroke of midnight, when everybody got up and sang, "The birthday is over . . . ." Much to everyone's delight, however, I remembered we were an hour ahead of G.M.T. so we went on dancing and celebrating again. Finally, Adams was escorted back to *Perula*, having had the birthday party of his life.

One afternoon Christiansen asked me if I would go and see the old sailors. Well, I know what sailors usually think about sailors' homes and, to be candid, I went not expecting to be impressed.

We arrived at a fine building and entered beneath an old compass to find ourselves "at the bottom of the sea"—the ground floor being decorated to represent the ocean bed, with fish, rocks, seaweed, etc., painted on the walls. As we climbed the stairs the "ocean" lightened until we came to the "surface", to look on a typical Norwegian seascape. The next storey took us into the "heavens"; to the moon and amongst the stars the old sailors had worked by and loved.

Each man has his own little flat where he could live in comfort and privacy with his wife. General rooms were also provided, and the one I liked best was the little workroom; so typical of the sea and ships. Here, amidst the familiar scent of tarry ropes, the old skippers sat, pipe in mouth, yarning together of the old days, splicing ropes, making lines and nets for those who are still at sea.

I thoroughly enjoyed that afternoon as I talked, as best I could, to the old men. Some of them showed me their flats, bedroom, sitting-room-kitchen, with all the latest cooking appliances. Many had their own furniture and on the walls hung souvenirs they had brought from foreign lands. There were laundries and drying rooms for the use of the families and the gardens were beautiful. As we came out there was a little stone room, rather like a church. "They are old, you see," said Christiansen. "Sometimes we lose them; we have to provide for that, too." If the men can afford it they pay a little to live in this home: a home that is a home. If they cannot afford it Aalesund looks after them.

To-night we have been to the cinema with the Solbjörg. We saw an English talkie with Norwegian captions. Just one picture and smoking strictly prohibited.

After the show we returned aboard for supper.

"I don't think you will ever get rid of us," I said.

"Welcome to Norway," Solbjorg replied cheerfully, a remark he makes at least a dozen times a day. In fact, most of our friends suggest we should lay *Perula* up and stay here for the winter! I am beginning to think we shall have to.

On Friday we ran out of money and we did not want to cash a cheque as we expected to sail at any moment. Solbjörg, hearing of this, lent us the necessary. A friend in need is a friend indeed. Everybody is the same, everything is done for us. My clothes were in a frightful mess, so Hr. Moa took them to a tailor friend and had them mended and pressed for me.

Now the wind is howling and shrieking outside and the rain pours down. I've just turned to Adams and said: "Anyway, Ron, we couldn't be held up in a better place than Aalesund."

The Saltstraum near Bodö

CHAPTER XII

ABSENCE MAKES THE HEART GROW FONDER

North Sea. August 25th. Position?

Don't know where we are and I don't care a damn. I've been at the wheel almost continually for three days and nights, never had my clothes off, never slept. But I better start at the beginning.

On the morning of August 22nd we were still at Aalesund. Adams had woken up decidedly off colour and I looked at him anxiously. He said it was nothing but I suspected he was in for what I call "one of his malaria bouts." He first got malaria when we were out East and then again in South America. I hoped that the telegram would not come telling us to sail, for while I knew what to do for him if he was ill, it is one thing in port and quite another in a small yacht crossing the North Sea.

Of course the telegram came; warning us to get ready as favourable weather might develop. "I'm all right—it's nothing," he persisted; so we went ashore to do the shopping.

At 1 p.m. I telephoned Hr. Petterssen from the Harbour Office. He thought we should be leaving, but was still in touch with various lighthouses and waiting for the latest reports to come in. He said he would wire a complete forecast in an hour or two.

Captain Christiansen took us back to his home to wait for it there. He is a great fisherman and his wife had prepared a very special salmon he had caught the previous day. As we sat at table with this charming Norwegian family, with whom we have spent such pleasant times, it seemed very like being at home.

I kept looking across at Adams; he looked like death. I did not know what to do. I kept saying to myself, "Ought we to sail?" Then the forecast came. It was blowing a "liten kuling" at Aalesund and to seaward, but Hr. Petterssen instructed me to sail south through the Indreled to Stadtlandet, where we would reach open water in moderate weather.

At 3.30 p.m. we sailed. The rain drove through our oilskins as we hauled the dinghy aboard, and we started wet through. We sailed south and, with darkness, came to a rather difficult part of the Indreled. Rain storms blotted out the lighthouses and I spent most of the time out on deck.

By midnight Svinö was abeam and we headed out to sea. I made Adams take a dose of whisky and quinine and sent him below. He had reached the cold shivery stage and his temperature was starting to rise. The wind was south-westerly, moderate, but a nasty swell from the nor'ard caused *Perula* to roll a good deal as we sailed on through the night under power and mizzen.

Next morning Adams was no better; his temperature was now about 105 and he was flushed and feverish. He tried to take an odd hour or two at the wheel but it wasn't much good.

At 10 a.m. I obtained a sight—intercept 4° "towards." At 2 p.m. the wind backed south, but the barometer had risen from 29.7 to 30 ins. and I hoisted the main and staysail. No sooner had I done so than the wind freshened and the glass began to fall.

That evening the weather forecast gave warning of a "liten kuling." It was already blowing pretty hard; I didn't know what the hell to do. I could not see myself getting the mainsail in alone and, in his condition, the deck was no place for Adams. I decided to risk carrying on; but by midnight I had to throttle back the engine and was faced with the prospect of having to heave-to under full sail.

At 4 a.m. Adams woke. The fever had gone but left him very weak. Of course, he would go and lower the mainsail which did not improve him. We proceeded for about ten hours under mizzen and staysail. The barometer was down to 28.9 and we were shipping a good deal of water. The saloon was soaking wet, for I think the heat in Norway, after the cold of Svalbard, has opened up the deck planking a little. The wheelhouse was the only dry place, so I brought "my patient" up from below and made him lie down on the settee, wrapping him up in rugs. "You will be warm and dry there," I remarked in my best bedside manner. At that moment a wave broke on the wheelhouse roof and water poured in, soaking us to the skin. "Sez you," groaned a feeble voice from beneath the rugs. I decided to back the staysail and try heaving-to.

It was not a big sea but one of the nasty short variety you get on the North Sea banks, where a wave will suddenly descend on you from a totally unexpected direction. There was no need to heave-to, but I had been at the wheel for practically 48 hours and was not sufficiently alert.

The staysail, not being reefed, the heaving-to was not very successful and as usual she went broadside. At length I found that by having the engine running slowly and lashing the wheel in a certain position, I could keep her more or less where I wanted. The only trouble was she occasionally decided to go over on the other tack and before I could free the wheel we were going back to Norway. My temper was naturally not improved and I was deep in the study of various books, for I thought I had very cleverly confined our drift to the westwards and Adams did not believe me.

While I was busy with my books (I'm never quite sure which is the port or starboard tack) Adams seized the opportunity to sneak below and oil the engine. When he returned I took one horrified look at him and said, "You bloody fool." For once I was not swearing. Being somewhat shaky on his legs, he had lost his balance and fallen, catching his hand on the flywheel. His little finger was skinned to the bone. Fortunately, I was a V.A.D. during the war and make a point of carrying a good first-aid kit. We spent last night, our third at sea, with Adams on the settee and "soft Alec" (that's me) on the floor. I tried to make a pillow out of the log box, but it was not successful. In any case, I did not want to fall asleep as I had to get up every so often and see that *Perula* had not decided to go back to Norway.

About 5 a.m. lights bore down on us. I think it must have been a fishery patrol boat with strong suspicions, for it cut across our bows, went round us in circles, and would not go away. In the end, fearing we would collide, I decided to get under way again, having been hove-to for 16 hours. In any case the wind was moderating. It is now 11 a.m. The morning weather-report was fresh breeze and a nice spot of fog thrown in for the Shetlands. The wind has fallen to light S.W. and the fog patches have arrived.

A few months ago I should have had a fit at finding myself at sea without any idea of our position. During this cruise I have been lost so frequently that I am quite used to it, and I really believe I can listen to a gale-warning now without getting unduly agitated. That is, of course, when Adams is fit and we have the necessary equipment. He has just asked me where we are.

"Near the Shetlands," I replied.

"How do you know?" he said, rudely.

"Because it is the only place the weather-report gave fog for," remarked the "navigator."

Lerwick. 10 p.m.: We sighted land at 1 p.m., and rather to my surprise, it was the Shetlands. We were slightly south of our course and Bressay was on the starboard bow. We took the southern entrance to the sound and anchored at 3 o'clock, having covered 268 miles by log.

Our friend of the Customs was out in a motor-launch, but kindly abandoned his trip and was alongside to welcome us before we had even dropped anchor. I have never seen our saloon in such a mess; the carpet squelched water and we had to lift off the settee cushions and mop up before he could sit down.

The business over, he asked if his friends might come aboard and see the boat. What they thought of the saloon I don't know, but I thoroughly enjoyed the welcome back.

We had been expected for some days, as mother had, of course, written to the Harbour Master and in a generous moment sent £10, instead of the usual £2 10s. or woollen underclothing. Captain Harrison had very kindly been writing back to her and allaying anxiety on our non-appearance by explaining that the bad weather conditions they had been experiencing here would be holding us up.

I really feel extremely grateful to Hr. Sverre Petterssen and the staff of Vervarslingi på Vestlandet, for we hear that while he was keeping us waiting in Aalesund, another British yacht attempted the crossing and was eventually towed into port badly damaged. There is no doubt that it pays every time to put yourself in the hands of the Met. Office. Our passage across may have been slightly uncomfortable, but this was more due to circumstances than actual weather.

I made an awful fool of myself ashore this evening. I could not realise I was back on British soil and would keep talking Norwegian, holding up my fingers and pointing to things I wanted in the shops. Adams only just prevented me from doing my sheep act in the butcher's. I am getting used to being back now, though. I must say it does feel rather good.

Stromness. August 27th: We left Lerwick yesterday after-noon at 5 o'clock, after a farewell tea ashore with Captain and Mrs. Harrison. I wish we could have seen more of the Shetlands, but it is getting late for rounding the north of Scotland.

It was a perfect day as we sailed south, and with Sumburgh Head abeam, Fair Island could be seen quite clearly. After Adams had turned in, the inspiration came to me: I decided to give him a nice surprise and proceed direct for Cape Wrath. Feeling very pleased with myself, I got busy with my charts, set course to pass north of the Orkneys and settled down to my novel.

It was a most interesting story, and I had just reached the point where I feared the heroine was about to do something she "shouldn't ought'er," when a light flashed right in my face. "Strike me pink," I yelled, and put the wheel hard to starboard: we were on the point of felling Fair Island.

There are two morals to this edifying episode. First, do not read at the wheel, and the second, watch the tide in the Röst.

At 8.55 p.m., Sumburgh Head abeam, I had set a compass course of 236°, 5° being added for tide. At that time I could see Fair Island, so I do not think the compass was out. At 10.15 p.m., on deciding to pass north of the Orkneys, I changed course to 260° compass, and 4½ hours later nearly hit Fair Island, after a distance of about 16 miles. Admittedly I was reading, but even so I do look at the compass frequently. I was thoroughly shaken and it took some minutes before I realised where we were and what had happened.

I consulted my C.D.C. (I had guessed the tide allowance before) and decided it was all quite feasible. It was springs and at Sumburgh Head the tide must have been running at about 7 knots on our beam, decreasing to about 4 knots on the starboard quarter and finally becoming slack.

"Confounded place," I groaned. "Might as well go to Holm Sound now." I looked up my original course and subtracted 20°, because the tide was now beginning to run in the opposite direction. At this point Adams relieved me and I turned in, leaving instructions about terrible tides that needed the utmost attention. Adams, however, was deep in solving the mystery of the "Murder at the Spotted Dog" and when at length I reappeared he had not the slightest idea where we were.

"Fair Island was astern a moment ago," he said, but that was little consolation to me for we had now run into rain and mist.

"I told you to watch the tides," I stormed.

We carried on for some hours and still there was no sign of land. "Now we're lost again," I remarked crossly. "It's all your fault—you and your blasted detective stories."

"You've no need to talk," he retorted hotly.

At 2 p.m. I changed course to the west and, shortly afterwards, we identified Auskerry. All this delay caused us to arrive at Holm Sound with the spring tide running at full strength. The prospect of negotiating the block ships at a good 8 knots did not improve my temper. We shot through Kirk Sound like a bat out of hell and proceeded across Scapa Flow.

"What's that?" asked Adams suddenly. A double row of large buoys stretched right across Bring Deep.

"Get the Sailing Directions," I replied, "and read up the regulations relating to a dockyard port."

Adams delved deeply into the book.

"Well?" I asked. "What does it say?"

"Apparently we are to consult the 'Edinburgh Gazette'," he replied.

Having been restored with a drink I again contemplated the buoys. "They are laying telegraph cables," I said, "I shall go through." Actually there was a channel marked, but there were so many buoys we did not notice it, and with Adams sitting forward to look for cables I headed *Perula* through in quite the wrong place.

On arrival at Stromness we were delighted to find Jimmy and, after greetings had been exchanged, I asked him why the channel had been littered in such a disgusting fashion.

"Did you come through?" he asked.

"Of course I did," I replied. "Why shouldn't I? "

"Oh, we are just laying submarine nets," he answered.

This is the first news we have received of the European situation. Jimmy is now attached to the Navy and Scapa is completely refortified. Troops and guns are everywhere and almost every sound guarded with blockships or nets.

"It is a good thing you came in to-day," continued Jimmy, indicating an old hull, "there is talk of sinking that in Kirk Sound on Monday." With visions of coming through Kirk Sound at 8 knots to find no channel I remarked faintly, "I think I need a drink."

"You don't drink, do you, Jimmy?" asked Adams, as he poured out some rum.

"Oh, yes, I do now," replied our friend, "since you and Miss Brown were here last time."

After he had gone I turned to Adams. "Now look what we've done, led a nice innocent lad astray."

"Perhaps it wasn't us," replied Adams. "Perhaps it was the Navy."

Loch Laxford. August 29th: We left Stromness at 5.35 this morning. Jimmy had been very emphatic that we must leave on the last of the ebb. Apparently the Röst in Hoy Sound can be very bad with the west-going stream and I had instructions to keep as close as possible to the southern shore. This is sound advice.

It was a perfect dawn and we sailed out of the harbour with a light northerly breeze. On rounding The Ness the water ahead was a mass of overfalls but, by making over to Oxan Point and across the entrance to Burra Sound, we missed the worst of them. Even so we got a bit of a ducking.

We proceeded under power and full sail and at 4.30 p.m. rounded Cape Wrath. There was a swell and we were again thrown about a bit. At 7.20 p.m. we anchored here in Fanagmore Bay. Must say I feel rather relieved to be round Wrath. The weather looks really settled and we are planning to push home as fast as we can.

Isle of Man. September 2nd. We spent the night of August 30th anchored off Kyle Atkin, close N.W. of the pier in 5 fathoms. Our arrival was somewhat spectacular, being made in the dark and nearly ending on the beach.

Next day we went on to Tobermory, also arriving in the dark. We did not intend to, it just happened that way.

The following morning I was ill and *Perula* sailed with the Captain lying on the settee, rubbing her tummy and feeling very sorry for herself. Adams had no sympathy. "You shouldn't have eaten seven cakes, three bananas, a tin of condensed milk, a box of chocolates," he said. I am, however, rather like an ostrich and by mid-day had recovered.

At midnight we rounded the Mull, wind N.W. moderate, and set course for Chicken Rock. At noon to-day I surveyed the chart.

"We'll go through Calf Sound," I announced.

"Do you think it is wise?" asked Adams. "It will be about low water."

"Don't be ridiculous," I replied. "We've been through far worse places in Norway."

When we arrived at Calf Sound I don't think I've ever been quite so scared. I really thought we were going on the rocks. "Whew!" I said. "It's the first and last time I come through this damn place."

We entered Douglas Harbour and were preparing to drop anchor and tie up astern to the mooring buoy when the usual gentlemen arrived in a rowing boat to assist us. We had moored in this fashion dozens of times in the last four months, yet with the aid of our "helpers" the procedure took about an hour and cost us 2s. 6d.

We had made the passage from Tobermory to Douglas in just over 31 hours and decided we were entitled to a night's rest in port. At 4.45 I tuned in to the Air Ministry weather forecast: a depression was approaching and the further outlook gave winds freshening from the S. "We'll sail to-night," I said. We hastened ashore to do some shopping and wire home. I learned that my father had been in Douglas and left the previous day, not realising we were so near.

While we were ashore Adams said to me, "Two ladies have been following us for ages, Win, do you know them?" I stopped and turned round. "It is Miss Brown, isn't it?" one said.

"Yes," I replied, feeling rather at a loss, for I had never met them before. Next moment they were wringing our hands and welcoming us as though we were long lost friends. They had been following our adventures in the newspaper and recognised us by photographs. Somehow there was something awfully nice about it; something that made us feel we really were home. "And how is your bullfight wound, my dear?" they asked. We took them back aboard to see *Perula* and, after they had gone, I found a little present of cigarettes hidden in my shopping basket.

Menai Straits. September 3rd: We are home. At 7.45 this morning we picked up moorings in the Straits, after an absence of 16 weeks, 3 days, 20 hours and 45 minutes, during which time we have covered 5,192 miles.

We left Douglas at 8.45 last night. We were both fairly tired, but too excited to sleep as we sailed on through the night, each minute taking us nearer and nearer home.

"Look, Ron it's Skerries—Skerries Light."

Shortly afterwards he cried, "Look, Win, it's Lynas— Lynas again."

Then at last we both yelled: "Menai Light." We throttled back, waiting for a misty grey dawn to reveal Puffin, the island that, on May 10th, I had looked back at wondering if I should ever see it again.

As we went down the Straits Adams said, "I suppose we better posh up a bit—do you think anyone will be there to meet us?"

"Well," I replied modestly, "it's early, I know, but I shouldn't be surprised if they turn the band out."

Eventually Glyn Garth came into view. "Can't see the band," said Adams. "In fact, I can't see anyone." But as we got nearer one lone figure with a black case over his shoulder was observed on shore.

"At least the Press is faithful," I remarked.

"There's someone on our moorings," said Adams. "What a home-coming!"

We circled round by the jetty, posed prettily for the cameraman and yelled, "We'll come ashore when we've found a mooring." At that moment a figure in pyjamas appeared aboard *Himeros* and a sleepy voice called: "Three cheers for *Perula*," after which the owner of the voice presumably returned to his bunk. We found a vacant mooring, lowered the dinghy and went ashore.

The unfortunate cameraman had been unearthed from his bed at 2 a.m., driven from Manchester, and inhabited the shore for the last two hours. He could have waited in his car, but several fishing boats had come in and, not knowing what we looked like, he had taken pictures of the lot.

"I do admire what you've done," he said to us.

"Thank you," I said feelingly. "That coming from you is sheer noble."

We walked up the jetty. "What shall we do for pictures of the reception?" he asked mournfully.

"Have you got to have them?" I asked.

"Lunch time edition," he groaned. "We'd better wake the hotel—then perhaps you could get me a beer." At this moment two ladies appeared. "I brought my wife and a friend," explained the cameraman. One of the ladies was tenderly nursing her finger. "I have been stung by a wasp," she announced then, with a withering look at me: "It will be a long time before I forget YOUR home-coming, Miss Brown."

Gradually the Gazelle was wakened to life. Maids started to appear, curtsied and shook hands with us, but it was far too early for anyone to be really pleased to see us. Poor Mrs. Owen and Mr. McNeil were dragged from their beds to pose on the doorstep, shaking my hand. At length the cameraman declared the reception pictures would have to do, and departed back to Manchester, very kindly promising to telephone my mother and save me a trunk call.

Adams and I rowed across to Dickie's yard and once again climbed the familiar office steps. I knocked and popped my head round Bill Campbell's door. "Good God!" said a startled voice then, with a yell of excitement: "Come in—jove, I'm glad to see you—you've had me scared to death."

"You're a B.F., Bill," I laughed. "Considering you designed *Perula*, you ought to have known she'd see us through." "How was she?" he asked.

"How was the rig?" "How did you find the mizzen?"

"You were right," I replied, "the 'bloody pocket handkerchief' was bloody useful." It was all very jolly and lots of fun to be back in his office again; the same old smelly oil stove and the drawing boards with designs of new ships.

"What sort of a reception did you get?" he asked.

"We didn't," said Adams. "Of course you've done the wrong thing in coming back at all," Bill said, with a grin.

"Why??"

"Oh, well, you know what people are," he explained. "Most of them have spent the summer saying you were mad and would drown yourselves; naturally they are a bit annoyed at being proved wrong."

Adams and I roared with laughter. "Oh, Bill," I gasped, "Do you really think we ought to be dead?"

"It would have been more considerate," he said, with a chuckle.

Menai Straits. September 10th: Bill was right, I am really beginning to feel we ought not to have come back. A friend in the newspaper world has just told me they actually had my obituary all ready prepared, waiting to go to press the moment news came through that we had perished in the deep. Still, I have a strong suspicion they have not wasted it, for last Monday an article appeared under the heading of "Britain's Adventure Girl, No. 1." It gave my life history and a selection of choice photographs, dating back some twenty years.

Last Wednesday we very nearly had to write an "obituary" ourselves. Adams says it was my fault, but I say it was his. The accident would never have happened if he had not decided to celebrate our return by falling into the Straits.

We were just going ashore. A nasty south-westerly was blowing against the tide and I was in the dinghy hanging on while he was attaching the outboard. Suddenly *Perula* swung round exposing us to the weather side. I looked aft to find Adams and the outboard had disappeared. "Where's the outboard?" I shouted in alarm, as a dark head rose from the water.

"It's sunk," gasped a voice.

"Then do something, you idiot," I shrieked.

"Blast the outboard, w-what about m-me?" replied the voice in an injured tone.

The affair annoyed me exceedingly. It was not so much the loss of the outboard, but the loss of dignity, just when it seemed we had at last collected a little. Of course, everybody pretended to be very sorry. Skippers shook their heads sadly in the bar parlour of the Gazelle and said we would never see it again; giving details of all the other out-boards that were lying at the bottom of the Straits. Men were supposed to be coming with grappling irons, but two days passed and they had not arrived. "We'll get that blasted thing up if it's the last thing we do," I said to Adams.

So yesterday evening mystified yachtsmen observed two figures emerge from *Perula's* wheelhouse, carrying an extraordinary implement. It consisted of two meat hooks, a flat iron, and a coil of rope. The figures got into the dinghy, the man took the oars and the woman sat aft, apparently "fishing". Fortunately we had taken bearings at the time of the disaster and, equally fortunately, the outboard had descended to the depths with its canvas cover on. Before long I got a "bite," and believe it or not, up came the outboard, with a meat hook firmly caught in the cover. Adams and I sat in the dinghy and laughed so much we drifted nearly to Beaumaris.

During the last week I have thought a good deal about our cruise. Once again I feel it is really *Perula* that has brought us safely home—to Bangor where she was built six years ago. We could not have had a better or sturdier little ship. We owe a great deal to Peter Dickie and Bill Campbell. Certainly they were working on a craft they had built themselves, but it was no easy job converting the old *Monavic* into a deep sea cruiser. Every alteration had to be carefully worked out; every little detail thought of, so that the new *Perula* could be managed by her small and inexperienced crew. I went to see Mr. Dickie.

"I've come to thank you," I said.

He smiled and replied: "As long as you are satisfied, Miss Brown, I am more than satisfied."

Since we got back we have remained solidly on our moorings. I think we both feel we have had sufficient sailing for one season. Next week *Perula* is to be laid up. "I shall be awfully sorry, Ron," I said, "but she does deserve a rest, doesn't she?"

Salford. December 21 st: Perula was laid up on September 24th. Half an hour before she was due up the slip it was discovered the self-starter would not "self start." We had been cheerfully sitting on our moorings for two weeks, lights blazing every night and quite forgetting that batteries do occasionally want charging.

"You're a damn fine engineer," remarked the Captain, in her usual laying-up temper.

"Nothing to worry about," said Adams, seizing the starting handle. "Just you pull down that compression lever when I say now." The engine started quite easily.

With our boat laid up we did not know what to do with ourselves.

"I can't sleep in my bed at home," I said to Adams.

"I can't in mine either: must be because there is no rocking," he replied.

As the English winter drags on I shiver with cold and ask for more blankets. Mother cannot understand it and seems to think I ought to walk around in summer clothes after being in Spitsbergen. Of course the climate there is drier than it is here and, although the temperatures were much the same as a winter's day in England, we did not seem to feel the cold as much as we do here.

The world is a small place. In November four people sat together in London. In June, three of them had sat together in Spitsbergen: the Governor, Adams and I, joined for this second meeting by Mrs. Marlow. Seems funny to have sailed so far, said good-bye, seemingly for ever, only to meet again a few months later.

Often our thoughts are back with our friends in Norway, and a little bit of *Perula* has been left behind as well. Hanging in the place of honour in the Aalesund Sailing Club is the tattered remains of a flag, the burgee of the Royal Mersey Yacht Club. From Wales to Aalesund, to Svalbard and back to Aalesund, *Perula* wore it at her mainmast head. It did not seem much to give, yet our friends appreciated it above anything else we could have offered.

Sometimes as I sit here in my Lancashire home, I turn the wireless on to the Norwegian weather reports. "Quick, Ron," I call, "it's 'sterk kuling' in Aalesund; maybe there's an 'orkan' at Isfjord."

Now snow covers the ground and, as I look at it, I feel kind of "homesick" for a foreign land. I think Adams feels it too. About an hour ago he got up and mixed two very large drinks.

"A toast to Norway," I said.

"Yes," he agreed, "to Norway—her sailing clubs, her port officials, the staff of her meteorological offices AND to the fishermen who helped us find our way."

"To all our friends," I cried. "To Schjelderup and the Spirit of the North; to Sverdrup and his Outside World." We rose to our feet. "Skaal," we said, drained our glasses and dashed them to the floor.

"That's torn it," I said as I looked at the broken glass. "You'll have to go to Woolworth's to-morrow."

"Hope your mother doesn't miss 'em in the meantime," he remarked feelingly.

We sat down in the evening twilight, looking into the fire: as people do

when thinking. Suddenly I looked up.
"Ron," I said. "Where shall we go next year?"

APPENDIX

THE BOAT.

Perula is 45 feet over-all and 40 feet on the water line. Her beam is 13 ft. 6 ins. and draft 5 ft. Gross tonnage 26 and registered 17. She was built by A. M. Dickie & Sons in 1932 as a fishing boat, and was at that time rigged with a single headsail and bermudian loose-footed mainsail without any boom. She is now rigged as a bermudian yawl with staysail, mainsail and mizzen, totalling 563 sq. ft. The mizzen, however, cannot be made to balance without the addition of a bowsprit (which I would be sure to stick into everything) and a small jib. It is at present used as a steadying sail and for riding out heavy weather.

Her hull is of pitch pine on grown oak frames. The wheelhouse is of teak with armour-plate glass; this latter we were often very thankful for. The steering is interchangeable wheel or tiller, and consists of rods and bevelled gears.

THE ENGINE.

Perula's engine is an R.N. 4-cylinder, 36 h.p. high-speed Diesel, with 2-1 reduction gear.

Our total engine hours for the cruise were 1,020; rather interesting to think that our R.N. ran for practically 1½ months of the four months we were away. She was running as sweetly at the end as she did at the beginning and never gave us a moment's anxiety. The parcel of spares lent to us by the makers, Russell Newbery & Co., was returned to them on the completion of our cruise, unopened. We never had to touch the engine apart from general maintenance, which included cleaning the valves three times, the injectors once, and changing the engine oil. Fuel and oil filters were cleaned every week.

In Svalbard the engine started at the first touch of our Bosch starter, although even after running for several hours no reading was apparent on the water temperature gauge. Fuel oil cost us about £15. We reckon to use 5/8 of a gallon at 5-6 knots. Current for the self-starter, lighting, etc., is obtained from a 12 volt 200 amp. Oldham battery, charged by the engine. We have also a small transformer that enables us to charge the wireless batteries.

ACCOMMODATION.

This consists of a galley-cum-cabin for'ard, a large saloon with two root bunks, an engine room, and a wheelhouse, aft of which is a small self-draining cockpit.

DECK GEAR.

We have both a main and a mast winch, the latter to enable the Captain to hoist the mainsail unaided. The staysail works on a horse. There is a handsome meat safe which has to be carried to the cockpit on the approach of bad weather. The dinghy problem is solved by a derrick, the boom fitting on to the mastband and being raised or lowered by the mast winch. This enables the dinghy to be hauled aboard singlehanded.

The running rigging was all new at the start of our cruise. Apart from the main halyard and mainsheet, which are 2 in. 4-strand yacht manila, it is 1¾ in. ship manila. Last season's running rigging was carried as spare and also half a coil of new rope. The only part of the running rigging replaced was the staysail sheet. We had four 3 in. warps of 15 fathoms each, and a 35 fathoms 3 in. lightly tarred Italian hemp for the kedge anchor. The main anchor is approximately 112 lbs., the kedge 70 lbs. and we have 30 fathoms of ½ in. chain.

One sea anchor was carried, and lost. I shall in future take two.

FOOD.

We did not take nearly sufficient tinned and dried goods. About the only thing I advise not taking in quantity is coffee, this is much better bought in Norway. Norwegians will often refuse an offer of a cup of coffee aboard a British ship: they know what we usually drink. Tinned milk and fish may also be bought in Norway. On the whole we found it more difficult to get fresh fruit and vegetables in the north of Scotland than we did in the Arctic.

I strongly advise dividing provisions into monthly supplies and keeping an emergency ration untouched. But do not 1 conceal the stores too cleverly, as I did: after having been desperately short a large supply was unearthed when laying up!

FINANCES.

Usually a sore point, but I think we covered expenses incurred during the cruise by writing, etc. We reckon to live on about £3 a week when we are aboard. Bonded stores materially assist. We usually have all meals on board, unless invited ashore and, for the most part, do all our own washing, etc. We carried travellers' cheques for the sake of convenience. Charts, Sailing Directions, etc., cost about £12. We did not have to pay any harbour dues and only once or twice were we asked to pay for water.

THE CREW.

The crew is always rather a problem aboard a small yacht and, on the whole, Adams and I got on about as well as two people could. Of course we swore at each other on occasions and the habits of one were apt to get on the nerves of the other. Adams used to get very annoyed all on account of a box of matches. Matches are his fad. Every morning he would walk round *Perula* and deposit three boxes of matches, one labelled "galley", the other "saloon" and the third "wheelhouse". Five minutes later I would walk along, put the galley matches in my pocket and absent-mindedly carry the saloon ones up to the wheelhouse. When Adams went below, there was not a match to be found.

He, on the other hand, annoyed me intensely by invariably deciding to write a letter home just when I had got into the dinghy all ready to go ashore. He also ate large quantities of honey at nearly every meal, until the very sight of the pot made me want to scream. It is silly things like these that do get on the nerves when people are confined together in a small space for any length of time.

I think in one way a man and a woman form an ideal crew. Each have an entirely different outlook on life and two sides to a problem are always better than one. Of course, there are people who may think it is hardly the thing for a single man and woman to sail the seas together. I remember on one occasion a newspaper reporter rang me up. "Don't you think it is a bit peculiar, Miss Brown—you and Mr. Adams sailing together?" "Peculiar," I repeated. "What do you mean?" "Well, er . . ." he said, "don't you think you ought to get married?" "Listen," I said cheerfully: "If Adams and I had evil minds like you, we'd choose some place other than a small yacht. Now put that in your blasted newspaper if you dare." A chuckle was heard at the other end of the line.

SUMMING UP.

Since we have returned many people have asked if we would tackle the passage to Spitsbergen again. When we first got back to Norway we both said that nothing would induce us to do so. Now we feel we would like to go back. I do not think there is much to worry about in such a passage, providing one has a sound ship and is prepared to face a few gales. The weather information is surprisingly good, considering the distance between the Met. stations. Of course, an accurate forecast on a seven-day passage is too much to hope for, but at least one would be warned of the approach of bad weather.

The outward passage, when we endeavoured to go to the North Pole by mistake, took 156 hours 40 minutes. The homeward passage, including the 36 hours' hove-to, took 163 hours 50 minutes. I should always reckon on taking about a week for the passage.

I think the navigation is the most difficult part. The compass is apt to be affected and as the sky is usually over-cast you cannot rely on getting a sight. The landfall also is difficult. I feel these problems could, however, be solved by D/F wireless, working with the stations at Bear Island and Isfjord. Echo sounding would be decidedly useful.

The constant daylight in summer is a great help. Ice can be seen and avoided—but I should hate to get amongst it in fog.

Although we made the passage earlier than advised in the first instance, I think we went at the right time of the year. Conditions, however, change from year to year; plans cannot definitely be made until reaching Tromsö. In fact, the weather appears to be going thoroughly mad. As we were snowed under here in England, Captain Johannessen wrote me that snow had not yet fallen in Tromsö and word came from Einar Sverdrup that Longyearbyen was "like spring."

On the whole, we had marvellous weather for our cruise, much better I think than it was here. In Spitsbergen we wore the same kind of clothes we would have worn on a clear frosty day in England. North Norway was almost tropically hot.

I found Norwegian charts excellent in every way—I would always use them again in preference to our own.

I would also use Norwegian Sailing Directions, if I could read the language. They give all the courses through the Indreled and are exceptionally cheap. The charts must, however, be watched as some give soundings in fathoms and others in metres.

Nowhere in the world have I received greater kindness and hospitality than that of the Norwegian people. To them Adams joins me in saying a very large and heartfelt: "Takk."

REPORT RECEIVED FROM HR. WINTHER-HANSEN VAERVARSLINGEN FOR NORD-NORGE, TROMSÖ

Ice and weather conditions along the route North Cape—Bear Island — Spitsbergen in the summer time, and some remarks about the most favourable time for a cruise in these waters.

1. *State of water in regard to ice.*

(a) Spitsbergen

The west coast of Spitsbergen is normally free from ice at Prince Carl's Foreland and northwards to the mouth of the Icefjord. South of Prince Carl's Foreland there is some ice. Normally this ice disappears at the beginning of the summer. Some years, however, the ice drifts in summer from the east coast round the South Cape and northwards along the west coast, and makes navigation difficult, may even block the Icefjord completely. This, for instance, happened in 1915. Then the ships had great difficulties in forcing the ice and penetrating into the Icefjord. Some of them had to give it up, and a couple of them stuck in the ice and must be left by the crew. We deal here with ships specially built for going in the ice. The north coast of Spitsbergen is normally free from ice in summer. The east coast of Spitsbergen (Storfjord) is often blocked by the ice all the summer. When it happens that the N.E. winds force the ice towards the South Cape the Storfjord becomes free from ice. The fjords are normally frozen every winter, but this fjord-ice breaks up and disappears in the spring. But it may happen that the drifting ice drifts into the fjords and fills them after the firm fjord-ice has disappeared.

(b) Bear Island

Easterly winds are most frequent and force the Polar ice towards the island, so that it becomes blocked for periods of variable duration. Under normal conditions the waters are free from ice at the end of May. In bad years the ice may lie round the island until July. But under favourable conditions the sea may be free from ice even all the winter, or ice and open water may alternate.

There is now every summer a somewhat regular steamship traffic between Norway and Spitsbergen. Normally it begins in May and sets forth until October.

2. Approximate temperatures.
The monthly mean temperatures C are:

	May	June	July	August
Spitsbergen (Green Hbr)	-4.8	2	5.4	4.6
Bear Island	-2.3	1.7	4.2	3.6
North Cape (Gjesvar)	2.6	7	9.9	10

3. Best time of the year to make the crossing.

It is considered most important to choose a time when the risk to meet ice is small, and in that respect the months July or August are recommended. July is also the month when heavy storms are rarest. On the other hand the months July and August are very foggy. But I think one must consider the ice to be considerably more dangerous than the fog. We shall give some mean numbers.

Frequency of wind direction in per cent.

(Mean of 5 years)

Ebeltofhafen—Quade Hook (Spitsbergen)									
	N	NE	E	SE	S	SW	W	NW	Calm
May	12	11	14	19	11	5	3	8	17
June	9	8	8	10	18	7	8	14	18
July	8	9	14	9	17	13	9	9	12
August	10	11	17	12	12	10	3	15	10

Bear Island									
	N	NE	E	SE	S	SW	W	NW	Calm
May	11	22	21	14	6	7	8	8	3
June	11	18	16	16	9	6	10	9	5
July	6	13	14	19	8	12	16	9	3
August	13	17	13	13	8	9	13	13	1

North Cape (Gjesvar)									
	N	NE	E	SE	S	SW	W	NW	Calm
May	9	11	11	11	9	8	15	11	15
June	9	10	7	6	5	7	24	13	19
July	8	16	10	6	4	4	20	8	24
August	7	10	10	10	9	7	19	8	20

Mean number of days with fog.				
	May	June	July	August
Spitsbergen (Green Hbr)	0.5	2.4	3.5	2.6
Bear Island	6.7	9.1	18.7	15.3
North Cape (Gjesvar)	0.9	3	5	3.4

It must be considered that the frequency of fog is probably much greater over the open sea than at Green Harbour.

Mean number of days with strong gale or more. (9 Beaufort or more—18.3 metres per second or more)				
	May	June	July	August
Spitsbergen (Green Hbr)	0.3	0.2	0.1	0.3
Bear Island	0	0.1	0	0.2
North Cape (Gjesvar)	0.9	0.4	0.3	0.4

It must be considered that the frequency of strong gales is probably much greater over the open sea than at Green Harbour.

Mean number of days with ice at Green Harbour
is in
May, 17.9; June, 0.9; July, 0; August, 0.1; September, 8.0

The time with continuous Daylight (Midnight Sun)
Green Harbour . . . . . . 21st April — 23rd August
Bear Island . . . . . . 1st May — 11th August
North Cape . . . . . . 12th May — 30th July 4.

4. Direction and strength of prevailing winds, etc.

In addition to what is already said about this we will add that the observations at Bear Island are probably the ones that are most representative. It is seen from these that in May, June and August north-easterly winds are prevailing, and in July south-easterly winds. Regarding strong gales there is no great difference between the summer months. It must be considered that the conditions vary very much from year to year, and may diverge considerably from the statistical mean values given above. Particularly we will emphasize the following facts:

(a) Though "the mean number of days with strong gale" at Bear Island is 0 in the months May and July, it is not allowed to conclude that strong gales will never occur in these months. It only means that it has not occurred during the relatively short period in which observations have been made.

(b) The same caution must be used regarding the number 0 for "mean number of days with ice at Green Harbour" in the month of July.

There are now meteorological stations at Bear Island and Cape Linné (Icefjord Radio) on Spitsbergen. Before leaving Norway, it will therefore be possible to get a survey of the present weather conditions along the route by telephoning "Vaervarslingen for Nord-Norge" (the weather forecasting station) at Tromsö. "Vaervarslingen for Nord-Norge" also issues weather forecasts for the coast of North Norway (the forecast period is about 24 hours) and for Bear Island (forecast period 12 hours). If there is a radio station and a telegraphist on board the yacht, it will be possible to take up the meteorological telegrams (containing the present weather conditions) sent from the meteorological stations at Bear Island and Spitsbergen. These are sent in international code. In case this might be of interest the necessary informations will be attained at "Vaervarslingen for Nord-Norge" in Tromsö.

DRAWINGS OF *PERULA*

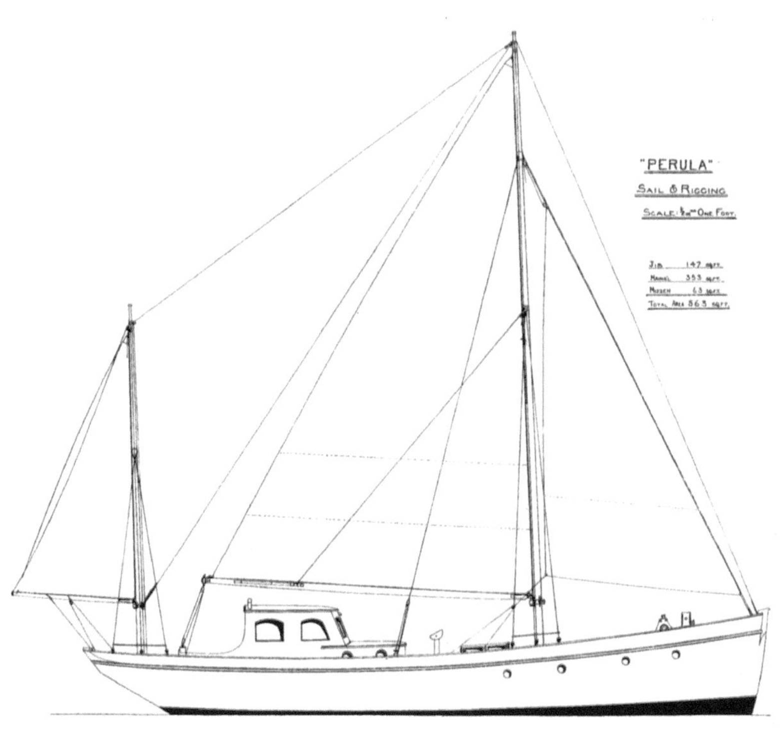

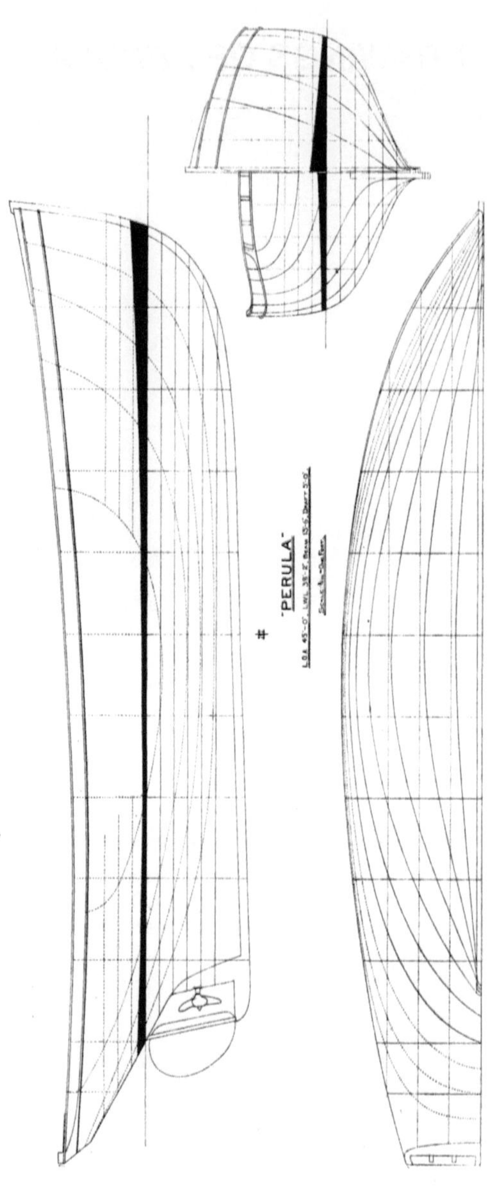
'PERULA'

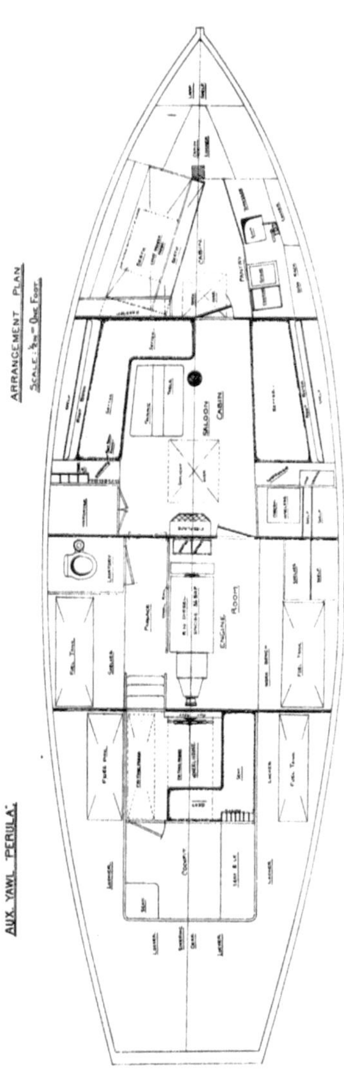
ARRANGEMENT PLAN
AUX. YAWL "PERULA"
SALOON CABIN
ENGINE ROOM

INDEX

Aalesund.74, 76, 80, 82, 84, 85, 136, 138-140, 142, 241, 247-250, 252, 255, 263
Aandalsnes.....80-82
asking the way.....181
astro-navigation.....170
Balholmen.....91, 92, 94, 95
basking sharks.....121
Bear Island.....173
Bilbao, man from.....98
Bodö....153-156, 160, 167, 178, 214, 234, 237, 238
Bömmelfjord.....62
Britain's Adventure Girl, No. 1.. 261
Brönnöysund.....148-150, 242, 243
bull fighting.....239, 242
Caledonian Canal.....46
charts.....39
circus ship.....140
compass adjustment.....36
Coronation Week.....31
cruise ships.....65, 94
customs clearance.....50, 110, 135
Dash, Captain.....33
Dickie's, boatyard 4-6, 20-22, 24, 34, 83, 101, 107, 118, 175, 260, 262, 265
diver.....221
Dobson, Captain W.A.....23
Edshaug.....145, 146, 148, 149, 243
engine problems.....63
Falmouth.....16
Fjaerland.....92
Florö.....88-90, 134, 136
fog.....131, 231
Forlandsund.....181
funeral, Norwegian.....93
gales.....177, 178, 206
Geiranger.....82-84
Hammerfest.....226, 228
Haugesund.....57, 58, 60, 61
Hell.....246
Holyhead solo.....13
ice.....163, 179, 205
Indreled....62, 69, 74, 133, 142, 144, 145, 149, 153, 157, 158, 168, 228, 234, 237, 241, 244, 252, 268
Isle of Man.....11
Johannssen, Captain....162, 220, 222
King's Cup Race.....23
Kinn.....89, 90
Klöven.....158
Lapps.....224
Laxford.....123-125, 257
Lerwick.....129, 130, 254, 255
Liverpool.....18
Longyearbyen.....185-188, 190-192, 195, 198, 199, 202, 203, 209, 212, 217, 220, 268
Manchester Nautical Academy.....23
Maraak.....83
mascots.....177
meat-safe.....177
Menai Straits.....3, 11, 116, 155, 179, 259, 261
Molde.....80
Morecambe Bay.....14
Namsos.....145
navigation...9, 16, 19, 23, 33, 46, 48, 54, 55, 103, 104, 123, 127, 145, 158, 170, 172, 173, 241, 242, 247, 268, 269
Noren.....133
North Cape.....227

Norway......................................22, 36
Norway, first arrival.......................56
Norway, first voyage......................40
Norway, leaving............................252
Norwegian buoyage.......................57
painting...106
Percy the whistler............85, 91, 135
Perula. .4-7, 11, 13-22, 24-26, 31, 32, 34, 36-39, 41, 42, 45-49, 51-54, 56-59, 61, 62, 65, 66, 69, 70, 72, 74, 75, 80-83, 85, 86, 88, 89, 91, 92, 94, 95, 97-100, 103, 106-111, 116-124, 128, 131, 132, 139, 140, 142, 146-151, 153-156, 158, 159, 161, 162, 165-169, 174, 176, 181, 186-193, 202, 203, 205-211, 214, 216, 217, 220-223, 225, 226, 229, 235-243, 247, 249, 253, 254, 257-263, 265, 267
Perula, purchase.................................4
pink undergarments.........................8
Portree..................................119, 120
Press, the34, 91, 105, 156, 185, 237, 260
propellor fouled...........................208
Rosendal............................63, 65, 69
Saltstraum......................................238
Scapa Flow...................................127
Schjelderup, Captain. 156, 159, 162-167, 171, 177, 193, 202, 220, 263
sea anchor............................208, 210
seagulls..30
sighting land.................................216
Sognefjord.........63, 91, 95, 133, 134
Sörvik...150
Spitsbergen conditions................102
Stornoway...................120, 122, 123
Storsund.............................62, 63, 65
Stromness............126, 128, 255, 257
Svalbard, setting off for..............167
Svartisen..151
Sverdrup, Einar. .189, 194-203, 263, 268
Sysselmann...................188, 190-192
Tafjord......................................84-86
Torghatten....................................149
Tromsö.......102, 154, 156, 158, 159, 161, 164, 165, 167, 185, 194, 202, 217, 220, 223, 226, 227, 231, 232, 234, 268, 272
Trondheim..................143, 245, 246
Vegsund..139
visitors, types of............................26
weather forecasts. 15, 40, 51, 95, 96, 100, 102, 111, 117, 119, 128, 143, 150, 154, 155, 159, 164, 166, 169, 174, 176, 193, 195, 214, 226, 227, 248, 252, 254, 258, 263, 269, 272
Westminster, Duke of.................228
"The wind is blowing..."............209

www.ingramcontent.com/pod-product-compliance
Ingram Content Group UK Ltd.
Pitfield, Milton Keynes, MK11 3LW, UK
UKHW041948190726
13854UKWH00004B/1863